taste of home
FRESH&EASY

HEARTY VEGGIE SANDWICHES, PAGE 87

A TASTE OF HOME/READER'S DIGEST BOOK

© 2010 Reiman Media Group, Inc.
5400 S. 60th St., Greendale WI 53129
All rights reserved.

Editor in Chief: Catherine Cassidy
Vice President, Executive Editor/Books: Heidi Reuter Lloyd
Creative Director: Howard Greenberg
North American Chief Marketing Officer: Lisa Karpinski
Food Director: Diane Werner RD
Senior Editor/Books: Mark Hagen
Art Director: Rudy Krochalk
Content Production Supervisor: Julie Wagner
Design Layout Artist: Kathy Crawford
Recipe Asset System Manager: Coleen Martin
Premedia Supervisor: Scott Berger
Recipe Testing & Editing: Taste of Home Test Kitchen
Food Photography: Taste of Home Photo Studio
Administrative Assistant: Barb Czysz

THE READER'S DIGEST ASSOCIATION, INC.
President and Chief Executive Officer: Mary G. Berner
President, North American Affinities: Suzanne M. Grimes
President/Publisher Trade Publishing: Harold Clarke
Associate Publisher: Rosanne McManus
Vice President, Sales and Marketing: Stacey Ashton

International Standard Book Number (10): 0-89821-827-6
International Standard Book Number (13): 978-0-89821-827-5
Library of Congress Control Number: 2010930052

COVER PHOTOGRAPHY
Photographer: Rob Hagen
Food Stylist: Kaitlyn Besasie
Set Stylist: Stephanie Marchese

Pictured on front cover: Bruschetta Pizza (p. 124).

Pictured on back cover from left to right: Grilled Greek Potato Salad (p. 58),
Gingered Cranberry Pear Crisp (p. 219) and French Tarragon Burgers (p. 83).

Stock Photography: Asparagus Border (p. 3) maya13/shutterstock.com, Tomatoes (p. 4)
Ekaterina Shlikhunova/shutterstock.com, Brambles (p. 5) Ivonne Wierink/shutterstock.com,
Zucchini (back cover) sarsmis/shutterstock.com, Produce (inside left flap)
Christina Richards/shutterstock.com, Fruit (spine) yamix/shutterstock.com.

For other Taste of Home books and products, visit us at tasteofhome.com.

For more Reader's Digest products and information, visit
rd.com (in the United States) or see rd.ca (in Canada).

Printed in U.S.A.
3 5 7 9 10 8 6 4

191

111

TABLE OF CONTENTS

set the table with a
harvest *of* flavor

With *Fresh & Easy* you have 390 ways to serve the season's best produce...even on your busiest night!

For many family cooks, visiting a farmers market, picking homegrown items from a garden or even shopping at the produce department is sheer heaven. They know that the intense flavors that fresh vegetables and fruits deliver, coupled with the satisfaction of serving healthy meals, just can't be beat. And with *Taste of Home Fresh & Easy,* taking advantage of the season's best is a cinch!

With 390 no-fuss recipes to choose from, it's a snap to find the perfect dish to use up ripe veggies and fruits...no matter what the season! Best of all, each recipe comes together without much effort, so you can whip up hearty veggie-filled dishes and sweet berry desserts even on hectic weeknights.

Many of the dishes in *Fresh & Easy* are table-ready in just 30 minutes! Better yet, 95 recipes are ready in less than half an hour. We've marked those items with this handy icon. Other recipes call for just a few moments of trouble-free prep work, then simmer or bake to mouthwatering perfection on their own.

13

132

THE CREAM OF THE CROP

Whether you need a fast fix for dinner or you're planning a holiday menu, *Fresh & Easy* offers hundreds of ways to enhance your meal with the robust taste of vegetables, fruits, berries and even herbs.

See the chapter "Main Dishes" (p. 100), where beef, poultry, pork and seafood are paired with your favorite produce for effortless entrees bursting with flavor. You'll even find some meatless dinners that are sure to become harvesttime specialties in your home.

When time's tight, try beefy Southwest Stuffed Peppers (p. 111), savory Greek Spinach Pizza (p. 134) or even colorful Asparagus Cashew Stir-Fry (p. 144). They're each ready in less than 30 minutes—start to finish!

Hosting a special occasion? Consider Roast Chicken with Veggies (p. 104), Spiral Ham with Cranberry Glaze (p. 107) or impressive Fennel Stuffed Cod (p. 109). They call for a few minutes of preparation, and then bake to perfection on their own...freeing up your time in the kitchen.

When you want to surprise your gang with golden muffins, coffee cakes, scones and more, simply see the chapter "Breads & Baked Goods" (p. 148). There you'll find quick Pineapple Nut Bread (p. 153), speedy Zucchini Cheddar Biscuits (p. 155), change-of-pace Kiwifruit Muffins (p. 163) and 28 other no-stress baked delights.

Fresh & Easy is also your source for tooth-tingling treats that don't call for excessive kitchen time. See "Desserts" (p. 198) for Saucy Poached Pears (p. 203) Tangy Lemon-Nut Tart (p. 206) and Sweet Berry Bruschetta (p. 232). You won't believe that fruity desserts so succulent can be so quick to assemble.

In addition, you can perfectly round out family meals with 50 veggie side dishes and dozens of salads and soups bursting with garden goodness. You'll even find swift appetizer ideas and satisfying sandwiches! Simply turn the page, and discover how *Fresh & Easy* can help you serve your family the best nature has to offer.

APPETIZERS

Everyone loves a savory nibble now and then, and with the effortless bites in this chapter, whipping up impressive finger food has never been easier. Turn here when you want an easy hors d'oeuvre that takes advantage of the best nature has to offer.

SMOKED SALMON CUCUMBER CANAPES | PAGE 10

PEPPER STEAK QUESADILLAS | PAGE 31

FRESH HERB FLATBREAD
prep/total time: 25 min.

1 tube (8 ounces) refrigerated crescent rolls	1-1/2 teaspoons minced fresh rosemary
1/4 cup fresh basil leaves, thinly sliced	1 egg, lightly beaten
	1 tablespoon grated Parmesan cheese

Unroll crescent dough and separate into two rectangles. On a lightly floured surface, roll each into a 10-in. x 7-in. rectangle, sealing seams and perforations.

Place one rectangle on an ungreased baking sheet. Sprinkle basil and rosemary to within 1/2 in. of edges. Top with remaining dough; pinch edges to seal. Brush with egg; sprinkle with cheese.

Bake at 375° 10-12 minutes or until golden brown. Cut into slices. Serve warm. **YIELD: 10 SERVINGS.**

BEV CREDLE
HAMPTON, VIRGINIA

Since I grow so many herbs, I always look for ways to use them in my cooking. This recipe calls for two of my favorites, but it's also delicious with thyme and marjoram or oregano and basil.

ROASTED RED PEPPER HUMMUS
prep: 30 min. + standing

2 large sweet red peppers	1 teaspoon curry powder
2 cans (15 ounces *each*) garbanzo beans *or* chickpeas, rinsed and drained	1/2 teaspoon ground coriander
	1/2 teaspoon ground cumin
1/3 cup lemon juice	1/2 teaspoon pepper
3 tablespoons tahini	Pita bread, warmed and cut into wedges, and reduced-fat wheat snack crackers
1 tablespoon olive oil	
2 garlic cloves, peeled	Additional garbanzo beans *or* chickpeas, optional
1-1/4 teaspoons salt	

Broil red peppers 4 in. from heat until skins blister, about 5 minutes. With tongs, rotate peppers a quarter turn. Broil and rotate until all sides are blistered and blackened. Immediately place peppers in a bowl; cover and let stand for 15-20 minutes.

Peel off and discard charred skin. Remove stems and seeds. Place the peppers in a food processor. Add beans, lemon juice, tahini, oil, garlic and seasonings; cover and process until blended. Transfer to a serving bowl. Serve with pita bread and crackers. Garnish with additional beans if desired. **YIELD: 3 CUPS.**

NANCY WATSON-PISTOLE
SHAWNEE, KANSAS

My son taught me how to prepare hummus, which is a great alternative to calorie-filled dips. Fresh roasted red bell peppers make this really special.

**MARCIA MARCOUX
CHARLTON,
MASSACHUSETTS**

*This dip is popular
with family and
friends, especially
when we can feature
our homegrown
vegetables. Serving
it in eggplant shells
makes for a fun
presentation.*

STUFFED EGGPLANT DIP

prep: 20 min. | cook: 20 min.

1 large eggplant	2 tablespoons minced fresh cilantro
1 tablespoon lemon juice	1 tablespoon red wine vinegar
1 medium green pepper, diced	1 garlic clove, minced
2 celery ribs, diced	1 teaspoon salt
1 medium onion, diced	1/4 teaspoon dried basil
1 medium carrot, diced	1/8 teaspoon cayenne pepper
1/4 cup olive oil	Pita breads, cut into wedges
2 large tomatoes, chopped	

Cut eggplant in half lengthwise. Remove pulp, leaving a 1/2-in. shell. Brush inside of shell with lemon juice; set aside.

Place eggplant pulp in a steamer basket; place in a saucepan over 1 in. of water. Bring to a boil; cover and steam for 5-8 minutes or until tender. Set aside.

In a large skillet, saute the green pepper, celery, onion and carrot in oil for 4-6 minutes or until tender. Stir in the tomatoes, cilantro, vinegar, garlic, salt, basil, cayenne and eggplant pulp. Cook and stir over medium heat for 10-15 minutes or until thickened.

Spoon dip into eggplant shells. Serve with pita wedges. **YIELD: 3 CUPS.**

JUDY GREBETZ
RACINE, WISCONSIN

This is the one appetizer that I'm always asked to bring to parties. It's simple, comes together quickly and is a real winner!

SMOKED SALMON CUCUMBER CANAPES
prep: 25 min. + chilling

2	medium cucumbers, peeled	1	tablespoon capers, drained
4	ounces smoked salmon, flaked	1	tablespoon minced fresh parsley
2	tablespoons lemon juice	1/2	teaspoon Dijon mustard
1	tablespoon finely chopped onion	1/8	teaspoon pepper

Cut cucumbers in half lengthwise; remove and discard seeds. In a small bowl, combine remaining ingredients. Spoon into cucumber halves. Wrap in plastic wrap. Refrigerate for 3-4 hours or until filling is firm. Cut into 1/2-in. slices. **YIELD: ABOUT 3-1/2 DOZEN.**

TERI ALBRECHT
MT. AIRY, MARYLAND

I love to serve these savory wrapped vegetable sticks for special occasions. They are an easy but impressive appetizer.

VEGETABLE SPIRAL STICKS
prep/total time: 30 min.

3	medium carrots	1	egg white, lightly beaten
12	fresh asparagus spears, trimmed	1/4	cup grated Parmesan cheese
1	tube (11 ounces) refrigerated breadsticks	1/2	teaspoon dried oregano

Cut carrots lengthwise into quarters. In a large skillet, bring 2 in. of water to a boil. Add carrots; cook for 3 minutes. Add asparagus; cook 2-3 minutes longer. Drain; immediately place in an ice water bath. Drain and pat dry.

Cut each piece of breadstick dough in half. Roll each piece into a 7-in. rope. Wrap one rope in a spiral around each vegetable. Place on a baking sheet coated with cooking spray; tuck ends of dough under vegetables to secure.

Brush with egg white. Combine cheese and oregano; sprinkle over sticks. Bake at 375° for 12-14 minutes or until golden brown. Serve warm. **YIELD: 2 DOZEN.**

ZUCCHINI PATTIES WITH DILL DIP

prep: 25 min. | cook: 10 min.

3/4	cup sour cream	1/4	teaspoon garlic powder
2	tablespoons minced fresh dill	1	egg, lightly beaten
1	teaspoon lemon juice	2	tablespoons butter, melted
1/8	teaspoon salt	1	large carrot, chopped
1/8	teaspoon pepper	1/4	cup finely chopped onion
2-1/2	cups shredded zucchini	1/4	cup all-purpose flour
1	cup seasoned bread crumbs	1/2	cup canola oil
1	teaspoon seafood seasoning		

For dip, in a small bowl, combine the first five ingredients. Cover and refrigerate until serving.

Place zucchini in a colander to drain; squeeze to remove excess liquid. Pat dry; set aside.

In a large bowl, combine the bread crumbs, seafood seasoning and garlic powder. Stir in egg and butter until blended. Add the carrot, onion and zucchini.

Place flour in a shallow bowl. Shape zucchini mixture into 24 small patties; coat with flour.

Heat oil in a large skillet; fry patties, a few at a time, for 3-4 minutes on each side or until lightly browned. Drain on paper towels. Serve with dip. **YIELD: 2 DOZEN (3/4 CUP DIP).**

**KELLY MAXWELL
PLAINFIELD, ILLINOIS**

These crisp-tender patties are a nice alternative to crab cakes and taste very similar, thanks to the seafood seasoning. They're sure to get gobbled up.

PEAR PIZZA WEDGES

prep/total time: 25 min.

2	whole pita breads	1/4	cup coarsely chopped walnuts
2	teaspoons olive oil	1	tablespoon honey
1/2	cup crumbled Gorgonzola cheese	1	teaspoon balsamic vinegar
1	medium ripe pear, thinly sliced		

Place pita breads on an ungreased baking sheet. Brush with oil; sprinkle with Gorgonzola cheese. Top with pear slices and walnuts.

Bake at 400° for 12-15 minutes or until bread is crisp and cheese is melted. Combine honey and vinegar; drizzle over pitas. Cut each into four wedges. **YIELD: 8 APPETIZERS.**

**MIMI MERTA
DUNEDIN, FLORIDA**

I guarantee you won't be able to stop eating this appetizer once you start. The recipe makes just the right amount for a small gathering.

TOMATO GUACAMOLE DIP

prep/total time: 15 min.

2	medium ripe avocados, peeled and chopped	3	tablespoons sour cream
1	tablespoon lime juice	1/2	teaspoon salt
1	small tomato, seeded and chopped	1/2	teaspoon minced garlic
		Tortilla chips	

In a small bowl, mash avocados and lime juice with a fork. Stir in the tomato, sour cream, salt and garlic. Cover and refrigerate for 5 minutes. Serve with tortilla chips. **YIELD: 2-1/3 CUPS.**

JILL PEREZ
RACINE, WISCONSIN

With just six ingredients, this refreshing dip is a snap to whip up. Light and fresh, it's a terrific way to start any dinner.

GRILLED POTATO SKINS

prep/total time: 30 min.

2	medium potatoes	**TOPPING:**	
1-1/2	teaspoons butter, melted	3	tablespoons mayonnaise
2	tablespoons picante sauce	2	tablespoons sour cream
1/4	cup shredded cheddar cheese	1	tablespoon prepared ranch salad dressing
1	tablespoon real bacon bits	1-1/2	teaspoons real bacon bits
1/4	cup chopped tomato	1/4	teaspoon garlic powder
2	tablespoons chopped green onion		

Cut each potato lengthwise into four wedges. Cut away the white portion, leaving 1/4 in. on the potato skins. Place skins on a microwave-safe plate.

Microwave, uncovered, on high for 8-10 minutes or until tender. Brush butter over shells; top with picante sauce, cheese and bacon bits.

Grill potatoes, skin side down, uncovered, over medium heat for 4-6 minutes or until lightly browned. Cover and grill 2-3 minutes longer or until cheese is melted. Sprinkle with tomato and onion. In a small bowl, combine topping ingredients. Serve with potato skins. **YIELD: 4 SERVINGS.**

EDITOR'S NOTE: This recipe was tested in a 1,100-watt microwave.

STEPHANIE MOON
BOISE, IDAHO

The creamy topping on these potato skins is so delicious. They make an excellent summertime treat alongside your favorite grilled meat.

CANADIAN BACON-STUFFED MUSHROOMS

prep: 30 min. | bake: 20 min.

30	to 35 large fresh mushrooms	1/2	teaspoon pepper
1/4	pound Canadian bacon, diced	2	tablespoons canola oil
		1	teaspoon minced garlic
1/3	cup chopped sweet red pepper	1/2	cup crumbled goat cheese *or* feta cheese
1/4	cup chopped red onion	1/2	cup shredded cheddar cheese
1/2	teaspoon salt		

Remove stems from mushrooms and finely chop; set caps aside. In a large skillet, saute the mushrooms, bacon, red pepper, onion, salt and pepper in oil until vegetables are crisp-tender. Add garlic; cook 1 minute longer.

Remove from the heat. Stir in cheeses. Fill each mushroom cap with about 1 tablespoon of filling.

Place on foil-lined baking sheets. Bake at 400° for 16-20 minutes or until mushrooms are tender. **YIELD: 30-35 APPETIZERS.**

JOAN AIREY
RIVERS, MANITOBA

I served this to company during the holidays and their response was great. For extra color, I sometimes sprinkle the mushrooms with fresh parsley after they're baked.

CRAN-APPLE SALSA

prep/total time: 15 min.

1	package (12 ounces) fresh *or* frozen cranberries, thawed	1/3	cup unsweetened apple juice
3	medium apples, cut into wedges	3	tablespoons minced fresh cilantro
1	medium sweet red pepper, cut into pieces	2	tablespoons chopped jalapeno pepper
1	small red onion, chopped	1	teaspoon grated lime peel
1/2	cup sugar		Tortilla chips

In a food processor, process the cranberries, apples, red pepper and onion in batches until coarsely pureed.

Transfer to a serving bowl. Stir in the sugar, apple juice, cilantro, jalapeno and lime peel. Refrigerate until serving. Serve with tortilla chips. **YIELD: 5 CUPS.**

EDITOR'S NOTE: When cutting hot peppers, disposable gloves are recommended. Avoid touching your face.

JODY BAUER
BALATON, MINNESOTA

Here's a festive twist on traditional holiday cranberry relish. This salsa packs a tart-sweet blend of flavors, goes together in minutes and the colors are simply beautiful! We think it makes the perfect party dip to celebrate the season.

**KENDRA DOSS
KANSAS CITY,
MISSOURI**

*Filled with
chicken,
mushrooms,
water chestnuts
and carrots,
these wraps are
both healthy
and yummy.
The gingerroot,
rice vinegar
and teriyaki
sauce give them
delicious
Asian flair.*

CHICKEN LETTUCE WRAPS

prep/total time: 25 min.

1-1/2	pounds boneless skinless chicken breasts, cubed
1	tablespoon plus 1-1/2 teaspoons peanut oil, *divided*
3/4	cup chopped fresh mushrooms
1	can (8 ounces) water chestnuts, drained and diced
1	tablespoon minced fresh gingerroot
2	tablespoons rice vinegar
2	tablespoons reduced-sodium teriyaki sauce
1	tablespoon reduced-sodium soy sauce
1/2	teaspoon garlic powder
1/4	teaspoon crushed red pepper flakes
1-1/2	cups shredded carrots
1/2	cup julienned green onions
12	Bibb *or* Boston lettuce leaves
1/3	cup sliced almonds, toasted

In a large nonstick skillet coated with cooking spray, cook chicken in 1 tablespoon oil for 3 minutes; drain. Add the mushrooms, water chestnuts and ginger; cook 4-6 minutes longer or until chicken is no longer pink. Drain and set aside.

In a small bowl, whisk the vinegar, teriyaki sauce, soy sauce, garlic powder, red pepper flakes and remaining oil. Stir in the carrots, onions and chicken mixture.

Spoon onto lettuce leaves; sprinkle with almonds. If desired, fold sides of lettuce over filling and roll up. **YIELD: 6 SERVINGS.**

FRUIT SALSA
prep/total time: 20 min.

1 quart fresh strawberries, hulled and chopped	2 tablespoons brown sugar
2 medium apples, peeled and chopped	2 tablespoons apple jelly
2 medium kiwifruit, peeled and chopped	1/4 cup orange juice
	Graham crackers

In a large bowl, combine the strawberries, apples and kiwi. In a small bowl, combine the brown sugar, jelly and orange juice; drizzle over the fruit and toss gently to coat. Serve with the graham crackers. **YIELD: 6 CUPS.**

KELLY HARBAUGH
YORK, PENNSYLVANIA

Fruit salsa is a nice change of pace from traditional tomato-based salsa. Kids love the sweet fruit and graham crackers.

JAMAICAN SHRIMP
prep: 35 min. + marinating

3 quarts water	4 teaspoons honey
1 teaspoon salt	3 teaspoons Caribbean jerk seasoning
2 pounds uncooked medium shrimp, peeled and deveined	1 medium mango or 2 medium peaches, peeled and cubed
1/3 cup olive oil	1 small red onion, thinly sliced and separated into rings
1/4 cup white wine vinegar	
3 tablespoons lime juice	1 medium lime, quartered and sliced
1 jalapeno pepper, seeded and finely chopped	

In a large saucepan, bring water and salt to a boil. Add shrimp; boil for 3 minutes or until shrimp turn pink, stirring occasionally. Drain and rinse with cold water; transfer to a large resealable plastic bag.

In a jar with a tight-fitting lid, combine the oil, vinegar, lime juice, jalapeno, honey and jerk seasoning; shake well. Pour 3/4 cup marinade over shrimp. Seal bag and turn to coat; refrigerate for 1-2 hours. Refrigerate remaining marinade.

Just before serving, drain and discard marinade from shrimp. On a large serving platter, layer the shrimp, mango, onion and lime. Drizzle with remaining marinade. **YIELD: 15-20 SERVINGS.**

EDITOR'S NOTE: When cutting hot peppers, disposable gloves are recommended. Avoid touching your face.

MARY LOU WAYMAN
SALT LAKE CITY, UTAH

Zesty jerk seasoning complements sweet mango in this crowd-pleasing appetizer. Although it takes time to prepare, this flavorful dish can conveniently be made ahead and refrigerated until ready to serve.

DIANNE WERDEGAR
NAPERVILLE, ILLINOIS

This is one of my all-time favorite appetizers. Fast and easy, the golden bites are always a huge hit. I make and freeze batches of them during asparagus season for dinner parties throughout the year.

DIANE HIXON
NICEVILLE, FLORIDA

This snack is both sweet and savory. The apples add a fresh touch to the robust sausage dish.

ASPARAGUS IN PUFF PASTRY
prep: 30 min. + chilling | bake: 10 min.

2	cups water	1/2	teaspoon salt
24	fresh asparagus spears (about 1 pound), trimmed	1	package (17-1/4 ounces) frozen puff pastry dough, thawed
1	package (8 ounces) reduced-fat cream cheese	1/4	cup egg substitute

In a large nonstick skillet, bring water to a boil. Add asparagus; cover and cook for 3 minutes. Drain asparagus and immediately place in ice water; drain and pat dry. In a bowl, beat cream cheese and salt until smooth; set aside.

Unfold the dough on a lightly floured surface. Cut each sheet in half widthwise. For each rectangle, spread cream cheese mixture lengthwise over half of the dough to within 1/2 in. of edges. Arrange two rows of three asparagus spears lengthwise in a single layer over cream cheese.

Brush edges of dough with some of the egg substitute; fold dough over filling and press edges together to seal. Cover and refrigerate for 1 hour.

Cut widthwise into 1-1/4-in. pieces. Place 1 in. apart on a baking sheet coated with cooking spray. Brush with the remaining egg substitute. Bake at 425° for 8-12 minutes or until golden. Serve warm. **YIELD: 28 SERVINGS.**

APPLE SAUSAGE APPETIZERS
prep: 10 min. | cook: 25 min.

1	small onion, chopped	8	ounces miniature smoked sausage links
1-1/2	teaspoons butter	1	small apple, peeled and sliced
2	tablespoons apple jelly	3/4	teaspoon cornstarch
2	tablespoons brown sugar	1-1/2	teaspoons water

In a small saucepan, saute onion in butter until tender. Stir in apple jelly and brown sugar; add sausage links. Cook, uncovered, over medium-low heat for 15-20 minutes or until thickened, stirring occasionally. Add apple.

Cover and cook over medium-low heat for 8-10 minutes or until apples are tender. Combine cornstarch and water until smooth; stir into saucepan. Bring to a boil; cook and stir for 1 minute or until thickened. Serve warm. **YIELD: 2-4 SERVINGS.**

SPINACH FETA PIZZA
prep/total time: 30 min.

- 1 tube (13.8 ounces) refrigerated pizza crust
- 1 tablespoon olive oil
- 1 teaspoon minced garlic
- 1 can (15 ounces) pizza sauce
- 2 cups chopped fresh spinach
- 3/4 cup sliced red onion, separated into rings
- 1 cup sliced fresh mushrooms
- 1 cup (4 ounces) shredded part-skim mozzarella cheese
- 1/2 cup crumbled feta cheese
- 1 teaspoon dried basil
- 1 teaspoon Italian seasoning
- Crushed red pepper flakes, optional

Unroll crust into a greased 15-in. x 10-in. x 1-in. baking pan; flatten dough and build up edges slightly. Brush with oil; sprinkle with garlic. Spread with pizza sauce.

Layer with spinach, onion, mushrooms and cheeses. Sprinkle with basil, Italian seasoning and pepper flakes if desired. Bake at 400° for 15-18 minutes or until golden brown. **YIELD: 12 PIECES.**

**CONNIE CLEGG
FREDERICK, MARYLAND**

My husband and I enjoy this pizza as a quick, hearty meal, which is perfect for us on busy work nights. We eat more meatless meals now, and this fits the bill!

CHEESY CHIVE CRISPS
prep: 10 min. + chilling | bake: 20 min./batch

- 1 cup butter, softened
- 3 cups (12 ounces) shredded sharp cheddar cheese
- 2 cups all-purpose flour
- 1/4 cup minced chives
- 1/2 teaspoon salt
- 1/2 teaspoon hot pepper sauce
- Dash garlic salt
- 2 cups crisp rice cereal

In a large bowl, cream the butter and cheese until light and fluffy. Beat in the flour, chives, salt, pepper sauce and garlic salt. Stir in the cereal. Shape into four 6-1/2-in. x 1-1/2-in. logs. Wrap tightly in plastic wrap and freeze.

Remove cheese logs from freezer 2 hours before baking. Unwrap; cut into 1/4-in. slices. Place on ungreased baking sheets. Bake at 325° for 20-25 minutes or until edges are crisp and lightly browned. Remove to wire racks to cool. Refrigerate leftovers. **YIELD: ABOUT 9 DOZEN.**

**EVE MCNEW
ST. LOUIS, MISSOURI**

These crisp bites are great to keep on hand for guests. Since the recipe makes a lot, you might want to freeze some of the cheese logs for future use. Be sure to thaw them in the refrigerator for 2 to 3 hours before slicing and baking.

BARBARA MCCALLEY
ALLISON PARK,
PENNSYLVANIA

Black pepper and garlic perk up this out-of-the-ordinary spread that hits the spot on a crisp cracker or toasted bread slice. It's excellent!

ROASTED EGGPLANT SPREAD

prep: 20 min. | bake: 45 min. + cooling

2	large sweet red peppers, cut into 1-inch pieces	3	tablespoons olive oil
1	medium eggplant, cut into 1-inch pieces	1/2	teaspoon salt
1	medium red onion, cut into 1-inch pieces	1/2	teaspoon pepper
3	garlic cloves, minced	1	tablespoon tomato paste

Toasted bread slices *or* assorted crackers

In a large bowl, combine the red peppers, eggplant, onion and garlic. Drizzle with oil; sprinkle with salt and pepper. Toss to coat.

Transfer to a 15-in. x 10-in. x 1-in. baking pan coated with cooking spray. Bake, uncovered, at 400° for 45-50 minutes or until lightly browned and tender, stirring once. Cool slightly.

Place vegetables and tomato paste in a food processor; cover and process until chopped and blended. Transfer to a serving bowl; cool to room temperature. Serve with bread. **YIELD: 2 CUPS.**

STEPHANIE SHERIDAN
PLAINFIELD, VERMONT

These salad-filled potato skins are packed with the kind of down-home goodness everyone loves. Let them chill for a few hours to enhance the flavor.

POTATO SALAD BITES

prep: 30 min. | cook: 15 min. + chilling

10	small red potatoes	1/2	cup mayonnaise
1/4	cup chopped pimiento-stuffed olives	1-3/4	teaspoons Dijon mustard
2	teaspoons minced fresh parsley	1/8	teaspoon pepper
1	teaspoon finely chopped onion	1/4	teaspoon salt

Paprika

Parsley sprigs, optional

Place the potatoes in a large saucepan and cover with water. Bring to a boil. Reduce heat; cover and cook for 12-15 minutes or until tender. Drain; immediately place the potatoes in ice water. Drain and pat dry.

Peel two potatoes; finely dice and place in a small bowl. Cut the remaining potatoes in half. With a melon baller, scoop out pulp, leaving a 3/8-in. shell; set shells aside. Dice pulp and add to the bowl. Stir in the olives, parsley and onion. Combine the mayonnaise, mustard and pepper; gently stir into potato mixture.

Sprinkle potato shells with salt; stuff with potato salad. Sprinkle with paprika. Chill for at least 1 hour before serving. Garnish with parsley if desired. **YIELD: 16 APPETIZERS.**

ARTICHOKE CAPRESE PLATTER

prep/total time: 15 min.

2 jars (7-1/2 ounces *each*) marinated artichoke hearts	2 balls (8 ounces *each*) fresh mozzarella cheese, halved and sliced
2 tablespoons red wine vinegar	2 cups loosely packed fresh basil leaves
2 tablespoons olive oil	
6 plum tomatoes, sliced	

Drain artichokes, reserving 1/2 cup marinade; cut artichokes in half. In a small bowl, whisk vinegar, oil and reserved marinade.

On a large serving platter, arrange artichokes, tomatoes, mozzarella cheese and basil. Drizzle with the vinaigrette. Serve immediately. **YIELD: 10-12 SERVINGS.**

EDITOR'S NOTE: Fresh mozzarella can be found in the deli section of most grocery stores.

MARGARET WILSON
SUN CITY, CALIFORNIA

This classic Italian combination of mozzarella, tomatoes and basil is dressed up with marinated artichokes. Using fresh mozzarella is the key to its great taste.

GREEK CHICKEN WINGS

prep: 15 min. + marinating | bake: 35 min.

3 tablespoons lemon juice	**CUCUMBER SAUCE:**
2 tablespoons olive oil	1/2 cup plain yogurt
2 tablespoons honey	1/2 cup chopped peeled cucumber
1 teaspoon dried oregano	1/2 cup crumbled feta cheese
1 garlic clove, minced	2 tablespoons snipped fresh dill *or* 2 teaspoons dill weed
1/4 teaspoon salt	
4 pounds frozen chicken wingettes, thawed	1 garlic clove, peeled
	Dash salt

In a large resealable plastic bag, combine the lemon juice, oil, honey, oregano, garlic and salt. Add chicken wings; seal bag and toss to coat. Refrigerate overnight.

In a blender, combine the sauce ingredients; cover and process until smooth. Transfer to a small bowl; cover and refrigerate until serving.

Drain and discard marinade. Place wings on a rack in a greased 15-in. x 10-in. x 1-in. baking pan. Bake, uncovered, at 400° for 35-40 minutes or until juices run clear, turning once. Serve with cucumber sauce. **YIELD: ABOUT 3 DOZEN (1 CUP SAUCE).**

LORRAINE CALAND
THUNDER BAY, ONTARIO

Your guests will be delighted to munch on these herb chicken wings. Just be sure to make plenty of cucumber dipping sauce.

MARIAN PLATT
SEQUIM, WASHINGTON

Canned crab and chive cream cheese combine to turn ordinary celery sticks into special appetizers. I keep this recipe's ingredients on hand for anytime snacking.

BRIDGETTA EALY
PONTIAC, MICHIGAN

I wasn't sure what to expect when I first made these, but they're fantastic. The jalapenos balance out the other ingredients perfectly. If you don't have shaved turkey, shaved chicken works just as well.

CRAB-STUFFED CELERY

prep/total time: 15 min.

1	carton (8 ounces) whipped chive cream cheese	1	tablespoon mayonnaise
		1/2	teaspoon lemon juice
1/2	cup crabmeat, drained, flaked and cartilage removed *or* imitation crabmeat	1/8	teaspoon onion salt
		1/8	teaspoon garlic salt
		6	celery ribs, cut into serving-size pieces

In a small bowl, combine the first six ingredients. Transfer to a small resealable plastic bag. Cut a small hole in the corner of the bag; pipe mixture into celery sticks. Store in the refrigerator. **YIELD: 2 DOZEN.**

CRANBERRY TURKEY CROSTINI
prep: 30 min. + chilling

1	package (12 ounces) fresh *or* frozen cranberries	1/4	teaspoon pepper
		30	slices French bread (1/4 inch thick)
1	medium tangerine, peeled and seeded	Cooking spray	
1/2	cup red wine vinegar	1	package (8 ounces) reduced-fat cream cheese
1/4	cup chopped shallots		
1/2	cup sugar	1/2	pound shaved deli smoked turkey
1/4	cup chopped seeded jalapeno peppers		

Place cranberries and tangerine in a food processor; cover and process until coarsely chopped. Set aside.

In a small saucepan, bring vinegar and shallots to a boil. Reduce heat; simmer, uncovered, for 5 minutes or until mixture is reduced to 1/3 cup, stirring occasionally. Stir in the sugar, jalapenos, pepper and reserved cranberry mixture. Cook for 5 minutes over medium heat, stirring frequently. Transfer to a small bowl; refrigerate until chilled.

Place bread on ungreased baking sheets; lightly spray bread on both sides with cooking spray. Broil 3-4 in. from the heat for 1-2 minutes on each side or until lightly browned. Spread each slice with 1-1/2 teaspoons cream cheese; top with turkey and 1 tablespoon cranberry mixture. **YIELD: 2-1/2 DOZEN.**

EDITOR'S NOTE: When cutting hot peppers, disposable gloves are recommended. Avoid touching your face.

ANNE BENNETT DELMAR, MARYLAND

The flavors of this tasty dip complement each other very nicely. It is a pleasant and colorful change from traditional salsa.

Fresh & Easy Tip

This Bean and Pineapple Salsa is delicious served with tortilla chips, but it also tastes great spooned over grilled pork or chicken. It can also be used as a topping for tacos, burritos or enchiladas. Yum!

BEAN AND PINEAPPLE SALSA

prep/total time: 15 min.

- 1/2 cup canned black beans, rinsed and drained
- 1/4 cup unsweetened pineapple tidbits, drained
- 1/4 cup chopped green pepper
- 1/4 cup chopped sweet red pepper
- 2 tablespoons finely chopped sweet onion
- 2 tablespoons chopped green chilies
- 1/2 to 1 teaspoon chopped seeded jalapeno pepper
- 1 tablespoon rice vinegar
- 1-1/2 teaspoons minced fresh cilantro
- 1/2 teaspoon ground coriander
- 1/2 teaspoon ground cumin
- Tortilla chips

In a small bowl, combine the first 11 ingredients. Refrigerate until serving. Serve with tortilla chips. **YIELD: 1-1/4 CUPS.**

EDITOR'S NOTE: When cutting hot peppers, disposable gloves are recommended. Avoid touching your face.

VEGGIE HAM CRESCENT WREATH

prep: 20 min. | bake: 15 min. + cooling

2	tubes (8 ounces *each*) refrigerated crescent rolls	1/4	cup finely chopped green pepper
1/2	cup spreadable pineapple cream cheese	1/2	cup chopped fresh broccoli florets
1/3	cup diced fully cooked ham	6	grape tomatoes, quartered
1/4	cup finely chopped sweet yellow pepper	1	tablespoon chopped red onion

Remove crescent dough from tubes (do not unroll). Cut each roll into eight slices. Arrange in an 11-in. circle on an ungreased 14-in. pizza pan.

Bake at 375° for 15-20 minutes or until golden brown. Cool for 5 minutes before carefully removing to a serving platter; cool completely.

Spread cream cheese over wreath; top with ham, peppers, broccoli, tomatoes and onion. Store in refrigerator. **YIELD: 16 APPETIZERS.**

DIXIE LUNDQUIST
CHANDLER, ARIZONA

Impress your guests with the look and flavor of this pretty crescent roll appetizer. The pineapple cream cheese adds a special touch.

 # FRIED SHOESTRING CARROTS

prep/total time: 25 min.

2	cups self-rising flour	1/2	teaspoon pepper, *divided*
1-1/2	cups water		
1	teaspoon salt, *divided*	10	cups shredded carrots
3/4	teaspoon cayenne pepper, *divided*		Oil for deep-fat frying

In a large bowl, whisk the flour, water, 1/2 teaspoon salt, 1/4 teaspoon cayenne and 1/4 teaspoon pepper until smooth. Stir in carrots. In a small bowl, combine remaining salt, cayenne and pepper; set aside.

In an electric skillet or deep-fat fryer, heat oil to 375°. Drop spoonfuls of carrot mixture, a few at a time, into oil; cook for 3-4 minutes or until golden brown, stirring frequently. Drain on paper towels; sprinkle with reserved seasoning mixture. **YIELD: 10 SERVINGS.**

EDITOR'S NOTE: As a substitute for each cup of self-rising flour, place 1-1/2 teaspoons baking powder and 1/2 teaspoon salt in a measuring cup. Add all-purpose flour to measure 1 cup.

KIM GAMMILL
RAYMONDVILLE, TEXAS

I came up with these fun snacks as an alternative to french fries. We like to serve them hot with ranch-style dressing as a dipping sauce.

APPLE-NUT BLUE CHEESE TARTLETS

prep: 25 min. | bake: 10 min.

1	large apple, peeled and finely chopped	4	tablespoons finely chopped walnuts, toasted, *divided*
1	medium onion, finely chopped	1/2	teaspoon salt
2	teaspoons butter	1	package (1.9 ounces) frozen miniature phyllo tart shells
1	cup (4 ounces) crumbled blue cheese		

In a small nonstick skillet, saute apple and onion in butter until tender. Remove from the heat; stir in the blue cheese, 3 tablespoons walnuts and salt. Spoon a rounded tablespoonful into each tart shell.

Place on an ungreased baking sheet. Bake at 350° for 5 minutes. Sprinkle with remaining walnuts; bake 2-3 minutes longer or until lightly browned. **YIELD: 15 APPETIZERS.**

**TRISHA KRUSE
EAGLE, IDAHO**

These attractive appetizers taste gourmet, but they're easy to make and have loads of blue cheese flavor. The phyllo shells and filling can be made in advance.

BAKED JALAPENOS

prep: 20 min. | bake: 25 min.

1	package (3 ounces) cream cheese, softened	1	teaspoon minced fresh cilantro
1/4	teaspoon ground cumin	8	jalapeno peppers, halved lengthwise and seeded
2/3	cup shredded Monterey Jack cheese	1	egg, lightly beaten
		3/4	cup cornflake crumbs

In a small bowl, beat cream cheese and cumin until smooth. Beat in Monterey Jack cheese and cilantro. Spoon into jalapeno halves.

Place egg and cornflake crumbs in separate shallow bowls. Dip filling side of jalapenos in egg, then coat with crumbs.

Place on a greased baking sheet with crumb side up. Bake at 350° for 25-30 minutes or until top is golden brown. Serve immediately. **YIELD: 16 APPETIZERS.**

EDITOR'S NOTE: When cutting hot peppers, disposable gloves are recommended. Avoid touching your face.

TASTE OF HOME TEST KITCHEN

The crunchy topping of these baked jalapeno poppers pairs well with the creamy filling.

CRAB BRUSCHETTA
prep/total time: 20 min.

1/2	cup finely chopped shallots
2	tablespoons plus 1/4 cup olive oil, *divided*
2	garlic cloves, minced
2	cans (6 ounces *each*) lump crabmeat, drained
1	cup chopped seeded plum tomatoes
1-1/2	teaspoons minced fresh basil *or* 1/2 teaspoon dried basil
3/4	teaspoon minced fresh oregano *or* 1/4 teaspoon dried oregano
8	slices Italian bread (1/2 inch thick)

In a large skillet, saute shallots in 2 tablespoons oil until tender. Add garlic; cook 1 minute longer. Add the crab, tomatoes, basil and oregano; cook and stir for 5-6 minutes or until heated through. Remove from the heat.

Brush both sides of each slice of bread with remaining oil. In another large skillet, toast bread for 1-2 minutes on each side. Cut each slice in half; top with crab mixture. **YIELD: 16 APPETIZERS.**

MARY PETRARA
LANCASTER, PENNSYLVANIA

Usually, I use only vegetables on bruschetta, but I wondered how crab would taste, because my family loves crab cakes. The appetizers are delicious and a winner with my family!

SNOW PEA HOLIDAY WREATH
prep/total time: 25 min.

1	package (3 ounces) cream cheese, softened
1/4	teaspoon garlic powder
1/4	teaspoon seasoned salt
1/2	pound fresh snow peas, strings removed
2	cups grape tomatoes

In a small bowl, combine the cream cheese, garlic powder and seasoned salt. Place mixture in a pastry bag or heavy-duty plastic bag with a small star tip.

Pipe about 1/4 teaspoon of mixture onto the wide end of each pea pod. Arrange pods on a serving platter with cheese mixture toward outside of platter; fill center with tomatoes. **YIELD: 20 SERVINGS.**

CAROL SCHNECK
LODI, CALIFORNIA

Santa himself might stop to sample this pretty-as-a-picture finger food! Crunchy green pea pods and juicy red tomatoes add a naturally fresh and festive holiday note to my buffet table.

VEGETABLE TORTILLA STACK
prep: 30 min. | bake: 10 min.

3/4 cup chopped green pepper	1 can (16 ounces) refried beans
3/4 cup chopped sweet red pepper	2 cups (8 ounces) shredded Monterey Jack cheese
1 small onion, chopped	2 cups (8 ounces) shredded cheddar cheese
2 tablespoons canola oil	
1/2 cup picante sauce	
1 package (16 ounces) frozen broccoli-cauliflower blend	Minced fresh cilantro, sliced ripe olives, sour cream and additional picante sauce
6 flour tortillas (8 inches)	

In a large skillet, saute peppers and onion in oil until tender. Stir in picante sauce; set aside. Meanwhile, cook frozen vegetables according to package directions; drain. Cool slightly; coarsely chop the vegetables.

Place two tortillas on an ungreased baking sheet. Spread each with 1/3 cup refried beans and sprinkle with 1/3 cup of the pepper mixture. Top each with another tortilla. Spoon 1-1/2 cups vegetables over each tortilla and sprinkle with Monterey Jack cheese. Top the last two tortillas with remaining beans and pepper mixture; place one on each stack. Sprinkle with cheddar cheese.

Bake at 375° for 10-15 minutes or until heated through and cheese is melted. Garnish with cilantro and olives. Cut into wedges. Serve with sour cream and sauce. **YIELD: 2 STACKS (4-6 SERVINGS EACH).**

IRENE MULLER
WRAY, COLORADO

These tasty layered tortillas are a hit with my children and grandchildren. Nutritious vegetables are deliciously disguised in this snack.

ROSEMARY ZUCCHINI STICKS
prep/total time: 30 min.

2 medium zucchini, peeled	1 tablespoon minced fresh rosemary or 1 teaspoon dried rosemary, crushed
1 cup seasoned bread crumbs	1 egg
	1 tablespoon water

Cut each zucchini in half widthwise, then cut each half lengthwise into quarters. In a shallow bowl, combine bread crumbs and rosemary. In another bowl, beat egg and water.

Dip zucchini in egg mixture, then coat with crumb mixture. Coat again in egg and crumbs. Arrange on a baking sheet coated with cooking spray. Bake at 375° for 20-25 minutes or until tender and golden, turning once. **YIELD: 4 SERVINGS.**

BETTY JACKSON
WHITE PINE, TENNESSEE

Our family loves zucchini, so I baked these one day and everybody raved about them! I like to serve these with a low-fat ranch dressing.

**SARA
LONGWORTH
BRISTOL,
CONNECTICUT**

The roasted veggies and goat cheese make this an elegant party food. We love to top the wedges with our favorite salsa for extra kick.

GOAT CHEESE 'N' VEGGIE QUESADILLAS

prep: 55 min. | bake: 5 min.

1	small eggplant, peeled, quartered and cut into 1/2-inch slices	2	tablespoons olive oil
1	medium zucchini, cut into 1/4-inch slices	1	tablespoon lemon juice
1	medium sweet red pepper, chopped	1/2	teaspoon chili powder
1	medium onion, chopped	1/2	teaspoon cayenne pepper
1/4	cup chopped ripe olives	1	tablespoon minced fresh cilantro
2	garlic cloves, minced	1/2	cup crumbled goat cheese
		8	whole wheat tortillas (8 inches)

Place the first six ingredients in an ungreased 15-in. x 10-in. x 1-in. baking pan. Combine the oil, lemon juice, chili powder and cayenne; drizzle over vegetables and toss to coat. Bake, uncovered, at 400° for 35-40 minutes or until tender, stirring once. Stir in cilantro.

Spread 1 tablespoon goat cheese over one side of each tortilla. Place two tortillas, plain side down, on an ungreased baking sheet; spread each with 2/3 cup vegetable mixture. Top each with another tortilla. Repeat. Bake at 400° for 5-10 minutes or until golden brown. Cut each quesadilla into six wedges. Serve warm. **YIELD: 2 DOZEN APPETIZERS.**

MELON WITH MINTED LIME DIP

prep: 15 min. + marinating

1/4 cup sugar	8 cups melon balls *or* cubes
1/4 cup water	**MINTED LIME DIP:**
6 tablespoons lime juice	1 cup (8 ounces) sour cream
2 tablespoons minced fresh mint	2 tablespoons sugar
2 teaspoons grated lime peel	1 tablespoon lime juice
2 tablespoons minced fresh gingerroot	2 teaspoons grated lime peel

In a large bowl, combine the sugar, water, lime juice, mint, lime peel and ginger. Add melon balls. Cover and refrigerate for 1-6 hours.

Thread melon onto wooden skewers or toothpicks. In a small bowl, combine dip ingredients. Serve with melon. **YIELD: 8 CUPS FRUIT (1 CUP DIP).**

**TASTE OF HOME
TEST KITCHEN**

For a refreshing summer side dish for any meal, try these marinated melon balls with a cool, creamy dip. You can also serve this fruity treat as a light dessert.

BROCCOLI CHEDDAR SPREAD

prep: 15 min. | bake: 20 min.

4 cups chopped fresh broccoli	1 envelope vegetable soup mix
1 tablespoon water	Pita chips *or* reduced-fat crackers
2 cups (16 ounces) reduced-fat sour cream	
1/2 cup plus 1 tablespoon shredded reduced-fat cheddar cheese, *divided*	

Place broccoli and water in a 1-1/2-qt. microwave-safe dish. Cover and microwave on high for 3-4 minutes or until crisp-tender; drain. In a large bowl, combine the sour cream, 1/2 cup cheese and soup mix. Gently stir in broccoli.

Transfer to an ungreased shallow 1-qt. baking dish. Sprinkle with remaining cheese. Bake, uncovered, at 350° for 20-25 minutes or until heated through. Serve with pita chips or crackers. **YIELD: 3 CUPS.**

EDITOR'S NOTE: This recipe was tested in a 1,100-watt microwave.

**BETH PARKER
GRAYSVILLE, ALABAMA**

People sure like this good-for-you broccoli spread. Using reduced-fat products lightens it up without sacrificing flavor.

PROSCIUTTO PHYLLO ROLL-UPS
prep: 30 min. | bake: 10 min.

24	sheets phyllo dough (14 inches x 9 inches)		2	ounces cream cheese, softened
1/4	cup butter, melted		1/4	cup chopped roasted sweet red peppers, drained
8	thin slices prosciutto, cut into 1-inch strips		3	tablespoons grated Parmesan cheese
24	fresh asparagus spears, trimmed		2	green onions, chopped
24	fresh green beans, trimmed		1	garlic clove, peeled

ARTICHOKE SAUCE:

1/4	cup sour cream		1/4	teaspoon white pepper
1/2	teaspoon lemon juice		1/4	teaspoon cayenne pepper
1	jar (6 ounces) marinated artichoke hearts, drained			

MICHAELA ROSENTHAL
WOODLAND HILLS,
CALIFORNIA

These elegant finger foods use delicate phyllo dough. With artichoke sauce on the side, the cheesy rolls make extra-special hors d'oeuvres.

Line baking sheets with parchment paper; set aside. Place one sheet of phyllo dough on a work surface (keep remaining dough covered with plastic wrap and a damp towel to avoid drying out). Brush with butter; fold in half lengthwise. Brush with butter; fold in half widthwise.

Brush with butter; top with a prosciutto strip. Place an asparagus spear and a green bean at a diagonal on bottom right corner; roll up. Repeat with remaining dough, butter, prosciutto and vegetables.

Place roll-ups on prepared baking sheets. Bake at 400° for 6-8 minutes or until golden brown. Meanwhile, in a blender, combine the sauce ingredients; cover and process until smooth. Transfer to a small bowl; serve with roll-ups. **YIELD: 2 DOZEN (1 CUP SAUCE).**

RADISH-STUFFED CHERRY TOMATOES
prep/total time: 30 min.

18	cherry tomatoes		2	tablespoons mayonnaise
1/2	cup chopped radishes		1	tablespoon minced fresh parsley
2	tablespoons chopped almonds, toasted		1	teaspoon grated onion

SANDY MAREK
GRAND MARAIS,
MINNESOTA

Christmas appetizer buffets get a refreshing lift with stuffed cherry tomatoes. Plus, the color is appropriate for the season!

Cut a thin slice off the top of each tomato. Scoop out and discard pulp; invert tomatoes onto paper towels to drain. In a small bowl, combine the remaining ingredients. Spoon into tomatoes. Refrigerate until serving. **YIELD: 1-1/2 DOZEN.**

MOZZARELLA BASIL BRUSCHETTA
prep/total time: 25 min.

6	slices Italian bread (1/2 inch thick)	1/4	teaspoon pepper
2	tablespoons olive oil	1/8	teaspoon salt
1	large tomato, seeded and chopped	6	slices part-skim mozzarella cheese, halved
3	tablespoons minced fresh basil		

Cut each slice of bread in half; place on an ungreased baking sheet. Brush with oil.

In a small bowl, combine the tomato, basil, pepper and salt. Spoon 1 tablespoonful over each piece of bread; top with cheese and remaining tomato mixture. Bake at 375° for 10-12 minutes or until cheese is melted. **YIELD: 1 DOZEN.**

CYNTHIA BENT
NEWARK, DELAWARE

This simple recipe makes a quick and light appetizer for hungry guests or family. Just like pizza, you can add whatever you desire each time you make it.

CHRISTMAS FRUIT KABOBS
prep: 10 min. + chilling | cook: 5 min. + cooling

1/2	fresh pineapple, trimmed and cut into 1-inch chunks	1	jar (10 ounces) maraschino cherries, drained
4	kiwifruit, peeled and cut into 1-inch pieces	SAUCE:	
3	navel oranges, peeled and sectioned	1	egg yolk
3	medium apples, cut into 1-inch pieces	1/4	cup maple syrup *or* honey
3	medium firm bananas, cut into 1-inch pieces	2	tablespoons lemon juice
		3/4	cup heavy whipping cream, whipped

Alternately thread fruit onto wooden skewers. Cover and refrigerate until serving.

In a small saucepan over low heat, cook and stir the egg yolk and syrup until a thermometer reads 160° and is thick enough to coat the back of a metal spoon. Remove from the heat; stir in lemon juice. Cool completely. Fold in the whipped cream. Serve with fruit. Refrigerate any leftovers. **YIELD: 20 KABOBS (ABOUT 1 CUP SAUCE).**

LOIS RUTHERFORD
ST. AUGUSTINE, FLORIDA

My chunky fruit skewers are always a hit for brunch, whether served with pastries, quiche or eggs and bacon. They're also excellent potluck additions. Feel free to use whatever fruits are in season.

REBEKAH SOUED
CONIFER, COLORADO

I usually use leftover spiral ham for the centers these light and flaky pastry triangles. With the white sauce and sprinkling of parsley, they are a crowd-pleaser.

Fresh & Easy Tip

Phyllo (pronounced FEE-lo) is a tissue-thin pastry that's made by gently stretching the dough into thin fragile sheets. It can be layered, shaped and baked in a variety of sweet and savory ways. Handling it quickly is the key! Follow the manufacturer's instructions for thawing phyllo in the unopened package.

HAM 'N' BROCCOLI TRIANGLES
prep: 40 min. | bake: 20 min.

2-1/2	cups diced fully cooked ham
2-1/2	cups chopped fresh *or* frozen broccoli, thawed
1	cup (4 ounces) shredded part-skim mozzarella cheese
2	eggs
1/2	cup heavy whipping cream
1/2	teaspoon minced fresh basil
1/2	teaspoon pepper
1/4	teaspoon Italian seasoning, optional

Dash cayenne pepper

1	package (16 ounces, 14-inch x 9-inch sheet size) frozen phyllo dough, thawed
3/4	cup butter, melted

SWISS CHEESE SAUCE:

1/4	cup butter
1/4	cup all-purpose flour
2	cups whole milk
1/2	teaspoon salt
1/2	cup shredded Swiss cheese

Minced fresh parsley, optional

In a large bowl, combine the ham, broccoli and mozzarella cheese. In a small bowl, beat eggs; stir in the cream, basil, pepper, Italian seasoning if desired and cayenne. Stir into ham mixture; set aside.

On a work surface, carefully remove one sheet of phyllo dough and fold into thirds lengthwise (keep remaining phyllo covered with plastic wrap and a damp towel to prevent it from drying out). Lightly brush phyllo strip with butter. Place a rounded tablespoonful of filling in lower right corner of strip. Fold dough over filling, forming a triangle. Fold triangle up, then fold over, forming another triangle. Continue folding, like a flag, until you come to the end of the strip.

Repeat with remaining phyllo sheets and filling. Place triangles on ungreased baking sheets. Brush with butter. Bake at 375° for 20-25 minutes or until golden brown.

Meanwhile, in a small saucepan, melt butter over medium heat. Whisk in flour until smooth; add milk and salt. Bring to a boil; cook and stir for 2 minutes or until thickened. Remove from the heat; stir in Swiss cheese until melted. Sprinkle with parsley if desired. Serve with triangles. **YIELD: 40 APPETIZERS.**

PEPPER STEAK QUESADILLAS
prep/total time: 30 min.

1/2 pound beef top sirloin steak	1/4 teaspoon dried rosemary, crushed
1/2 each medium green, sweet red and yellow pepper, julienned	4 flour tortillas (6 inches)
1 tablespoon chopped red onion	6 cherry tomatoes, halved
1 garlic clove, minced	1/4 cup sliced fresh mushrooms
1 tablespoon minced fresh cilantro	1 cup (4 ounces) shredded part-skim mozzarella cheese

Using long-handled tongs, dip a paper towel in cooking oil and lightly coat the grill rack. Grill steak, covered, over medium heat or broil 4 in. from the heat for 4 minutes on each side or until meat reaches desired doneness (for medium-rare, a meat thermometer should read 145°; medium, 160°; well-done, 170°). Let stand for 10 minutes.

Meanwhile, in a large skillet coated with cooking spray, saute peppers and onion for 5-6 minutes or until tender. Add garlic; cook 1 minute longer. Sprinkle with cilantro and rosemary.

Place two tortillas on a baking sheet coated with cooking spray. Cut steak into thin strips; place on tortillas. Using a slotted spoon, place pepper mixture over steak. Top with tomatoes, mushrooms, cheese and remaining tortillas; lightly coat tops of tortillas with cooking spray.

Bake at 425° for 5-10 minutes or until golden brown and cheese is melted. Cut each into four wedges. **YIELD: 16 APPETIZERS.**

BARBARA MOORE
FARMINGTON, NEW MEXICO

I came up with this savory snack when my family needed a quick lunch before running off in several directions. I threw together what I had in the fridge and it was a big hit!

HERBED CHEESE SPREAD
prep: 10 min. + chilling

1-1/2 cups (12 ounces) 4% cottage cheese	1-1/2 teaspoons minced fresh thyme or 1/2 teaspoon dried thyme
1 package (3 ounces) cream cheese, softened	3/4 teaspoon minced fresh basil or 1/4 teaspoon dried basil
1 tablespoon minced chives	3/4 teaspoon minced fresh savory or 1/4 teaspoon dried savory
1 tablespoon minced fresh parsley	1/8 to 1/4 teaspoon salt
	Assorted crackers

Place cottage cheese and cream cheese in a blender; cover and process until smooth. Transfer to a small bowl; stir in the chives, parsley, thyme, basil, savory and salt. Cover and chill for 2 hours. Serve with crackers. **YIELD: ABOUT 1-1/2 CUPS.**

SHIRLEY GLAAB
HATTIESBURG, MISSISSIPPI

This tasty herb spread is terrific on top of crackers or served with fresh veggies. Preparing it in the blender yields a creamy concoction.

SALADS

Add a bit of sunshine to the dinner table with these super easy, but marvelous salads. It just takes a few minutes to create one of these delicious and colorful recipes. You'll find a variety of fruit, vegetable and green salads on the following pages.

GREEN GRAPE SALAD | PAGE 41

GRILLED GREEK POTATO SALAD | PAGE 58

MARIE MELCHERT
LAS VEGAS, NEVADA

*I was given this delightful recipe
many years ago by my mother, who
said it was oh, so good! It's
very attractive, and you
can make it ahead.*

RUTH TURPIN
CINCINNATI, OHIO

*For over 30 years, this recipe has
been a holiday tradition in my
family. With marshmallows,
cranberries, apples and grapes,
it has a sweet-tart flavor and
comforting creaminess that appeals
to all ages.*

PERKY PARSLEYED TOMATOES

prep/total time: 25 min. + chilling

8	medium tomatoes	2	teaspoons Dijon mustard
1/4	cup olive oil		
1/4	cup minced fresh parsley	1	garlic clove, minced
		1	teaspoon salt
2	tablespoons tarragon *or* cider vinegar	1	teaspoon sugar
		1/4	teaspoon pepper

Cut a thin slice off the bottom of each tomato so it sits flat. Cut each tomato into 1/2-in. horizontal slices; reassemble tomatoes, stacking slices on top of each other. Place the stacks in a 13-in. x 9-in. dish.

In a small bowl, whisk the remaining ingredients. Pour over tomatoes. Cover and refrigerate for 4 hours or overnight. Remove from the refrigerator 20 minutes before serving. **YIELD: 8 SERVINGS.**

CREAMY CRANBERRY APPLE SALAD

prep/total time: 20 min. + chilling

1	package (12 ounces) fresh *or* frozen cranberries, thawed	1/2	cup halved seedless red grapes
		1/2	cup chopped walnuts
3	cups miniature marshmallows	1/4	teaspoon salt
1	cup sugar	1	carton (8 ounces) frozen whipped topping, thawed
2	medium apples, diced		

Coarsely chop the cranberries; place in a large bowl. Stir in the marshmallows and sugar. Cover and refrigerate for several hours or overnight.

Just before serving, stir in the apples, grapes, walnuts and salt. Fold in whipped topping. **YIELD: 8-10 SERVINGS.**

Fresh & Easy Tip

A crumpled paper towel is a great way to gently brush the silk from corn. It works better than any vegetable brush because the towel isn't abrasive to the kernels.

GRILLED CORN PASTA SALAD
prep: 20 min. + soaking | grill: 25 min. + cooling

4	large ears sweet corn in husks	1	tablespoon minced fresh basil *or* 1 teaspoon dried basil
1-1/2	cups uncooked penne pasta	1	teaspoon sugar
2	cups cherry tomatoes	1	teaspoon salt
1	medium zucchini, thinly sliced	1/2	teaspoon ground mustard
1	can (2-1/4 ounces) sliced ripe olives, drained	1/4	teaspoon garlic powder
1/3	cup white wine vinegar	1/4	teaspoon pepper
2	tablespoons olive oil		

Carefully peel back corn husks to within 1 in. of bottom; remove silk. Rewrap corn in husks and secure with kitchen string. Place in a large kettle; cover with cold water. Soak for 20 minutes; drain.

Grill corn, covered, over medium heat for 25-30 minutes or until tender, turning often.

Meanwhile, cook pasta according to package directions; drain and rinse in cold water. When corn is cool enough to handle, remove kernels from cobs and place in a large bowl. Add pasta, tomatoes, zucchini and olives.

In a small bowl, whisk the remaining ingredients. Pour over salad and toss gently to coat. Cover and refrigerate until serving. **YIELD: 8 SERVINGS.**

PEAR CHICKEN SALAD
prep/total time: 15 min.

6	cups spring mix salad greens
1	medium ripe pear, sliced
1-1/2	cups cooked chicken strips
1/4	cup crumbled feta cheese
1/4	cup dried cranberries
1/4	cup chopped walnuts *or* pecans

DRESSING:

1/4	cup olive oil
2	tablespoons orange juice
2	tablespoons white wine vinegar
1-1/2	teaspoons sugar
1/2	teaspoon grated orange peel
1/8	teaspoon salt

Dash pepper

On each of four salad plates, arrange the greens, pear, chicken, feta cheese, cranberries and nuts. In a small bowl, whisk the dressing ingredients; drizzle over salads. **YIELD: 4 SERVINGS.**

REBECCA BAIRD
SALT LAKE CITY, UTAH

This beautiful salad is sprinkled with feta cheese, sweetened cranberries and walnuts for extra depth of flavor and crunch.

ZUCCHINI BEAN SALAD
prep/total time: 30 min.

1	cup cut fresh green beans
1	can (16 ounces) kidney beans, rinsed and drained
1-1/2	cups thinly sliced halved zucchini
1	medium green pepper, julienned

3	green onions, thinly sliced
3	tablespoons cider vinegar
2	tablespoons canola oil
3/4	teaspoon sugar
3/4	teaspoon seasoned salt
1/4	teaspoon pepper

Place green beans in a small saucepan and cover with water. Bring to a boil; cover and cook for 8-10 minutes or until crisp-tender. Drain and immediately place in ice water; drain and pat dry.

In a large bowl, combine the green beans, kidney beans, zucchini, green pepper and onions. In a small bowl, whisk the vinegar, oil, sugar, seasoned salt and pepper. Pour over bean mixture; toss to coat. Cover and chill until serving. **YIELD: 6 SERVINGS.**

CAROL WAUGH
BELLINGHAM, WASHINGTON

A fun combination of good-for-you ingredients makes up this Zucchini Bean Salad. It's fresh and tangy, thanks to the light coating of vinaigrette. You can make this salad ahead and chill for a few hours before serving.

FROZEN FRUIT SLUSH

prep/total time: 10 min. + freezing

3	medium firm bananas, sliced	1	can (20 ounces) crushed pineapple, undrained
1/2	cup thawed lemonade concentrate	2	cups sugar
6	medium ripe peaches, peeled and cubed	1-1/3	cups seedless red grapes, halved
3	cups water	1	cup thawed orange juice concentrate

In a large bowl, stir the bananas and lemonade concentrate until coated. Stir in remaining ingredients. Cover and freeze for 8 hours or until firm.

Remove from the freezer 1 to 1-1/4 hours before serving so mixture becomes slushy. **YIELD: 12 SERVINGS.**

BRENDA BEACHY
BELVIDERE, TENNESSEE

Our family loves this refreshing fruit-filled salad—it's pretty enough to serve to company, too. The salad combines pineapple, bananas, grapes and peaches along with lemonade and orange juice concentrates. It's so good, you'll want seconds.

GRILLED ROMAINE SALAD

prep/total time: 20 min.

1/3	cup plus 3 tablespoons olive oil, *divided*	1/8	teaspoon salt
2	tablespoons white wine vinegar	6	green onions
1	tablespoon dill weed	4	plum tomatoes, halved
1/2	teaspoon garlic powder	1	large cucumber, peeled and halved lengthwise
1/8	teaspoon crushed red pepper flakes	2	romaine hearts

In a small bowl, whisk 1/3 cup oil, vinegar and seasonings. Set aside.

Brush the onions, tomatoes, cucumber and romaine with remaining oil. Grill the onions, tomatoes and cucumber, uncovered, over medium heat for 4-5 minutes on each side or until onions are crisp-tender. Grill romaine for 30 seconds on each side or until heated through.

Chop the vegetables; place in a large bowl. Whisk dressing and pour over salad; toss to coat. Serve immediately. **YIELD: 12 SERVINGS.**

TASTE OF HOME
TEST KITCHEN

For a great salad, try this recipe on the grill. Add any dressing of your choice to complete it!

DANA HERBERT
GOSHEN, UTAH

This hearty side makes a nice change-of-pace salad. It's crunchy, creamy and simply delicious. You'd never guess it's light!

PRISCILLA GILBERT
INDIAN HARBOR BEACH,
FLORIDA

This salad is so refreshing because of the juicy ripe melon. The dressing pairs well with spinach.

FRESH BROCCOLI SALAD

prep/total time: 20 min.

6	cups fresh broccoli florets	1-1/2	teaspoons sugar
1	can (8 ounces) sliced water chestnuts, drained	1-1/2	teaspoons cider vinegar
		1-1/2	teaspoons Dijon mustard
1/2	cup dried cranberries	1/4	teaspoon salt
1/4	cup chopped red onion	1/8	teaspoon pepper
3/4	cup reduced-fat mayonnaise	1/4	cup slivered almonds, toasted
3/4	cup fat-free plain yogurt		

In a large bowl, combine the broccoli, water chestnuts, cranberries and onion. In a small bowl, whisk the mayonnaise, yogurt, sugar, vinegar, mustard, salt and pepper. Pour over salad; toss to coat. Just before serving, sprinkle with almonds. **YIELD: 9 SERVINGS.**

MELON SALAD WITH POPPY SEED VINAIGRETTE

prep/total time: 25 min.

1	cup *each* cubed cantaloupe, honeydew and seedless watermelon	1/2	teaspoon salt
		1/4	teaspoon ground mustard
1/2	cup chopped cucumber	1/4	cup canola oil
2	tablespoons coarsely chopped fresh mint	1	tablespoon plain yogurt
2	tablespoons sugar	1	teaspoon poppy seeds
2	tablespoons white wine vinegar	4	cups fresh baby spinach

In a large bowl, combine the melon, cucumber and mint; cover and refrigerate until serving.

For vinaigrette, in a small saucepan, combine the sugar, vinegar, salt and mustard. Cook and stir over medium heat until sugar is dissolved. Cool. Transfer to a blender. While processing, gradually add oil in a steady stream. Stir in yogurt and poppy seeds.

Pour half of the vinaigrette over melon mixture; toss to coat. Arrange spinach on a serving platter; top with melon mixture. Drizzle with remaining vinaigrette. **YIELD: 4 SERVINGS.**

PRETTY PEPPER SALAD

prep/total time: 20 min.

2 medium green peppers, cut into rings	1 can (2-1/4 ounces) sliced ripe olives, drained
1 medium sweet yellow pepper, cut into rings	1/4 cup canola oil
1 medium sweet red pepper, cut into rings	3 tablespoons lemon juice
1 medium red onion, cut into rings	1/2 to 1 teaspoon minced fresh oregano
1 jar (6-1/2 ounces) marinated quartered artichoke hearts, drained	1/2 teaspoon sugar
	1/2 teaspoon salt
	1/4 to 1/2 teaspoon paprika

In a large bowl, combine the peppers, onion, artichokes and olives. In a small bowl, whisk the remaining ingredients. Pour over pepper mixture and toss to coat. Chill until serving. Serve with a slotted spoon. **YIELD: 9 SERVINGS.**

**COLETTE GEROW
RAYTOWN, MISSOURI**

This terrific salad goes great with grilled chicken or ribs. Use a variety of sweet bell peppers—they come in different colors.

TOSSED SALAD WITH CARROT DRESSING

prep/total time: 25 min.

3/4 cup red wine vinegar	**SALAD:**
1 cup sugar	8 cups spring mix salad greens
2 celery ribs, cut into chunks	2 medium tomatoes, cut into wedges
1 small onion, cut into chunks	1 medium cucumber, sliced
1 small carrot, cut into chunks	2 green onions, sliced
1/2 teaspoon salt	1/2 cup chow mein noodles
3/4 cup canola oil	1/2 cup shredded cheddar cheese
	1/2 cup dried cranberries

In a blender, combine first six ingredients; cover and process until smooth. While processing, gradually add the oil in a steady stream. Transfer to bowl or small pitcher; cover and refrigerate until serving.

In a large bowl, combine the salad ingredients. Stir dressing and serve with salad. Refrigerate leftover dressing. **YIELD: 10 SERVINGS (3 CUPS DRESSING).**

**DARLIS WILFER
WEST BEND, WISCONSIN**

We love going to the farmer's market on summer Saturdays to buy homegrown lettuce and produce for salads. I hope you'll try my special dressing made with pureed vegetables. I've received compliments on its flavor and pretty color.

TASTE OF HOME TEST KITCHEN

Let these whimsical parfaits celebrate the end of a work week and the beginning of a wonderful weekend! Watermelon, bananas and raspberries make for a flavorful and healthy treat.

BANANA SPLIT FRUIT SALAD
prep/total time: 20 min.

2	medium bananas		1	cup fresh raspberries
1/4	medium seedless watermelon		1/4	cup chopped walnuts
1	carton (6 ounces) vanilla custard-style yogurt			

Cut each banana in half widthwise. Cut each half into quarters lengthwise. Using an ice cream scoop, scoop four balls from watermelon (save remaining melon for another use).

Arrange four banana quarters in each shallow dessert bowl; top with watermelon. Spoon yogurt over melon. Sprinkle with raspberries and walnuts. Serve immediately. **YIELD: 4 SERVINGS.**

MILDRED SHERRER FORT WORTH, TEXAS

When I had a large vegetable garden, I had fun creating recipes, depending on what was ready for picking. This salad can be served even if you have another vegetable as a side dish.

COLORFUL VEGETABLE SALAD
prep/total time: 15 min. + chilling

3	cups fresh *or* frozen corn	**DRESSING:**		
1	can (15 ounces) black beans, rinsed and drained	1/4	cup olive oil
3	medium tomatoes, seeded and diced	3	tablespoons lime juice
1	cup chopped green pepper	2	tablespoons minced fresh cilantro
1	cup chopped sweet red pepper	1	garlic clove, minced
		1	teaspoon salt
		1/2	teaspoon pepper

In a large bowl, combine the first five ingredients. In a small bowl, whisk the dressing ingredients together. Pour over the vegetables and toss to coat. Cover and refrigerate for at least 2 hours before serving. **YIELD: 8 SERVINGS.**

GREEN GRAPE SALAD
prep/total time: 10 min.

1 cup green grapes, halved	1/4 cup blue cheese salad dressing
1 large firm banana, sliced	3 tablespoons mayonnaise
1/2 cup chopped walnuts	2 teaspoons honey

In a small bowl, combine grapes, banana and walnuts. In a small bowl, whisk the salad dressing, mayonnaise and honey; pour over the grape mixture and toss to coat. Chill until serving. **YIELD: 2 SERVINGS.**

**MARJORIE GREEN
SOUTH HAVEN, MICHIGAN**

This is an easy, great recipe for any time of the year. The sweetness of the fruit and the crunchy texture from the nuts, topped with blue cheese salad dressing, make for a tasty salad.

VEGGIE BOW TIE SALAD
prep/total time: 30 min.

2 cups uncooked bow tie pasta	1/4 cup unsalted sunflower kernels
2 cups fresh broccoli florets	1/4 cup minced fresh basil
1 cup fresh cauliflowerets	1/4 cup oil-packed sun-dried tomatoes, chopped, optional
1 medium sweet red pepper, chopped	**VINAIGRETTE:**
1/2 cup cherry tomatoes, halved	1/2 cup olive oil
1/2 cup chopped pitted green olives	1/4 cup balsamic vinegar
1 jar (4-1/2 ounces) marinated artichoke hearts, drained	2 tablespoons lemon juice
	1 teaspoon sugar
	1/2 teaspoon salt
	1/4 teaspoon pepper

Cook pasta according to package directions. Meanwhile, in a small saucepan, bring 1 in. of water to a boil. Add broccoli and cauliflower; cook for 2-3 minutes. Drain and immediately place vegetables in ice water; drain and pat dry. Drain pasta and rinse in cold water.

In a large salad bowl, combine the pasta, broccoli mixture, red pepper, cherry tomatoes, olives, artichokes, sunflower kernels, basil and sun-dried tomatoes if desired.

In a small bowl, whisk the vinaigrette ingredients. Pour over salad; toss to coat. Cover and refrigerate until serving. **YIELD: 9 SERVINGS.**

**ELEKTRA HARRIS
VANCOUVER,
BRITISH COLUMBIA**

Here's a special salad full of fresh vegetables, tender pasta and zippy, homemade vinaigrette dressing. It's a perfect accompaniment for lean meat or fish.

FRUIT 'N' SPINACH SALAD
prep/total time: 15 min.

1	pound fresh spinach, torn
4	cups whole strawberries, sliced
1	can (11 ounces) mandarin oranges, drained
1	star fruit, sliced

GINGER SALAD DRESSING:

1/3	cup lemon juice
2	tablespoons olive oil
2	tablespoons sugar
1	tablespoon minced fresh gingerroot
2	teaspoons grated lemon peel

Arrange spinach and fruit on salad plates. In a small bowl, whisk the dressing ingredients. Drizzle over salads. **YIELD: 4 SERVINGS.**

REBECCA BAIRD
SALT LAKE CITY, UTAH

A hint of fresh ginger in the dressing accents the fruits in this delightful salad.

PARSNIP CARROT SALAD
prep/total time: 25 min.

3	cups sliced peeled parsnips
3/4	cup sliced peeled carrots
3	tablespoons orange juice
1	tablespoon olive oil

1-1/2	teaspoons lemon juice
3/4	teaspoon Dijon mustard
3	tablespoons minced chives
3/4	teaspoon celery seed

Place the parsnips and carrots in a large saucepan; cover with water. Bring to a boil. Reduce heat; cover and simmer for 8-10 minutes or until crisp-tender. Meanwhile, in a small bowl, whisk the orange juice, oil, lemon juice and mustard until blended.

Drain vegetables; add orange juice mixture and toss to coat. Sprinkle with chives and celery seed. Serve warm. **YIELD: 4 SERVINGS.**

MARGE CAMPBELL
WAYMART, PENNSYLVANIA

Because my husband's garden produced an overabundance of parsnips, I experimented and came up with this combination that can be served as a sit-down appetizer, salad or side dish.

GRILLED STEAK TOSSED SALAD
prep/total time: 20 min.

4	cups Italian-blend salad greens	1/2	cup fresh whole kernel corn
1/2	pound cooked beef sirloin steak, thinly sliced	1/3	cup prepared balsamic vinaigrette
4	tomato wedges	1/4	cup shredded Romano cheese

In a large bowl, combine the salad greens, steak, tomato wedges and corn. Drizzle with vinaigrette and toss to coat; sprinkle with cheese. **YIELD: 2 SERVINGS.**

**WARREN PAULSON
MESA, ARIZONA**

My grandmother gave me this recipe. It's great for hot summer nights and takes only a few minutes to prepare.

BLUEBERRY CHICKEN SALAD
prep/total time: 15 min. + chilling

2	cups fresh blueberries	3/4	cup (6 ounces) lemon yogurt
2	cups cubed cooked chicken breast	3	tablespoons mayonnaise
3/4	cup chopped celery	1/2	teaspoon salt
1/2	cup diced sweet red pepper		Bibb lettuce leaves, optional
1/2	cup thinly sliced green onions		

Set aside a few blueberries for garnish. In a large bowl, gently combine the chicken, celery, red pepper, onions and remaining blueberries. Combine the yogurt, mayonnaise and salt; drizzle over chicken mixture and gently toss to coat.

Cover and refrigerate for at least 30 minutes. Serve on lettuce-lined plates if desired. Top with reserved blueberries. **YIELD: 4 SERVINGS.**

**KARI CAVEN
POST FALLS, IDAHO**

This excellent combination goes together quickly in the morning to take for lunch or makes a nice, light main-dish salad supper.

MILDRED SHERRER FORT WORTH, TEXAS

If your idea of tuna salad is laden with mayo, kick the can and make a tuna steak salad instead. The steaks are delicious on a bed of greens and can be easily replaced with another favorite fish.

DRESSED-UP TUNA SALAD

prep/total time: 30 min.

3	tablespoons plus 1/2 cup olive oil, *divided*	1	tablespoon Dijon mustard
3	tablespoons chopped shallots, *divided*	1-1/2	teaspoons sugar
1/2	teaspoon salt, *divided*	1	package (5 ounces) spring mix salad greens
1/4	teaspoon pepper, *divided*	1	cup cut fresh thin asparagus (1-inch pieces)
1	pound tuna steaks (1 inch thick)	1	cup grape tomatoes, halved
1/4	cup cider vinegar	2	tablespoons minced chives

In a large resealable plastic bag, combine 3 tablespoons oil, 1 tablespoon shallots, 1/4 teaspoon salt and 1/8 teaspoon pepper. Cut tuna steaks into quarters; add to bag. Seal and turn to coat; marinate for 10 minutes.

Meanwhile, for dressing, combine the vinegar, mustard, sugar, and remaining shallots, salt and pepper in a small bowl; slowly whisk in remaining oil. Set aside.

Drain and discard marinade. In a large nonstick skillet, cook tuna over medium heat for 4-5 minutes on each side for medium-rare or until slightly pink in the center.

On individual salad plates, arrange the greens, asparagus and tomatoes. Top with flaked tuna; drizzle with dressing. Sprinkle with chives. **YIELD: 4 SERVINGS.**

GREENS AND ROASTED BEETS

prep: 10 min. | bake: 1 hour + cooling

2	whole fresh beets	2	teaspoons orange juice concentrate
3	cups torn mixed salad greens	1/4	teaspoon ground mustard
1	can (11 ounces) mandarin oranges, drained	1/4	teaspoon dried thyme
		1/8	teaspoon pepper
2	tablespoons cider vinegar	5	teaspoons canola oil
		1	teaspoon sesame oil

Spray beets with cooking spray. Place in an ungreased 8-in. square baking dish. Cover and bake at 350° for 60-70 minutes or until tender; cool. Peel and cut into 1/2-in. cubes.

In a large salad bowl, combine the greens, beets and oranges. In a blender, combine vinegar, orange juice concentrate, mustard, thyme and pepper; cover and process until blended. While processing, gradually add canola oil and sesame oil. Drizzle over salad and toss to coat. **YIELD: 4 SERVINGS.**

TASTE OF HOME TEST KITCHEN

A refreshing from-scratch dressing tops off this colorful salad, featuring roasted beets, mixed greens and mandarin oranges. The dish is a dressy addition to any special-event menu you might have.

GINGERED GREEN BEAN SALAD

prep/total time: 30 min.

2	pounds fresh green beans, trimmed	2	tablespoons sesame oil
1	cup thinly sliced red onion, separated into rings	1	tablespoon minced fresh gingerroot
1	cup canned bean sprouts, rinsed and drained	1	tablespoon reduced-sodium soy sauce
VINAIGRETTE:		2	teaspoons sesame seeds, toasted
1/4	cup rice vinegar	1	teaspoon honey
		1/2	teaspoon minced garlic

Place green beans in a large saucepan and cover with water. Bring to a boil. Cook, uncovered, for 4-7 minutes or until crisp-tender. Drain and immediately place in ice water; drain and pat dry.

In a large salad bowl, combine the beans, onion and bean sprouts. In a small bowl, whisk the vinaigrette ingredients. Pour over bean mixture and toss to coat. **YIELD: 8 SERVINGS.**

TRISHA KRUSE EAGLE, IDAHO

This crisp summer salad keeps well in the refrigerator.

KIWI-STRAWBERRY SPINACH SALAD

prep/total time: 10 min.

- 12 cups torn fresh spinach
- 2 pints fresh strawberries, halved
- 4 kiwifruit, peeled and cut into 1/4-inch slices
- 1/4 cup canola oil
- 1/4 cup raspberry vinegar
- 1/4 teaspoon Worcestershire sauce
- 1/3 cup sugar
- 1/4 teaspoon paprika
- 2 green onions, chopped
- 2 tablespoons sesame seeds, toasted
- 1 tablespoon poppy seeds

In a large salad bowl, combine the spinach, strawberries and kiwi. In a blender, combine the oil, vinegar, Worcestershire sauce, sugar and paprika; cover and process for 30 seconds or until blended. Add the onions, sesame seeds and poppy seeds. Pour over salad; toss to coat. **YIELD: 12 SERVINGS.**

**LAURA POUNDS
ANDOVER, KANSAS**

This pretty salad is always a hit when I serve it! The recipe came from a cookbook, but I "doctored" it to accommodate my tastes. A small change in ingredients can make a big difference.

PEACHY TOSSED SALAD

prep/total time: 20 min.

- 1 package (10 ounces) ready-to-serve salad greens
- 1 to 2 medium peaches, cut into wedges
- 1/2 cup thinly sliced cucumber
- 1/2 cup crumbled feta cheese
- 1/4 cup thinly sliced red onion, separated into rings

CREAMY POPPY SEED DRESSING:
- 2/3 cup canola oil
- 1/4 cup sugar
- 1/4 cup white vinegar
- 1/4 cup sour cream
- 2 teaspoons poppy seeds
- 1/2 teaspoon salt

In a large salad bowl, combine the greens, peaches, cucumber, feta cheese and onion. In a small bowl, whisk the dressing ingredients. Serve with salad. **YIELD: 8 SERVINGS.**

**TONIA BOOKER
GILBERT, ARIZONA**

A sweet homemade dressing flecked with poppy seeds coats this green salad. The combination of sweet peaches, salty feta cheese, and crunchy onion and cucumber offers a delightful array of flavors.

GREEN SALAD WITH HERB VINAIGRETTE

prep/total time: 15 min. + chilling

2/3 cup canola oil	1 teaspoon dill weed
1/4 cup red wine vinegar	1/4 teaspoon pepper
1/4 cup minced fresh parsley	6 cups torn mixed salad greens
2 green onions, chopped	6 medium tomatoes, cut into wedges
1 garlic clove, minced	6 large fresh mushrooms, sliced
1 teaspoon salt	
1 teaspoon dried basil	

In a small bowl, whisk the first nine ingredients. Cover and refrigerate for at least 8 hours.

Divide the salad greens, tomatoes and mushrooms among eight salad plates. Whisk dressing; drizzle over salads. **YIELD: 8 SERVINGS.**

AMY SAUSER
OMAHA, NEBRASKA

My mother-in-law regularly makes this for birthdays and holiday dinners. It is best in the summer when fresh, locally grown tomatoes are available.

LAYERED TORTELLINI SALAD

prep/total time: 30 min. + chilling

1/2 cup buttermilk	6 cups fresh baby spinach
1/2 cup plain yogurt	1 block (8 ounces) part-skim mozzarella cheese, cubed
1/4 cup mayonnaise	
1 teaspoon sugar	1 cup cherry tomatoes, halved
1/4 teaspoon salt	
1/4 teaspoon dill weed	1 small red onion, thinly sliced
1/4 teaspoon dried basil	
1/8 teaspoon white pepper	8 bacon strips, cooked and crumbled
SALAD:	
1 package (9 ounces) refrigerated cheese tortellini	1/2 cup crumbled feta cheese
2 cups shredded red cabbage	

For dressing, place the first eight ingredients in a blender. Cover and process until blended; process 1-2 minutes longer or until smooth.

Cook the tortellini according to package directions. Drain and rinse in cold water.

In a large glass bowl, layer the cabbage, spinach and tortellini. Top with mozzarella cheese, tomatoes, onion, bacon and feta cheese. Cover and refrigerate for at least 3 hours. Drizzle with dressing; toss to coat. **YIELD: 12 SERVINGS (1-1/2 CUPS DRESSING).**

NITA RAUSCH
DALLAS, TEXAS

My tempting tortellini salad combines layers upon layers of textures, and its colors are amazing. It's perfect for a luncheon. Other cheese options are Havarti, fontina or even Monterey Jack.

FRUITED CABBAGE SALAD
prep/total time: 15 min. + chilling

4	cups shredded cabbage	1	can (20 ounces) pineapple tidbits
2	medium firm bananas, sliced	3	tablespoons mayonnaise
2	medium tangerines, peeled, sectioned and seeded		

In a large bowl, layer the cabbage, bananas and tangerines. Drain the pineapple, reserving 2 tablespoons of the juice. Place pineapple over tangerines.

In a small bowl, combine mayonnaise and reserved pineapple juice until smooth; drizzle over salad. Cover and refrigerate for at least 2 hours. Toss just before serving. **YIELD: 10-12 SERVINGS.**

**RITA RIAL
ROCHESTER,
NEW HAMPSHIRE**

This refreshing salad is a hit when I take it to summer picnics, family get-togethers, church suppers and potlucks.

BRUSSELS SPROUTS SALAD
prep/total time: 20 min.

1-1/2	pounds fresh brussels sprouts, trimmed and halved	1/2	teaspoon salt
2	green onions, chopped	1/2	teaspoon dried thyme
1/2	cup olive oil	1/4	teaspoon pepper
2	tablespoons lemon juice	1	large bunch red leaf lettuce or radicchio, torn
1	to 1-1/2 teaspoons Dijon mustard	2	tablespoons slivered almonds, toasted

Place 1 in. of water in a saucepan; add brussels sprouts. Bring to a boil. Reduce heat; cover and simmer for 8-10 minutes or until tender. Drain; rinse with cold water and pat dry. Place sprouts and onions in a bowl; set aside.

In a small bowl, whisk the oil, lemon juice, mustard, salt, thyme and pepper. Toss the lettuce with 2 tablespoons of dressing; place in a large shallow serving bowl. Pour the remaining dressing over brussels sprouts and toss to coat; mound on lettuce. Sprinkle with almonds. **YIELD: 6-8 SERVINGS.**

**NANCY KORONDAN
YORKVILLE, ILLINOIS**

My husband and I like brussels sprouts, so I'm always looking for new ways to use them. I most often serve this colorful salad with roast pork or duck.

RASPBERRY TOSSED SALAD

prep/total time: 10 min.

4	cups torn red leaf lettuce	1/4	cup pecan halves, toasted
1	package (5 ounces) spring mix salad greens	2	tablespoons 100% raspberry fruit spread, melted
1	cup fresh raspberries	2	tablespoons raspberry vinegar
1	cup sliced fresh mushrooms	2	tablespoons canola oil
1/2	cup julienned red onion	1/8	teaspoon salt
1/4	cup crumbled feta cheese		Dash pepper

In a large salad bowl, combine the first seven ingredients. In a small bowl, whisk the fruit spread, vinegar, oil, salt and pepper. Pour over salad and toss gently to coat. **YIELD: 8 SERVINGS.**

TASTE OF HOME TEST KITCHEN

Our home economists tossed together mixed greens, fresh raspberries, mushrooms, feta cheese and more in this pretty salad. Toasted pecan halves add fun crunch, and a homemade raspberry dressing adds a great flavor!

COLORFUL CAULIFLOWER SALAD

prep/total time: 20 min. + chilling

6	cups fresh cauliflowerets	1/2	cup sliced pimiento-stuffed olives
3	plum tomatoes, chopped	1/2	cup mayonnaise
1	cup thinly sliced green onions	12	bacon strips, cooked vand crumbled
1	cup (4 ounces) shredded cheddar cheese		

In a large bowl, combine the cauliflower, tomatoes, onions, cheese and olives. Add the mayonnaise; toss to coat. Cover and refrigerate for at least 1 hour. Just before serving, sprinkle with the bacon. **YIELD: 10 CUPS.**

DOROTHY JOINER WARSAW, MISSOURI

Bacon, cheese, tomatoes and olives really dress up plain old cauliflower. Even my husband had to admit this salad is simply delicious!

BERRY GELATIN MOLD
prep/total time: 15 min. + chilling

2	packages (3 ounces *each*) strawberry gelatin	1	cup *each* fresh blueberries, raspberries and sliced strawberries
2	cups boiling cranberry juice		Lettuce leaves
1-1/2	cups club soda, chilled		Additional mixed fresh berries, optional
1	teaspoon lemon juice		

In a large bowl, dissolve gelatin in boiling cranberry juice. Let stand for 10 minutes. Stir in the club soda and lemon juice; refrigerate for 45 minutes or until partially set.

Fold in berries. Pour into a 6-cup ring mold coated with cooking spray. Refrigerate for 4 hours or until set. Unmold the gelatin onto a lettuce-lined platter and fill the center with additional berries if desired. **YIELD: 8 SERVINGS.**

ANNE MARIE PAPINEAU
HANOVER, CONNECTICUT

This refreshing gelatin mold is delicious and always a big hit! For a patriotic buffet, I fill the center with frozen whipped topping, strawberries and blueberries for festive red-white-and-blue flair.

FRESH VEGETABLE SALAD
prep/total time: 15 min.

3	cups thinly sliced cucumbers	1/2	cup cider vinegar
3/4	cup chopped red onion	2	tablespoons sugar
1/2	cup *each* chopped green, sweet red and yellow peppers		

In a large serving bowl, combine the cucumbers, onion and peppers. In a small bowl, whisk vinegar and sugar. Pour over the vegetables; toss to coat. Refrigerate until serving. Serve with a slotted spoon. **YIELD: 6 SERVINGS.**

NANCEE MAYNARD
BOX ELDER, SOUTH DAKOTA

This crisp and colorful salad is an ideal way to use up extra produce. It's especially good on hot summer evenings. I've even added chopped zucchini for a little variety.

SHIRLEY JOAN HELFENBEIN LAPEER, MICHIGAN

There's plenty of crunch in this salad that's perfect for autumn when apples are ripe for picking. The simple milk and sugar dressing allows the fruit and veggie flavors to shine. You could use vanilla yogurt in place of the cooked dressing.

DUTCH APPLE SALAD

prep/total time: 30 min. + chilling

2 tablespoons all-purpose flour	2 large Red Delicious apples, chopped
1 tablespoon sugar	1/2 cup finely chopped celery
1 cup whole milk	1/2 cup seedless red grapes, quartered
1 egg	1/2 cup chopped walnuts, toasted
2 large Golden Delicious apples, chopped	

In a small heavy saucepan, combine the flour and sugar. Gradually whisk in milk until smooth. Cook and stir over medium-high heat until thickened and bubbly. Reduce heat; cook and stir 2 minutes longer. Remove from the heat. Stir a small amount of hot mixture into egg; return all to the pan, stirring constantly. Bring to a gentle boil; cook and stir 2 minutes longer. Remove from the heat. Transfer to a small bowl. Cool to room temperature without stirring. Cover surface of salad dressing with waxed paper; refrigerate until cooled.

Just before serving, combine the apples and celery in a large salad bowl. Drizzle with dressing; gently toss to coat. Sprinkle with grapes and walnuts. **YIELD: 8 SERVINGS.**

KATE SELNER
ST. PAUL, MINNESOTA

A colorful blend of apples, strawberries, peaches and pears simmers in a simple lemon-and-honey sauce for a fantastic fruit salad. Top off servings with low-fat vanilla yogurt, granola or try some of both.

DONNA NOEL
GRAY, MAINE

The old standby Waldorf salad is simply too good to let slip away! Here's a new slant featuring fresh fennel. Try Braeburn apples for a fresh, crisp taste.

FRESH FRUIT COMPOTE
prep: 10 min. | cook: 30 min. + chilling

1/2	medium lemon	1/3	cup apricot spreadable fruit
1/2	cup water	2	cups sliced strawberries
1/4	cup honey		
2	cups sliced peeled apples	1	cup seedless red grapes
2	cups sliced peeled peaches	7	tablespoons vanilla yogurt
1	cup sliced peeled pears		

Cut two 1-in.-long strips from lemon peel. Squeeze juice from lemon. In a large saucepan, combine the water, honey, lemon juice and lemon peel strips. Add the apples, peaches and pears. Bring to a boil. Reduce heat; cook, uncovered, for 15-20 minutes or until fruit is softened.

Remove from the heat; discard lemon peel. Using a slotted spoon, transfer fruit to a large bowl; discard poaching liquid. Stir in spreadable fruit, strawberries and grapes. Cover and refrigerate for 4 hours or overnight. Serve with a slotted spoon. Top each serving with yogurt. **YIELD: 7 SERVINGS.**

FENNEL WALDORF SALAD
prep/total time: 25 min.

1-1/2	cups sliced fennel bulb	1-1/2	teaspoons grated onion
1-1/2	cups sliced apples		
3	tablespoons fat-free mayonnaise	1/8	teaspoon salt
		1/3	cup chopped pecans, toasted
1-1/2	teaspoons fat-free milk		

In a large bowl, combine fennel and apples. In a small bowl, whisk the mayonnaise, milk, onion and salt. Pour over fennel mixture and toss to coat. Chill until serving; stir in pecans. **YIELD: 4 SERVINGS.**

FLAVORFUL RICE SALAD

prep/total time: 15 min. + chilling

1	can (15 ounces) black beans, rinsed and drained
1-1/2	cups cold cooked long grain rice
1-1/2	cups chopped fresh tomatoes (about 4 medium)
4	green onions, chopped
1	celery rib, chopped
1/2	cup chopped fresh spinach
2	tablespoons minced fresh cilantro
1/2	cup fat-free Italian salad dressing
1	cup (4 ounces) crumbled feta cheese

In a large bowl, combine the beans, rice, tomatoes, onions, celery, spinach and cilantro. Drizzle with dressing; toss to coat. Cover and refrigerate for 1 hour.

Just before serving, sprinkle with cheese. **YIELD: 6 SERVINGS.**

KIM COOK
DADE CITY, FLORIDA

I started with a basic bean, rice and onion medley and added veggies and a lighter dressing to make it healthier. You can substitute brown rice for the long grain if you like.

ROASTED ONION SALAD

prep: 20 min. | bake: 40 min. + cooling

3	large sweet onions, cut into 1/2-inch slices
1/4	cup plus 1/2 teaspoon olive oil, *divided*
4	garlic cloves
8	cups torn mixed salad greens
1	cup (4 ounces) crumbled blue cheese
1/2	cup chopped walnuts, toasted

DRESSING:

2	tablespoons white wine vinegar
2	shallots, quartered
1/4	cup minced fresh parsley
1/2	teaspoon crushed red pepper flakes
2/3	cup olive oil

Place onions in a 15-in. x 10-in. x 1-in. baking pan. Drizzle with 1/4 cup oil; toss to coat. Place garlic on a double thickness of heavy-duty foil. Drizzle with remaining oil. Wrap foil around garlic; place on baking pan with onions.

Bake at 400° for 40-45 minutes or until onions are lightly browned and garlic is tender, turning onions occasionally. Cool for 10-15 minutes.

In a large salad bowl, combine the greens, cheese and walnuts; top with onions.

For dressing, place vinegar and shallots in a blender; squeeze softened garlic into blender. Cover and pulse until blended. Add parsley and pepper flakes. Cover and process, gradually adding oil in a steady stream. Serve with salad. **YIELD: 8 SERVINGS.**

JANICE MITCHELL
AURORA, COLORADO

Try this impressive salad at your next dinner party or during the holidays. Roasting the onions and garlic creates a depth of flavor you just can't get with any other cooking method!

TRISHA KRUSE
EAGLE, IDAHO

This fresh-tasting salad is such a treat! I like to serve it in the summer when it's too hot to cook. You can also use it as a sandwich filling stuffed into a pita bread.

FAVORITE TURKEY SALAD

prep/total time: 20 min.

1	can (8 ounces) unsweetened pineapple chunks	1/3	cup chopped walnuts, toasted
2	cups cubed cooked turkey	3/4	cup mayonnaise
1	medium apple, thinly sliced	1	tablespoon brown sugar
1	cup seedless red *or* green grapes, halved	1	teaspoon curry powder
1	celery rib, thinly sliced	1/2	teaspoon salt
4	green onions, thinly sliced	16	radicchio *or* other lettuce leaves
		1/4	cup flaked coconut, toasted

Drain pineapple, reserving 2 tablespoons juice (save remaining juice for another use). In a large bowl, combine the pineapple, turkey, apple, grapes, celery, onions and walnuts.

In a small bowl, combine the mayonnaise, brown sugar, curry, salt and reserved pineapple juice. Fold into the turkey mixture. Spoon onto lettuce-lined plates and sprinkle with coconut. Serve immediately. **YIELD: 8 SERVINGS.**

HASEL KING
NACOGDOCHES, TEXAS

I combine spinach tortellini and carrots to bring color and variety to this tasty chilled pasta recipe. Italian dressing and fragrant basil add lively flavor with minimal effort.

CARROT TORTELLINI SALAD
prep/total time: 20 min. + chilling

1	package (9 ounces) refrigerated cheese-filled spinach tortellini	2/3	cup Italian salad dressing
		2	green onions, sliced
1	package (9 ounces) refrigerated cheese-filled tortellini	8	to 12 small fresh basil leaves
		1	tablespoon grated Parmesan cheese
2	medium carrots, thinly sliced	1/4	teaspoon pepper

Cook both types of tortellini according to package directions. Drain and rinse in cold water.

In a large bowl, combine the tortellini and remaining ingredients. Cover and refrigerate for 2 hours before serving, stirring occasionally. **YIELD: 7 SERVINGS.**

VEGGIE POTATO SALAD

prep: 20 min. | cook: 35 min. + standing

6	large potatoes (about 3 pounds)	2/3	cup chopped seeded peeled cucumber
1	cup Italian salad dressing	1	cup frozen peas, thawed
8	hard-cooked eggs, sliced	1	cup mayonnaise
1	bunch green onions, thinly sliced	2/3	cup sour cream
3	celery ribs, chopped	2	teaspoons prepared mustard
1	medium green pepper, chopped	1	teaspoon salt
		1/8	to 1/4 teaspoon pepper

Place potatoes in a Dutch oven and cover with water. Bring to a boil. Reduce heat. Cover and cook for 15-20 minutes or until tender. Cool for 15-20 minutes or until easy to handle.

Peel and dice potatoes into a large bowl. Add salad dressing; gently toss to coat. Let stand for 30 minutes.

Stir in the eggs, green onions, celery, green pepper, cucumber and peas. Combine the remaining ingredients. Add to potato mixture; gently toss to coat. **YIELD: 14 SERVINGS.**

**JAMES KORZENOWSKI
DEARBORN, MICHIGAN**

Growing up with a huge family of relatives, large gatherings were the norm. Mom always brought her "famous" potato salad, and now I'm carrying on the tradition.

CUCUMBER SALAD

prep/total time: 15 min.

1-1/2	cups thinly sliced cucumbers	1	teaspoon minced fresh parsley, *divided*
2	tablespoons sour cream	1	teaspoon snipped fresh dill, *divided*
2	tablespoons prepared ranch salad dressing	1	hard-cooked egg, sliced
1	green onion, chopped		

Arrange cucumbers on a serving plate. In a small bowl, combine the sour cream, salad dressing, onion, 1/2 teaspoon parsley and 1/2 teaspoon dill. Spoon over cucumbers. Garnish with egg slices and sprinkle with remaining parsley and dill. **YIELD: 2 SERVINGS.**

**YULIA BAGWELL
PHILADELPHIA,
PENNSYLVANIA**

This is a good salad for folks who are watching their weight because it's very light but filling. Go easy on the dressing so the natural goodness of the cucumbers shines through.

JENNIFER KLANN CORBETT, OREGON

After using fresh mozzarella for the first time, I tried to incorporate it into as many dishes as possible and came up with this salad. It has quickly become a mainstay at my house.

Fresh & Easy Tips

Greek olives, also known as kalamata olives, are dark eggplant in color, almond-shaped and range in size from 1/2 to 1 inch long. Kalamata olives are found packed in vinegar or olive oil.

TOMATO-CUCUMBER MOZZARELLA SALAD

prep/total time: 20 min. + chilling

3	medium tomatoes, chopped	1/3	cup olive oil
1	English cucumber, quartered and cut into 1/4-inch slices	2	tablespoons red wine vinegar
1	small green pepper, chopped	2	tablespoons balsamic vinegar
1/4	cup thinly sliced onions	1	teaspoon sugar
12	pitted Greek olives, sliced	1/2	teaspoon salt
2	tablespoons minced fresh parsley	1/2	teaspoon dried oregano
1	tablespoon minced fresh basil	1/4	teaspoon pepper
		4	ounces fresh mozzarella cheese, cubed

In a large bowl, combine the tomatoes, cucumber, green pepper, onions, olives, parsley and basil.

For dressing, in a small bowl, whisk the oil, vinegars, sugar, salt, oregano and pepper. Pour over salad and toss to coat.

Cover and refrigerate for at least 15 minutes. Just before serving, stir in cheese. Serve with a slotted spoon. **YIELD: 8 SERVINGS.**

TANGY ASPARAGUS POTATO SALAD
prep/total time: 25 min.

- 4 small red potatoes, cut into 1/4-inch wedges
- 1 pound fresh asparagus, trimmed
- 1 tablespoon Dijon mustard
- 1 tablespoon lemon juice
- 1/4 cup olive oil
- 2 tablespoons minced chives
- 1/8 teaspoon salt
- Dash pepper

Place potatoes in a large saucepan; cover with water. Bring to a boil; cook for 15-20 minutes or until tender.

Meanwhile, in a large skillet, bring 1/2 in. of water to a boil. Add asparagus; cover and boil for 3 minutes. Drain and immediately place asparagus in ice water. Drain and pat dry. Cut into 1-in. pieces.

Drain the potatoes and place in a large bowl; add the asparagus. In a small bowl, combine the mustard and lemon juice; whisk in the oil until combined. Add the chives, salt and pepper. Pour over the vegetables and toss to coat. Serve warm or at room temperature. **YIELD: 4 SERVINGS.**

DEBBIE KONIETZKI
NEENAH, WISCONSIN

I look forward to making this whenever asparagus season rolls around. The recipe has been a family favorite for years.

MIXED FRUIT WITH LEMON-BASIL DRESSING
prep/total time: 15 min.

- 2 tablespoons lemon juice
- 1/2 teaspoon sugar
- 1/4 teaspoon salt
- 1/4 teaspoon ground mustard
- 1/8 teaspoon onion powder
- Dash pepper
- 6 tablespoons olive oil
- 4-1/2 teaspoons minced fresh basil
- 1 cup cubed fresh pineapple
- 1 cup sliced fresh strawberries
- 1 cup sliced peeled kiwifruit
- 1 cup cubed seedless watermelon
- 1 cup fresh blueberries
- 1 cup fresh raspberries

In a blender, combine the lemon juice, sugar, salt, mustard, onion powder and pepper; cover and process for 5 seconds. While processing, gradually add oil in a steady stream. Stir in basil.

In a large bowl, combine the fruit. Drizzle with dressing and toss to coat. Refrigerate until serving. **YIELD: 8 SERVINGS.**

DIXIE TERRY
GOREVILLE, ILLINOIS

A slightly savory dressing really complements the sweet fruit in this recipe. I also use the dressing on salad greens.

ROBIN JUNGERS
CAMPBELLSPORT,
WISCONSIN

My most requested summer recipe, this salad is wonderful served warm, cold or at room temperature. It's dressed with a vinaigrette, not mayonnaise, so it's ideal for outdoor occasions.

TASTE OF HOME
TEST KITCHEN

This refreshing salad pairs well with roasted meats and poultry. The avocado, red onion and garlic-mustard dressing complement the tart fruit just beautifully.

GRILLED GREEK POTATO SALAD

prep: 30 min. | grill: 20 min.

3 pounds small red potatoes, halved	1-1/4 cups grape tomatoes, halved
2 tablespoons olive oil	1/2 pound fresh mozzarella cheese, cubed
1/2 teaspoon salt	3/4 cup Greek vinaigrette
1/4 teaspoon pepper	1/2 cup halved Greek olives
1 large sweet yellow pepper, chopped	1 can (2-1/4 ounces) sliced ripe olives, drained
1 large sweet red pepper, chopped	2 tablespoons minced fresh oregano *or* 1 teaspoon dried oregano
1 medium red onion, halved and sliced	
1 medium cucumber, chopped	

Drizzle potatoes with oil and sprinkle with salt and pepper; toss to coat. Grill potatoes, covered, over medium heat or broil 4 in. from the heat for 20-25 minutes or until tender.

Place in a large bowl. Add the remaining ingredients; toss to coat. Serve salad warm or cold. **YIELD: 16 SERVINGS (3/4 CUP EACH).**

 # GRAPEFRUIT AVOCADO SALAD

prep/total time: 15 min.

1/4 cup olive oil	Freshly ground pepper to taste
2 tablespoons lemon juice	Lettuce leaves
2 tablespoons orange juice	2 large red grapefruit, peeled and sectioned
1 teaspoon Dijon mustard	1 small red onion, thinly sliced and separated into rings
1 garlic clove, minced	1 medium ripe avocado, peeled and sliced
1/2 teaspoon salt	

In a small bowl, whisk the first seven ingredients. On four salad plates, arrange the lettuce, grapefruit, onion, and avocado. Drizzle with the dressing. **YIELD: 4 SERVINGS.**

RANCH COLESLAW
prep/total time: 15 min.

3	cups coleslaw mix	1/2	cup shredded cheddar cheese
1/4	cup Mexicorn, drained	1/2	cup ranch salad dressing
1	jalapeno pepper, seeded and chopped	1-1/2	teaspoons lime juice
2	tablespoons chopped red onion	1/2	teaspoon ground cumin
1	tablespoon minced fresh cilantro		

In a large bowl, combine the first six ingredients. In a small bowl, whisk the salad dressing, lime juice and cumin. Pour over the coleslaw; toss to coat. Refrigerate until serving. **YIELD: 6 SERVINGS.**

EDITOR'S NOTE: When cutting hot peppers, disposable gloves are recommended. Avoid touching your face.

LAUREL LESLIE
SONORA, CALIFORNIA

Lime and cilantro add refreshing accents to this tangy, yummy slaw. It's perfect for a summer get-together.

WARM ASPARAGUS-SPINACH SALAD
prep/total time: 30 min.

1-1/2	pounds fresh asparagus, trimmed and cut into 1-inch pieces	6	tablespoons white wine vinegar
2	tablespoons plus 1/2 cup olive oil, *divided*	2	tablespoons soy sauce
1/4	teaspoon salt	1	package (6 ounces) fresh baby spinach
1-1/2	pounds uncooked penne pasta	1	cup coarsely chopped cashews
3/4	cup chopped green onions	1/2	cup shredded Parmesan cheese

Place the asparagus in a 13-in. x 9-in. baking dish. Drizzle with 2 tablespoons oil; sprinkle with salt. Bake, uncovered, at 400° for 8-10 minutes or until crisp-tender, stirring after 5 minutes. Meanwhile, cook pasta according to package directions; drain.

For dressing, combine onions, vinegar and soy sauce in a blender; cover and process. While processing, gradually add the remaining oil in a steady steam.

In a large salad bowl, combine pasta, spinach and asparagus. Drizzle with dressing; toss to coat. Sprinkle with cashews and Parmesan cheese. **YIELD: 12 SERVINGS.**

KATHLEEN LUCAS
TRUMBULL, CONNECTICUT

Fresh spinach, crunchy cashews and penne pasta are tossed with roasted asparagus to create this delightful spring salad.

SOUPS

The perfect chill chaser when days turn gray, a piping hot bowl of soup is sure to warm the heart and soothe the soul. Best of all, soups and chowders make it easy to enjoy a harvest of seasonal produce no matter what time of year.

FRESH CORN AND TOMATO SOUP | PAGE 67

CARROT BROCCOLI SOUP | PAGE 71

ELAINE KRUPSKY
LAS VEGAS, NEVADA

Chock-full of veggies, ham and cheese in every spoonful, this thick, creamy chowder will take the chill off even the nippiest of autumn evenings. I like to serve the soup with crusty French bread.

DAWN ROHN
RIVERTON, WYOMING

This is my family's favorite soup, and I can have it on the table in 30 minutes. I like to double the recipe so there are leftovers. The next day, the soup is even better because the flavors had time to blend.

MUSHROOM CORN CHOWDER
prep/total time: 30 min.

1-1/4 cups sliced fresh carrots	1-1/3 cups whole milk
1 cup chopped celery with leaves	1-1/2 cups frozen corn, thawed
3/4 cup sliced fresh mushrooms	1/2 cup cubed fully cooked ham
3 green onions, sliced	1/2 teaspoon seasoned salt
1/4 cup butter, cubed	1/2 cup cubed process cheese (Velveeta)
1 can (10-3/4 ounces) condensed cream of mushroom soup, undiluted	

In a large saucepan, saute the carrots, celery, mushrooms and onions in butter until tender. Stir in the soup, milk, corn, ham and seasoned salt. Bring to a boil. Reduce the heat; stir in cheese. Cook and stir 3-5 minutes longer or until cheese is melted. **YIELD: 8 SERVINGS.**

SAUSAGE AND KALE SOUP
prep: 15 min. | cook: 25 min.

3 medium Yukon Gold *or* red potatoes, chopped	1 can (14-1/2 ounces) diced tomatoes, undrained
2 medium onions, chopped	1 can (15 ounces) garbanzo beans *or* chickpeas, rinsed and drained
2 tablespoons olive oil	
1 bunch kale, trimmed and torn	1 pound smoked kielbasa *or* Polish sausage, cut into 1/4-inch slices
4 garlic cloves, minced	
1/4 teaspoon pepper	1 carton (32 ounces) chicken broth
1/4 teaspoon salt	
2 bay leaves	

In a Dutch oven over medium-low heat, cook potatoes and onions in oil for 5 minutes, stirring occasionally. Add kale and garlic; cover and cook for 2-3 minutes or until kale is wilted.

Add the remaining ingredients. Bring to a boil. Reduce heat; cover and simmer for 9-12 minutes or until the potatoes are tender. Discard the bay leaves. **YIELD: 14 SERVINGS (3-1/2 QUARTS).**

**MARIE HATTRUP
THE DALLES,
OREGON**

*If you're looking
for something
special to fix on
a holiday, look
no further. This
velvety soup is
accented with
tarragon, and
the toasted bread
topped with
melted Brie is the
crowning touch.*

LEEK SOUP WITH BRIE TOASTS

prep: 15 min. | cook: 25 min.

6	medium leeks (white portion only), thinly sliced	7-1/2	teaspoons all-purpose flour
1/2	pound sliced fresh mushrooms	4	cups chicken broth
1/2	teaspoon dried tarragon	1/2	cup heavy whipping cream
1/4	teaspoon white pepper	12	slices French bread *or* bread of your choice (1/2 inch thick)
2	tablespoons plus 6 teaspoons butter, softened, *divided*	1	round (8 ounces) Brie cheese, cut into 1/4-inch slices
1	garlic clove, minced		

In a Dutch oven, saute the leeks, mushrooms, tarragon and pepper in 2 tablespoons butter for 8-10 minutes or until vegetables are tender. Add garlic; cook 1 minute longer. Stir in flour until blended; gradually add broth and cream. Bring to a boil; cook and stir for 2 minutes or until thickened.

Place bread slices on an ungreased baking sheet. Broil 3-4 in. from the heat for 1-2 minutes or until golden brown. Spread one side of each slice with 1/2 teaspoon butter. Place Brie on buttered side of toasts.

Broil 3-4 in. from the heat for 1-2 minutes or until the cheese is melted. Ladle soup into six 8-oz. bowls; place two toasts in each bowl. **YIELD: 6 SERVINGS.**

SARAH TRAVIS
EDINA, MINNESOTA

Fresh basil perks up the flavor in this creamy from-scratch tomato soup. My aunt gave me the recipe years ago, and it's been one of my favorites ever since.

JENNIFER BLACK
SAN JOSE, CALIFORNIA

Cooking with vegetables is quick and healthy. This meatless soup makes a great dinner with a salad or slice of bread.

BASIL TOMATO SOUP

prep: 20 min. | cook: 20 min.

1	medium onion, chopped	1/4	teaspoon salt
1	medium carrot, shredded	1/8	teaspoon coarsely ground pepper
1-1/2	teaspoons butter	1/4	cup loosely packed fresh basil leaves
4	medium tomatoes, peeled and seeded	1	cup reduced-sodium chicken broth *or* vegetable broth
1/4	teaspoon sugar		

In a small saucepan, saute onion and carrot in butter until tender. Stir in the tomatoes, sugar, salt and pepper. Bring to a boil. Reduce heat; cover and simmer for 10 minutes. Cool slightly.

Transfer to a blender; add the basil. Cover and process until smooth. Return to pan; stir in broth and heat through. **YIELD: 2 SERVINGS.**

GARDEN VEGETABLE SOUP

prep: 25 min. | cook: 20 min.

1-1/2	teaspoons minced garlic	1/2	cup thinly sliced fresh carrots
2	tablespoons olive oil	1	teaspoon salt
1/4	cup uncooked long grain rice	1/2	teaspoon dried basil
2	cans (14-1/2 ounces *each*) chicken broth	1/4	teaspoon dried rosemary, crushed
1	cup chopped sweet red pepper		Dash pepper
1	cup chopped green pepper	2	medium zucchini, sliced
		6	plum tomatoes, chopped

In a large saucepan, cook the garlic in oil for 1 minute. Stir in the rice; cook and stir for 1 minute. Add the broth, peppers, carrots and seasonings. Bring to a boil. Reduce the heat; cover and simmer for 15-20 minutes or until rice is tender.

Stir in zucchini and tomatoes; cook for 3 minutes. Cool. Transfer to freezer containers. May be frozen for up to 3 months.

To serve immediately, cook soup 3-5 minutes longer or until zucchini is tender. **YIELD: 8 SERVINGS (2 QUARTS).**

TO USE FROZEN SOUP: Thaw the soup in the refrigerator overnight. Transfer to a saucepan. Cover and cook over medium heat until it is heated through.

CURRIED TURKEY VEGETABLE SOUP

prep: 15 min. | cook: 20 min.

2 medium onions, chopped	2 tablespoons minced fresh parsley
2 tablespoons canola oil	1-1/2 teaspoons minced fresh sage
2 to 3 tablespoons all-purpose flour	2 cups cubed cooked turkey breast
1 teaspoon curry powder	1-1/2 cups fat-free half-and-half cream
3 cups reduced-sodium chicken broth	1 package (9 ounces) fresh baby spinach, coarsely chopped
1 cup diced red potatoes	
1 celery rib, sliced	1/4 teaspoon salt
1/2 cup thinly sliced fresh carrots	1/4 teaspoon pepper

In a Dutch oven, saute onions in oil until tender. Stir in flour and curry until blended. Gradually stir in the broth. Add the potatoes, celery, carrots, parsley and sage. Bring to a boil. Reduce heat; cover and simmer for 10-12 minutes or until vegetables are tender.

Stir in the turkey, half-and-half, spinach, salt and pepper. Cook and stir until the spinach is wilted and the soup is heated through. **YIELD: 6 SERVINGS (2 QUARTS).**

**VIRGINIA ANTHONY
JACKSONVILLE, FLORIDA**

Chock-full of veggies, this aromatic soup has just the right hint of curry. It's a delicious way to use your leftover holiday turkey.

CREAMY ZUCCHINI SOUP

prep: 10 min. | cook: 25 min.

2 tablespoons chopped onion	1/2 teaspoon salt
3 tablespoons butter	1/4 teaspoon pepper
3 tablespoons all-purpose flour	1 large zucchini, shredded
2 cups whole milk	1 cup (4 ounces) shredded cheddar cheese
1 cup water	
1 teaspoon chicken bouillon granules	

In a large saucepan, saute onion in butter until tender. Stir in the flour until blended. Gradually stir in the milk, water, bouillon, salt and pepper. Bring to a boil; cook and stir for 2 minutes or until thickened. Add zucchini. Simmer, uncovered, for 10 minutes or until zucchini is tender. Stir in cheese until melted. **YIELD: 4 SERVINGS.**

**MRS. THOMAS MAUST
BERLIN, PENNSYLVANIA**

One day I decided to try a new recipe that called for zucchini, and my family really liked the results.

JANET ONDRICH THAMESVILLE, ONTARIO

The fennel in this bisque is so refreshing— I usually serve it in the spring as a side dish.

Fresh & Easy Tip

Fennel is an aromatic herb with a large pale green bulb, celery-like stems and feathery leaves. Uncooked fennel has a mild licorice flavor and is crunchy. Cooked fennel has a delicate flavor and soft texture.

GARLIC FENNEL BISQUE
prep: 30 min. | cook: 40 min.

4	cups water	2	tablespoons chopped fennel fronds
2-1/2	cups half-and-half cream	1/2	teaspoon salt
24	garlic cloves, peeled and halved	1/8	teaspoon pepper
3	medium fennel bulbs, cut into 1/2-inch pieces	1/2	cup pine nuts, toasted

In a Dutch oven, bring the water, cream and garlic to a boil. Reduce heat; cover and simmer for 15 minutes or until garlic is very soft. Add fennel and fennel fronds; cover and simmer 15 minutes longer or until fennel is very soft.

Cool slightly. In a blender, process soup in batches until blended. Return all to the pan. Season with salt and pepper; heat through. Sprinkle each serving with pine nuts. **YIELD: 14 SERVINGS.**

ZIPPY CHICKEN MUSHROOM SOUP

prep: 15 min. | cook: 25 min.

1/2	pound fresh mushrooms, chopped		Pinch dried tarragon
1/4	cup *each* chopped onion, celery and carrot	1/2	teaspoon hot pepper sauce
1/4	cup butter, cubed	3	cups half-and-half cream
1/2	cup all-purpose flour	2-1/2	cups cubed cooked chicken
5-1/2	cups chicken broth	1	tablespoon minced fresh parsley
1	teaspoon pepper	1-1/2	teaspoons lemon juice
1/2	teaspoon white pepper	1/2	teaspoon salt
1/4	teaspoon dried thyme		

In a Dutch oven, saute the mushrooms, onion, celery and carrot in butter until tender. Stir in flour until blended. Gradually add the broth and seasonings. Bring to a boil. Reduce heat; simmer, uncovered, for 10 minutes.

Stir in the cream, chicken, parsley, lemon juice and salt; heat through (do not boil). **YIELD: 11 SERVINGS (2-3/4 QUARTS).**

JULIA THORNELY
LAYTON, UTAH

My sister-in-law telephoned me because she was looking for a good cream of mushroom soup recipe. I gave her this one, which gets its boost from a splash of pepper sauce.

FRESH CORN AND TOMATO SOUP

prep: 30 min. | cook: 30 min.

1	celery rib, chopped	1/2	teaspoon salt
1	small onion, chopped	1/8	teaspoon white pepper
1/4	cup chopped green pepper	2	cups fresh sweet corn
2	tablespoons butter	1	tablespoon minced fresh basil
4	cups chopped seeded peeled tomatoes	2	tablespoons minced fresh parsley
2	cups chicken broth	1	green onion, finely chopped
1	teaspoon sugar		

In a large saucepan, saute celery, onion and green pepper in butter until tender. Stir in tomatoes and broth. Bring to a boil. Reduce heat; cover and simmer for 20 minutes.

Press through a sieve or food mill; return to the pan. Add the sugar, salt and white pepper. Bring to a boil. Stir in corn and basil. Reduce the heat; simmer, uncovered, for 3-5 minutes or until corn is tender. Garnish with parsley and green onion. **YIELD: 6 SERVINGS.**

CLYDA CONRAD
YUMA, ARIZONA

This light, fresh soup is excellent. Pressing the tomatoes, celery, onion and green pepper through a sieve offers silky smoothness and lets the corn flavor stand out nicely.

STRAWBERRY SOUP
prep/total time: 15 min.

1	pound fresh strawberries	2	tablespoons orange juice concentrate
1-1/4	cups vanilla yogurt, *divided*	1/8	teaspoon almond extract *or* 1/2 teaspoon lemon juice
3	tablespoons confectioners' sugar		

In a food processor, combine strawberries, 1 cup yogurt, confectioners' sugar, orange juice concentrate and extract; cover and process until blended. Garnish each serving with a dollop of remaining yogurt. **YIELD: 3 SERVINGS.**

PHYLLIS HAMMES
ROCHESTER, MINNESOTA

I enjoyed a cool berry soup at a restaurant several years ago. Although the manager wouldn't give me amounts, he did list the ingredients. I tinkered around with variations until I came up with this refreshing rendition.

TWO-BEAN CHILI
prep: 40 min. | cook: 8 hours

1/2	pound sliced fresh mushrooms	1	can (16 ounces) red beans, rinsed and drained
1	large green pepper, chopped	1	can (15 ounces) black beans, rinsed and drained
1	large sweet red pepper, chopped	1	large carrot, chopped
2	celery ribs, chopped	1/2	cup water
1	medium onion, chopped	1/2	cup barbecue sauce
1	jalapeno pepper, seeded and chopped	1/4	cup chili powder
1	tablespoon olive oil	1	teaspoon Liquid Smoke, optional
4	garlic cloves, minced		
2	teaspoons ground cumin		
1	teaspoon dried oregano		
1	can (28 ounces) diced tomatoes, undrained		

OPTIONAL TOPPINGS:
Reduced-fat sour cream, hot pepper sauce, shredded cheddar cheese, chopped onion *and/or* crushed baked tortilla chip scoops

In a large skillet over medium heat, cook and stir mushrooms, peppers, celery, onion and jalapeno in oil until onion is lightly browned. Add the garlic, cumin and oregano; cook and stir 1 minute longer.

Transfer to a 5-qt. slow cooker. Stir in the tomatoes, beans, carrot, water, barbecue sauce, chili powder and Liquid Smoke if desired. Cover and cook on low for 8 hours or until vegetables are tender. Serve with sour cream, pepper sauce, cheese, onion and/or chips if desired. **YIELD: 6 SERVINGS (2 QUARTS).**

EDITOR'S NOTE: When cutting hot peppers, disposable gloves are recommended. Avoid touching your face.

RONALD JOHNSON
ELMHURST, ILLINOIS

The first time I had this chili at a Super Bowl party, I was eating my second bowl before I realized it had no meat! It's so hearty and chock-full of flavor that it's hard to believe it's meatless.

**SANDY LUND
BROOKINGS,
SOUTH DAKOTA**

I put together this appetizing soup almost every Sunday during our long, cold winters. Roasted vegetables and turkey meatballs perk up the broth. What a wonderful way to warm up!

ROASTED VEGGIE AND MEATBALL SOUP

prep: 45 min. | cook: 50 min.

5	medium red potatoes, cubed
4	large carrots, cut into 1/2-inch slices
1	large red onion, halved and cut into wedges
4	tablespoons canola oil, *divided*
1-1/4	teaspoons salt, *divided*
3	tablespoons minced fresh basil
3	garlic cloves, crushed
1	egg, lightly beaten
1/2	cup seasoned bread crumbs
1/4	cup grated Parmesan cheese
1/4	cup minced fresh parsley
1/2	teaspoon pepper
1	pound ground turkey
1	carton (32 ounces) reduced-sodium chicken broth
2	cups water
1	can (14-1/2 ounces) diced tomatoes, undrained

In a large bowl, combine the potatoes, carrots, onion, 2 tablespoons oil and 1/2 teaspoon salt. Place in a single layer in two greased 15-in. x 10-in. x 1-in. baking pans. Bake at 425° for 20 minutes. Add basil and garlic; toss to coat. Bake 10-15 minutes longer or until vegetables are tender.

In a large bowl, combine egg, bread crumbs, cheese, parsley, 1/2 teaspoon salt and pepper. Crumble turkey over mixture and mix well. Shape into 1-in. balls. In a Dutch oven, brown meatballs in remaining oil in batches; drain and set aside.

In the same pan, combine the broth, water, tomatoes, roasted vegetables and remaining salt. Return meatballs to pan. Bring to a boil. Reduce heat; cover and simmer for 45-55 minutes or until meatballs are no longer pink. **YIELD: 8 SERVINGS (3 QUARTS).**

CURRIED CARROT SOUP
prep: 15 min. | cook: 30 min.

1	large onion, chopped	1	bay leaf
2	teaspoons sesame oil	1	package (3 ounces) cream cheese, cubed
5	cups vegetable broth		
4	medium carrots, grated (about 1-3/4 cups)	5	tablespoons minced fresh parsley
1-1/2	teaspoons curry powder	1/4	teaspoon salt
1	teaspoon dried thyme		Dash cayenne pepper, optional

In a large saucepan, saute onion in oil. Stir in the broth, carrots, curry, thyme and bay leaf. Bring to a boil. Reduce heat; simmer, uncovered, for 25-30 minutes or until carrots are tender.

Discard bay leaf. Cool slightly. Transfer half of the soup to a blender; add half of the cream cheese.

Cover and process until smooth; repeat with remaining soup and cream cheese. Return all to the pan. Heat through. Stir in the parsley, salt and cayenne if desired. **YIELD: 4 SERVINGS.**

BETSY HEDEMAN
TIMONIUM, MARYLAND

This pretty pureed soup is perfect for a luncheon. It has wonderful flavor sparked by curry, herbs and, of course, the colorful carrots.

ROASTED RED PEPPER BISQUE
prep: 30 min. + standing | cook: 20 min.

8	medium sweet red peppers	2	cups half-and-half cream
1	large onion, chopped	1/2	teaspoon salt
2	tablespoons butter	1/2	teaspoon white pepper
3	cups chicken broth, *divided*	6	tablespoons shredded Parmesan cheese, *divided*

Broil peppers 4 in. from the heat until skins blister, about 5 minutes. With tongs, rotate peppers a quarter turn. Broil and rotate until all sides are blistered and blackened. Immediately place peppers in a large bowl; cover and let stand for 15-20 minutes.

Peel off and discard the charred skin. Remove stems and seeds; set peppers aside.

In a large saucepan, saute onion in butter until tender; cool slightly. In a blender, combine the onion mixture, 2 cups broth and roasted peppers; cover and process until smooth. Return to the pan.

Stir in cream and remaining broth; heat through (do not boil). Stir in salt and pepper. Sprinkle each serving with 1 tablespoon Parmesan cheese. **YIELD: 6 SERVINGS (2 QUARTS).**

MARY ANN ZETTLEMAIER
CHELSEA, MICHIGAN

Folks are sure to comment about the awesome roasted red pepper taste in this velvety soup. It's a fantastic first course for special occasions or even alongside sandwiches.

MEAT AND POTATO SOUP
prep/total time: 30 min.

4	cups water	2	teaspoons cider vinegar
3	cups cubed cooked beef chuck roast	1	teaspoon brown sugar
4	medium red potatoes, cubed	1	teaspoon Worcestershire sauce
4	ounces sliced fresh mushrooms	1/8	teaspoon ground mustard
1/2	cup chopped onion	1	cup coarsely chopped fresh spinach
1/4	cup ketchup		
2	teaspoons beef bouillon granules		

In a Dutch oven, combine the first 11 ingredients. Bring to a boil. Reduce heat; cover and simmer for 14-18 minutes or until potatoes are tender. Stir in spinach; cook 1-2 minutes longer or until tender. **YIELD: 6 SERVINGS (2 QUARTS).**

TASTE OF HOME TEST KITCHEN

Potatoes and roast beef come together in this rich and hearty soup. The result is a well-balanced, flavorful dish terrific for fall.

CARROT BROCCOLI SOUP
prep: 15 min. | cook: 20 min.

1	medium onion, chopped	3	cups fat-free milk, *divided*
2	medium carrots, chopped	3/4	teaspoon salt
2	celery ribs, chopped	1/2	teaspoon dried thyme
1	tablespoon butter	1/8	teaspoon pepper
3	cups fresh broccoli florets	3	tablespoons all-purpose flour

In a large saucepan coated with cooking spray, cook onion, carrots and celery in butter for 3 minutes. Add the broccoli; cook 3 minutes longer. Stir in 2-3/4 cups milk, salt, thyme and pepper.

Bring to a boil. Reduce heat; cover and simmer for 5-10 minutes or until vegetables are tender. Combine the flour and remaining milk until smooth; gradually stir into soup. Bring to a boil; cook 2 minutes longer or until thickened. **YIELD: 4 SERVINGS.**

SANDY SMITH LONDON, ONTARIO

This soup is a staple at my house. It's easy, fast, nutritious and oh-so yummy!

STONE SOUP

prep: 15 min. | cook: 40 min.

4	cans (14-1/2 ounces *each*) chicken broth	1/2	teaspoon pepper
4	medium red potatoes, cut into eighths	4	cups cubed cooked chicken
1	yellow summer squash, chopped	1	cup frozen cut green beans
2	medium carrots, chopped	1/2	cup quick-cooking barley
1	medium onion, chopped	1	can (14-1/2 ounces) diced tomatoes, undrained
2	celery ribs, chopped	4	cups salad croutons
1	teaspoon dried thyme	1	cup shredded Parmesan cheese

In a Dutch oven, combine the first eight ingredients. Bring to a boil. Reduce heat; cover and simmer for 10-15 minutes or until vegetables are crisp-tender.

Stir in the chicken, beans and barley. Bring to a boil. Reduce heat; cover and simmer for 10-12 minutes or until vegetables and barley are tender. Add tomatoes; heat through. Serve with croutons and cheese. **YIELD: 12 SERVINGS.**

TASTE OF HOME TEST KITCHEN

After reading the Stone Soup folktale, we enjoyed concocting this version based on the classic story. It's a hearty recipe that is full of vegetables and other wonderful ingredients.

ELISABETH HARDERS WEST ALLIS, WISCONSIN

To us, asparagus is the taste of spring, so we enjoy it in as many meals as we can. When this thick and creamy chowder is on the table, we know spring has arrived.

ASPARAGUS LEEK CHOWDER

prep/total time: 20 min.

1	pound fresh asparagus, trimmed and cut into 1-inch pieces	1/2	teaspoon salt
		Dash pepper	
3	cups sliced fresh mushrooms	2	cups chicken broth
3	large leeks (white portion only), sliced	2	cups half-and-half cream
6	tablespoons butter	1	can (11 ounces) whole kernel corn, drained
1/4	cup all-purpose flour	1	tablespoon chopped pimientos

In a large saucepan, saute the asparagus, mushrooms and leeks in butter for 10 minutes or until tender. Stir in the flour, salt and pepper until blended.

Gradually stir in broth and cream. Bring to a boil. Reduce heat; cook and stir for 2 minutes or until thickened. Stir in corn and pimientos; heat through. **YIELD: 7 SERVINGS.**

CHILLED RASPBERRY SOUP
prep/total time: 20 min. + chilling

1/3	cup cranberry juice	1-1/3	cups plus 2 tablespoons sour cream, *divided*
1/3	cup sugar		
5-1/3	cups plus 12 fresh raspberries, *divided*		

In a blender, combine the cranberry juice, sugar and 5-1/3 cups raspberries; cover and process until blended. Strain and discard seeds. Stir in 1-1/3 cups sour cream. Cover and refrigerate for at least 2 hours.

To serve, pour 1/4 cup of soup into 12 cordial glasses. Top each with a raspberry and 1/2 teaspoon sour cream. **YIELD: 12 SERVINGS.**

AMY WENGER
SEVERANCE, COLORADO

Family and friends enjoy sipping this lovely, chilled soup. To make it lighter, I often use sugar substitute and reduced-fat sour cream.

MOROCCAN CHICKPEA STEW
prep: 20 min. | cook: 30 min.

1	large onion, finely chopped	1	can (14-1/2 ounces) diced tomatoes, undrained
2	tablespoons olive oil	1	medium red potato, cut into 1-inch cubes
1	tablespoon butter	1	medium sweet potato, peeled and cut into 1-inch cubes
2	garlic cloves, minced		
2	teaspoons ground cumin	1	medium lemon, thinly sliced
1	cinnamon stick (3 inches)	1/4	teaspoon salt
1/2	teaspoon chili powder	2	small zucchini, cubed
4	cups vegetable broth	3	tablespoons minced fresh cilantro
2	cups cubed peeled butternut squash		
1	can (15 ounces) chickpeas *or* garbanzo beans, rinsed and drained		

In a Dutch oven, saute onion in oil and butter until tender. Add garlic, cumin, cinnamon stick and chili powder; saute 1 minute longer.

Stir in the broth, squash, chickpeas, tomatoes, potatoes, lemon and salt. Bring to a boil. Reduce heat; cover and simmer for 15-20 minutes or until potatoes and squash are almost tender.

Add zucchini; return to a boil. Reduce heat; cover and simmer for 5-8 minutes or until vegetables are tender. Discard cinnamon stick and lemon slices. Stir in cilantro. **YIELD: 9 SERVINGS (ABOUT 2 QUARTS).**

CINDY BEBERMAN
ORLAND PARK, ILLINOIS

When I served this spicy stew to guests, they were thrilled with the abundance of squash, potatoes, tomatoes and onion.

**TASTE OF HOME
TEST KITCHEN**

This hearty soup combines Swiss chard with other garden favorites. Its light broth tastes surprisingly rich and the grated Parmesan packs an additional punch.

**HEIDI WILCOX
LAPEER, MICHIGAN**

Delicate and lemony, this squash soup would set the stage for a memorable ladies luncheon. It's the best of late summer in a bowl.

SWISS CHARD BEAN SOUP
prep: 25 min. | cook: 30 min.

1	medium carrot, coarsely chopped	4	cups chopped Swiss chard
1	small zucchini, coarsely chopped	1	can (15-1/2 ounces) great northern beans, rinsed and drained
1	small yellow summer squash, coarsely chopped	1	can (14-1/2 ounces) diced tomatoes, undrained
1	small red onion, chopped	1	teaspoon dried thyme
2	tablespoons olive oil	1/2	teaspoon salt
2	garlic cloves, minced	1/2	teaspoon dried oregano
3	cans (14-1/2 ounces each) reduced-sodium chicken broth	1/4	teaspoon pepper
		1/4	cup grated Parmesan cheese

In a Dutch oven, saute the carrot, zucchini, yellow squash and onion in oil until tender. Add garlic; saute 1 minute longer. Add the broth, Swiss chard, beans, tomatoes, thyme, salt, oregano and pepper. Bring to a boil. Reduce heat; simmer, uncovered, for 15 minutes or until chard is tender. Just before serving, sprinkle with cheese. **YIELD: 10 SERVINGS (2-1/2 QUARTS).**

SUMMER SQUASH SOUP
prep: 35 min. | cook: 15 min.

2	large sweet onions, chopped	4	fresh thyme sprigs
1	medium leek (white portion only), chopped	1/4	teaspoon salt
2	tablespoons olive oil	2	tablespoons lemon juice
6	garlic cloves, minced	1/8	teaspoon hot pepper sauce
6	medium yellow summer squash, seeded and cubed	1	tablespoon shredded Parmesan cheese
4	cups reduced-sodium chicken broth	2	teaspoons grated lemon peel

In a large saucepan, saute onions and leek in oil until tender. Add garlic; cook 1 minute longer. Add squash; saute 5 minutes. Stir in the broth, thyme and salt. Bring to a boil. Reduce heat; cover and simmer for 15-20 minutes or until squash is tender.

Discard thyme sprigs. Cool slightly. In a blender, process soup in batches until smooth. Return all to the pan. Stir in lemon juice and hot pepper sauce; heat through. Sprinkle each serving with cheese and lemon peel. **YIELD: 8 SERVINGS (2 QUARTS).**

HEARTY MEATLESS CHILI
prep: 20 min. | cook: 55 min.

- 1 small onion, chopped
- 1 tablespoon olive oil
- 3 garlic cloves, minced
- 2 medium zucchini, finely chopped
- 2 medium carrots, finely chopped
- 3 tablespoons cornmeal
- 2 tablespoons chili powder
- 2 tablespoons paprika
- 1 tablespoon sugar
- 1/2 teaspoon ground cumin
- 1/4 to 1/2 teaspoon cayenne pepper
- 2 cans (one 28 ounces, one 14-1/2 ounces) diced tomatoes, undrained
- 2 cans (15 ounces *each*) pinto beans, rinsed and drained
- 1 can (16 ounces) kidney beans, rinsed and drained

TOPPINGS:
- 8 tablespoons fat-free sour cream
- 8 tablespoons thinly sliced green onions
- 8 teaspoons minced fresh cilantro

In a Dutch oven, saute the onion in oil until tender. Add the garlic; cook 1 minute longer. Stir in zucchini and carrots. Add the cornmeal, chili powder, paprika, sugar, cumin and cayenne; cook and stir for 1 minute.

Stir in tomatoes and beans. Bring to a boil. Reduce heat; cover and simmer for 45 minutes. Garnish each serving with sour cream, green onions and cilantro. **YIELD: 8 SERVINGS (2-1/2 QUARTS).**

**LOIS BEACH
COLLEGE STATION, TEXAS**

Years ago I found a recipe for chili con carne. I tried it and changed the spices, reduced the oil and added vegetables to make it more attractive. Dozens have enjoyed the results and asked for the recipe!

CUCUMBER SOUP
prep: 25 min. + chilling

- 3 medium cucumbers
- 3 cups chicken broth
- 3 cups (24 ounces) sour cream
- 3 tablespoons cider vinegar
- 2 teaspoons salt, optional
- 1 garlic clove, minced

TOPPINGS:
- 2 medium tomatoes, chopped
- 3/4 cup sliced almonds, toasted
- 1/2 cup chopped green onions
- 1/2 cup minced fresh parsley

Peel cucumbers; halve lengthwise and remove seeds. Cut into chunks. In a blender, cover and puree cucumbers and broth in small batches.

Transfer to a large bowl; stir in sour cream, vinegar, salt if desired and garlic until well blended. Cover and refrigerate for at least 4 hours. Stir before serving. Garnish with tomatoes, almonds, onions and parsley. **YIELD: 12 SERVINGS.**

**BEVERLY SPRAGUE
BALTIMORE, MARYLAND**

I dress up this smooth soup with a selection of savory toppings, such as crunchy almonds and green onions.

TASTE OF HOME
TEST KITCHEN

This refreshing tomato-based soup features shrimp, cucumber and avocados. Serve it as an appetizer or as a meal by itself.

LINDA REIS
SALEM, OREGON

I make this zippy, satisfying soup all the time. It's my dad's favorite. The recipe makes a lot, freezes well, and tastes just as great reheated!

SHRIMP GAZPACHO
prep/total time: 10 min. + chilling

6	cups spicy hot V8 juice	2	medium ripe avocados, diced
2	cups cold water	1/2	cup lime juice
1	pound cooked medium shrimp, peeled and deveined	1/2	cup minced fresh cilantro
2	medium tomatoes, seeded and diced	1/2	teaspoon salt
1	medium cucumber, seeded and diced	1/4	to 1/2 teaspoon hot pepper sauce

In a large bowl, combine all the ingredients. Cover and refrigerate for 1 hour. Serve cold. **YIELD: 12 SERVINGS (ABOUT 3 QUARTS).**

EDITOR'S NOTE: This recipe is best served the same day it's made.

MINESTRONE WITH ITALIAN SAUSAGE
prep: 25 min. | cook: 1 hour

1	pound bulk Italian sausage	3	cups shredded cabbage
1	large onion, chopped	1	teaspoon dried basil
2	large carrots, chopped	1	teaspoon dried oregano
2	celery ribs, chopped	1/4	teaspoon pepper
1	medium leek (white portion only), chopped	1	can (15 ounces) garbanzo beans *or* chickpeas, rinsed and drained
1	medium zucchini, cut into 1/2-inch pieces		
1/4	pound fresh green beans, trimmed and cut into 1/2-inch pieces	1/2	cup uncooked small pasta shells
3	garlic cloves, minced	3	tablespoons minced fresh parsley
6	cups beef broth	1/3	cup grated Parmesan cheese
2	cans (14-1/2 ounces *each*) diced tomatoes with basil, oregano and garlic		

In a Dutch oven, cook sausage and onion over medium heat until meat is no longer pink; drain. Stir in carrots, celery and leek; cook for 3 minutes. Add zucchini, green beans and garlic; cook 1 minute longer.

Stir in broth, tomatoes, cabbage, basil, oregano and pepper. Bring to a boil. Reduce heat. Cover; simmer for 45 minutes. Return to a boil.

Add chickpeas, pasta and parsley; cook until pasta is tender, 6-9 minutes. Serve with cheese. **YIELD: 11 SERVINGS.**

COLORFUL CHICKEN 'N' SQUASH SOUP

prep: 25 min. | cook: 1-1/2 hours

1	broiler/fryer chicken (4 pounds), cut up	1	bunch kale, trimmed and chopped
13	cups water	6	medium carrots, chopped
5	pounds butternut squash, peeled and cubed (about 10 cups)	2	large onions, chopped
		3	teaspoons salt

Place chicken and water in a stockpot. Bring to a boil. Reduce heat; cover and simmer for 1 hour or until chicken is tender.

Remove chicken from broth. Strain broth and skim fat. Return broth to the pan; add the squash, kale, carrots and onions. Bring to a boil. Reduce heat; cover and simmer for 25-30 minutes or until vegetables are tender.

When chicken is cool enough to handle, remove meat from bones and cut into bite-size pieces. Discard bones and skin. Add chicken and salt to soup; heat through. **YIELD: 14 SERVINGS (5-1/2 QUARTS).**

TRINA BIGHAM
FAIRHAVEN, MASSACHUSETTS

When I turned 40, I decided to live a healthier lifestyle, which included cooking better food for my family. I make this soup every week because everyone loves it!

SWEET POTATO AND PEAR SOUP

prep: 15 min. | cook: 30 min.

1-3/4	pounds sweet potatoes (about 4 medium), peeled and cubed	2	large pears, peeled and sliced
1-3/4	cups water	1	large onion, chopped
1	teaspoon salt, *divided*	2	tablespoons butter
1/4	teaspoon ground cinnamon	1/2	cup white grape juice
		1	cup half-and-half cream
		1/4	teaspoon white pepper

In a large saucepan, combine sweet potatoes, water, 3/4 teaspoon salt and cinnamon. Bring to a boil. Reduce heat; simmer, uncovered, for 20 minutes.

Meanwhile, in another large saucepan, cook and stir the pears and onion in butter over medium heat for 5 minutes. Stir in grape juice; bring to a boil. Reduce heat; simmer, uncovered, for 5 minutes. Stir into the sweet potato mixture. Cool slightly.

In a blender, cover and puree soup in batches; return all to the pan. Stir in the cream, pepper and remaining salt; heat through (do not boil). **YIELD: 5 SERVINGS.**

CRISTY SHANK
SUMMERSVILLE,
WEST VIRGINIA

I'm a family physician who enjoys trying new recipes. This tasty cold-weather soup has garnered many warm compliments from family and friends.

TASTE OF HOME TEST KITCHEN

Our home economists combined ready-made turkey meatballs with fresh and frozen vegetables to come up with this nicely seasoned soup. Small families can enjoy half now and freeze the rest for later. Large families can double the recipe, so there's plenty left over for later.

GWEN FRITSCH EASTLAKE, OHIO

When cold weather arrives, my family always asks when I'm going to make this hearty soup. Cabbage is a perfect partner for potatoes.

TURKEY MEATBALL SOUP

prep/total time: 30 min.

3	cups cut fresh green beans	2	cans (14-1/2 ounces *each*) Italian stewed tomatoes
2	cups fresh baby carrots	1	package (12 ounces) refrigerated fully cooked Italian turkey meatballs
2	cups chicken broth		
1	teaspoon dried oregano		
1	teaspoon dried basil	2	cups frozen corn
1	teaspoon minced garlic		

In a large saucepan, combine the first six ingredients. Bring to a boil. Reduce heat; cover and simmer for 10 minutes.

Add the tomatoes, meatballs and corn. Cover and cook over medium-low heat for 10 minutes or until meatballs are heated through. Serve immediately or transfer to freezer containers. May be frozen for up to 3 months. **YIELD: 6 SERVINGS.**

TO USE FROZEN SOUP: Thaw in the refrigerator overnight. Transfer the soup to a Dutch oven. Cover and cook over medium heat until heated through.

DILLED CABBAGE SOUP

prep: 20 min. | cook: 20 min.

2	cups shredded cabbage	2	tablespoons all-purpose flour
1	large onion, chopped	1/2	cup sour cream
1	celery rib, chopped	2	to 3 teaspoons snipped fresh dill
2	tablespoons butter		
1	can (49-1/2 ounces) chicken broth, *divided*	1/4	teaspoon pepper
3	medium potatoes, peeled, halved and sliced		

In a Dutch oven, saute the cabbage, onion and celery in butter for 1 minute. Cover and cook on low for 10 minutes. Set aside 1/2 cup broth. Add potatoes and remaining broth to cabbage mixture.

Whisk flour and reserved broth until smooth; stir into the cabbage mixture. Bring to a boil over medium heat. Reduce the heat; simmer, uncovered, for 20 minutes, stirring occasionally.

Stir a small amount of hot broth into sour cream; return all to pan, stirring constantly. Add dill and pepper; heat through (do not boil). **YIELD: 2 QUARTS.**

BECKY RUFF MCGREGOR, IOWA

This delectable soup feels like fall! Its golden color and satisfying flavor have made it a favorite recipe of mine.

Fresh & Easy Tip

Before using leeks, cut off the roots. Trim the tough leaf ends. Slit the leek from end to end and wash thoroughly under cold water to remove dirt trapped between the leaf layers. Chop or slice the white portion only.

GOLDEN SQUASH SOUP
prep/total time: 30 min.

5	medium leeks (white portion only), sliced	1/4	teaspoon dried thyme
2	tablespoons butter	1/4	teaspoon pepper
1-1/2	pounds butternut squash, peeled, seeded and cubed (about 4 cups)	1-3/4	cups shredded cheddar cheese
4	cups chicken broth	1/4	cup sour cream
		2	tablespoons thinly sliced green onion

In a large saucepan, saute leeks in butter until tender. Stir in the squash, broth, thyme and pepper. Bring to a boil. Reduce heat; cover and simmer for 10-15 minutes or until squash is tender. Cool slightly.

In a blender, cover and process squash mixture in small batches until smooth; return all to the pan. Bring to a boil. Reduce heat to low. Add cheese; stir until soup is heated through and cheese is melted. Garnish with sour cream and onion. **YIELD: 6 SERVINGS.**

SANDWICHES

When time's tight and hunger is high, there's no need to hit the fast food drive-through! Simply consider any of the quick fixes in this chapter. Whether you prefer hoagies, pitas, hamburgers or wraps, turn here for a fresh and easy handheld great.

HEARTY VEGGIE SANDWICHES | PAGE 87

SAUSAGE PEPPER SANDWICHES | PAGE 96

FRUITED TURKEY WRAPS

prep/total time: 15 min.

1/2 cup fat-free mayonnaise	2 cups finely shredded Chinese or napa cabbage
1 tablespoon orange juice	1/2 cup thinly sliced red onion
1 teaspoon grated orange peel	1 can (11 ounces) mandarin oranges, drained
3/4 teaspoon curry powder	2/3 cup dried cranberries
4 whole wheat tortillas (8 inches), room temperature	1/2 pound thinly sliced deli smoked turkey

Combine the mayonnaise, orange juice, peel and curry; spread over tortillas. Top with cabbage, onion, oranges, cranberries and turkey. Roll up. **YIELD: 4 SERVINGS.**

**LISA RENSHAW
KANSAS CITY, MISSOURI**

This colorful wrap tastes great and is so good for you. It's packed with lean protein, fruit and veggies and wrapped in whole grain goodness!

VEGGIE TUNA BURGERS

prep/total time: 30 min.

1/4 cup finely chopped onion	1 can (6 ounces) light water-packed tuna, drained and flaked
1 garlic clove, minced	1/4 teaspoon salt
1 cup *each* shredded zucchini, yellow summer squash and carrots	1/4 teaspoon pepper
	1 teaspoon butter
1 egg, lightly beaten	6 hamburger buns, split
2 cups soft whole wheat bread crumbs	6 slices reduced-fat cheddar cheese
	6 lettuce leaves
	6 slices tomato

In a large nonstick skillet coated with cooking spray, saute onion and garlic for 1 minute. Add the zucchini, yellow squash and carrots; saute until tender. Drain and cool to room temperature.

In a large bowl, combine egg, bread crumbs, tuna, salt and pepper. Add vegetable mixture. Shape into six 3-1/2-in. patties.

Coat the same skillet again with cooking spray; cook patties in butter for 3-5 minutes on each side or until lightly browned. Serve on buns with cheese, lettuce and tomato. **YIELD: 6 SERVINGS.**

**LAURA DAVIS
RUSTON, LOUISIANA**

You don't have to be a health nut to enjoy these moist and nutritious burgers. They're an easy way to get my children to eat their vegetables.

MICHAEL COHEN LOS ANGELES, CALIFORNIA

These French hamburgers are a twist on a lipsmacking traditional burger. The flavorful sauce and crunchy French bread are truly delicious.

Fresh & Easy Tip

Tarragon is an herb with slender, green leaves and a distinctive anise-like flavor. Widely used in French cooking, tarragon is most well-known for flavoring Bearnaise sauce and for making flavored vinegar.

FRENCH TARRAGON BURGERS

prep: 15 min. | grill: 20 min.

1 cup mayonnaise	2 loaves (1 pound and 20 inches *each*) unsliced French bread
2 tablespoons Dijon mustard	1 teaspoon salt
3 teaspoons chopped shallot, *divided*	1/2 teaspoon pepper
2 teaspoons minced fresh tarragon or 3/4 teaspoon dried tarragon	2 pounds ground beef
2 garlic cloves, minced	4 cups spring mix salad greens

In a small bowl, combine the mayonnaise, mustard, 1 teaspoon shallot, tarragon and garlic; cover and refrigerate.

Meanwhile, cut one loaf of bread into five 4-in. pieces. Cut one 4-in. piece from the second loaf; set aside remaining bread for another use. Cut bread pieces in half horizontally; set aside.

In a large bowl, combine the salt, pepper and remaining shallot. Crumble beef over mixture and mix well. Shape into six patties.

Grill burgers, covered, over medium heat for 6-8 minutes on each side or until a meat thermometer reads 160° and juices run clear.

Grill bread, cut side down, for 1-2 minutes or until toasted. Spread with mayonnaise mixture. Layer bread bottoms with greens and burgers. Replace tops. **YIELD: 6 SERVINGS.**

DARLYNE PLAISANCE
POPLARVILLE, MISSISSIPPI

I came across this recipe when I lived and worked in New Orleans, where po' boys are very popular. This meatless version featuring spinach and cheese can be served as an appetizer or sandwich, or try it as a side dish with a pasta casserole.

AMBER INDRA
THOUSAND OAKS,
CALIFORNIA

Creating this recipe was a way to get more veggies into my diet. I'm busy and on the go like many other mothers. These wraps give me energy and taste delicious.

SPINACH PO'BOYS
prep: 15 min. | bake: 25 min.

2	loaves (8 ounces *each*) French bread	1	teaspoon garlic powder
1	cup butter, softened, *divided*	1/4	teaspoon hot pepper sauce
3/4	cup chopped green onions	1	cup (4 ounces) shredded sharp cheddar cheese
1	package (10 ounces) fresh spinach, trimmed and coarsely chopped	1	cup (4 ounces) shredded part-skim mozzarella cheese

Cut each loaf of bread in half lengthwise. Spread the cut sides with 1/2 cup butter; set aside. In a large skillet, cook onions in remaining butter for 4-5 minutes or until tender. Add the spinach, garlic powder and the hot pepper sauce; cook and stir for 3 minutes or until the spinach is tender.

Spread spinach mixture over the bottom halves of bread. Sprinkle with cheeses; replace bread tops. Wrap each loaf in foil; place on a baking sheet. Bake at 375° for 20 minutes. Carefully open the foil and bake 5 minutes longer or until cheese is melted. Cut into slices. **YIELD: 12-16 SLICES.**

 # VEGETARIAN HUMMUS WRAPS
prep/total time: 10 min.

6	tablespoons hummus	1	cup fresh baby spinach
2	flour tortillas (8 inches), room temperature	6	slices tomato
1/2	cup shredded carrots	2	tablespoons green goddess salad dressing

Spread hummus over each tortilla. Layer with carrots, spinach and tomato; drizzle with dressing. Roll up tightly. **YIELD: 2 SERVINGS.**

TURKEY WALDORF PITA
prep/total time: 10 min.

1	cup cubed cooked turkey	1/4	cup chopped walnuts
2	celery ribs, chopped	1/4	cup mayonnaise
1/2	cup chopped tart apple	4	lettuce leaves
1/2	cup halved seedless grapes	2	pita breads (6 inches), halved

In a large bowl, combine the turkey, celery, apple, grapes, walnuts and mayonnaise. Place a lettuce leaf in each pita half; fill with turkey salad. **YIELD: 2 SERVINGS.**

RITA MILLER
HUNTINGDON, PENNSYLVANIA

We like to roast turkey all year long because we enjoy the leftovers. Several years ago, while nibbling on Waldorf salad and some cold turkey, I decided to combine the two. This pita was an instant hit.

ASPARAGUS CHICKEN SANDWICHES
prep/total time: 15 min.

1	pound fresh asparagus, trimmed and cut into 3-inch pieces	1/2	teaspoon salt
1-1/2	cups reduced-fat sour cream	8	ounces sliced cooked chicken breast
2	teaspoons lemon juice	4	English muffins, split and toasted
1-1/2	teaspoons prepared mustard	2	medium tomatoes, sliced
			Paprika, optional

In a large saucepan, bring 1/2 in. of water to a boil. Add asparagus; cover and boil for 3 minutes. Drain and immediately place asparagus in ice water. Drain and pat dry.

In the same pan, combine the sour cream, lemon juice, mustard and salt; cook on low until heated through. Remove from the heat.

Place the chicken on a microwave-safe plate; microwave on high for 30-40 seconds or until warmed.

Place two English muffin halves on each serving plate. Top with the chicken, tomatoes, asparagus and sauce. Sprinkle with paprika if desired. **YIELD: 4 SERVINGS.**

EDITOR'S NOTE: This recipe was tested in a 1,100-watt microwave.

ANCA CRETAN
HAGERSTOWN, MARYLAND

No one will be able to resist these lovely open-faced sandwiches that definitely say "spring." Served on toasted English muffins, slices of chicken and tomato are topped with fresh asparagus spears, then draped with a creamy lemon sauce.

JENNIFER WILKS THORNTON, COLORADO

These wraps are a family favorite because everyone raves about the fresh flavor. Plus, they're just as wonderful the second day!

STEAK VEGGIE WRAPS

prep: 25 min. | cook: 15 min.

1/2 teaspoon minced garlic	15 ounces beef top sirloin steak, cut into thin strips
1/4 teaspoon Italian seasoning	1/3 cup fat-free ranch salad dressing
1/4 teaspoon ground cumin	1/3 cup salsa
2 tablespoons olive oil, *divided*	2/3 cup shredded reduced-fat Mexican cheese blend
1-1/4 cups chopped yellow summer squash	
1 medium sweet red pepper, cut into strips	1/3 cup minced fresh cilantro
3/4 cup julienned carrot	1 large tomato, chopped
1/2 cup sliced onion	5 whole wheat tortillas (8 inches), warmed
1 jalapeno pepper, chopped	

In a large bowl, combine the garlic, Italian seasoning, cumin and 1 tablespoon oil. Add the summer squash, red pepper, carrot, onion and jalapeno; toss to coat.

Place in a single layer in an ungreased 15-in. x 10-in. x 1-in. baking pan. Broil 4-6 in. from the heat for 10-15 minutes or until tender and lightly browned, stirring once.

Meanwhile, in a large skillet, saute steak in remaining oil for 4-6 minutes or until no longer pink.

Combine the salad dressing and salsa. Sprinkle the cheese, cilantro and tomato over each tortilla; drizzle with dressing mixture. Top with vegetables and steak. Roll up tightly. **YIELD: 5 SERVINGS.**

EDITOR'S NOTE: When cutting hot peppers, disposable gloves are recommended. Avoid touching your face.

HEARTY VEGGIE SANDWICHES

prep/total time: 15 min.

2	tablespoons mayonnaise	1	medium ripe avocado, peeled and sliced
2	teaspoons Dijon mustard	2	large slices tomato
2	bagels, split	1	slice sweet onion, separated into rings
2	lettuce leaves		Salt and pepper to taste

In a small bowl, combine the mayonnaise and mustard; spread over cut sides of bagels. On the bagel bottoms, layer lettuce, avocado, tomato and onion. Sprinkle with salt and pepper. Replace bagel tops. **YIELD: 2 SERVINGS.**

CHICKEN 'N' BROCCOLI BRAID

prep: 25 min. | bake: 15 min.

2	cups cubed cooked chicken	1	garlic clove, minced
1	cup chopped fresh broccoli	1/4	teaspoon salt
		1/2	cup mayonnaise
1	cup (4 ounces) shredded sharp cheddar cheese	2	tubes (8 ounces *each*) refrigerated crescent rolls
1/2	cup chopped sweet red pepper	1	egg white, lightly beaten
2	teaspoons dill weed	2	tablespoons slivered almonds

In a large bowl, combine first seven ingredients. Stir in mayonnaise. Unroll both tubes of crescent dough onto an ungreased baking sheet; press together, forming a 15-in. x 12-in. rectangle. Seal the seams and perforations. Spoon filling lengthwise down the center third of dough.

On each long side, cut dough 3 in. toward the center at 1-1/2-in. intervals, forming strips. Bring one strip from each side over filling; pinch ends to seal. Repeat. Pinch ends of loaf to seal.

Brush with egg white; sprinkle with almonds. Bake at 375° for 15-20 minutes or until crust is golden brown and filling is heated through. **YIELD: 8 SERVINGS.**

CAROLINE MUNOZ
AUSTIN, MINNESOTA

My sister and I developed this sandwich one day when we had some "everything bagels" left over. I have often served it to my friends as a casual lunch. The total lack of fussiness allows me to spend quality time with guests.

DANA RABE
WEST RICHLAND, WASHINGTON

Beautiful braided breads really dress up events. It's full of chicken and veggies and surrounded by a buttery crust. I love to make this simple, tasty dish for my gang.

CARA NETH
FORT COLLINS, COLORADO

We love this recipe because it's easy and vegetarian. Family members assemble their own sandwiches to their liking.

EDWARD MEYER
ARNOLD, MISSOURI

Sliced fresh strawberries, Swiss cheese and a nutty cream cheese spread make this turkey sandwich different. Try it on whole wheat, oatmeal or sunflower seed bread. It's tasty and fast to put together.

SWEET PEPPER SANDWICHES
prep/total time: 25 min.

1	*each* small green, sweet red and yellow pepper, thinly sliced		1/4	cup fat-free mayonnaise
1	small onion, thinly sliced		1/2	teaspoon prepared horseradish
1	tablespoon olive oil		4	hard rolls, split and toasted
1	garlic clove, minced		8	fresh basil leaves
1	tablespoon balsamic vinegar		1	plum tomato, thinly sliced
2	ounces fresh mozzarella cheese			

In a large nonstick skillet, saute the peppers and onion in oil until crisp-tender. Add garlic; cook 1 minute longer. Drizzle with vinegar; toss to coat.

Cut mozzarella cheese into four slices. Combine the mayonnaise and horseradish; spread over cut sides of rolls. Spoon vegetable mixture onto bottom halves; top with cheese.

Broil 4-6 in. from the heat for 2-4 minutes or until cheese is melted. Top with basil and tomato. Replace roll tops. **YIELD: 4 SERVINGS.**

BERRY TURKEY SANDWICH
prep/total time: 5 min.

4	slices whole wheat bread		4	fresh strawberries, sliced
2	lettuce leaves		2	tablespoons reduced-fat spreadable cream cheese
2	slices reduced-fat Swiss cheese			
1/4	pound thinly sliced deli turkey breast		2	teaspoons finely chopped pecans

On two slices of bread, layer lettuce, Swiss cheese, turkey and strawberries. Combine the cream cheese and pecans; spread over remaining bread. Place over strawberries. **YIELD: 2 SERVINGS.**

DELI VEGETABLE ROLL-UPS

prep/total time: 10 min.

1/2 cup garden vegetable cream cheese spread	4 slices part-skim mozzarella cheese
4 flour tortillas (10 inches)	8 thick dill pickle slices
1 medium tomato, seeded and diced	1/4 cup ranch salad dressing
2 sweet banana peppers, seeded and julienned	4 lettuce leaves
1 cup sliced ripe olives	4 thinly sliced deli turkey
4 slices Colby cheese	4 thin slices salami
	Additional ranch salad dressing, optional

Spread about 2 tablespoons of the cream cheese spread over each tortilla. Layer with tomato, peppers, olives, cheeses and pickle slices. Drizzle with salad dressing. Top with lettuce, turkey and salami.

Roll up tightly; wrap in plastic wrap. Refrigerate until ready to serve. Serve with additional dressing if desired. **YIELD: 4 SERVINGS.**

NANCY DIVELBISS
LEO, INDIANA

I make these loaded tortilla sandwiches for my husband and son to take for lunch. My son thought I could peddle them on a street corner!

APPLE 'N' PROSCIUTTO SANDWICHES

prep/total time: 20 min.

1/4 cup olive oil	1 loaf (12 ounces) focaccia bread
1/2 cup chopped walnuts	8 thin slices prosciutto
2 tablespoons grated Parmesan cheese	1 medium apple, sliced
2 tablespoons minced fresh rosemary	6 ounces Brie cheese, rind removed and sliced

In a blender, combine the oil, walnuts, cheese and rosemary; cover and process until blended and nuts are finely chopped. With a bread knife, split focaccia into two horizontal layers. Spread the rosemary mixture over cut sides of bread.

On bottom of bread, layer the prosciutto, apple and Brie; replace bread top. Cut into quarters.

Cook on an indoor grill for 2-3 minutes or until bread is browned and cheese is melts. Cut each wedge in half. **YIELD: 8 SERVINGS.**

ELIZABETH BENNETT
MILL CREEK, WASHINGTON

Prepared on an indoor grill, these Italian-style sandwiches are spread with homemade rosemary pesto. They're wonderful on a cool day with a bowl of butternut squash soup.

CUCUMBER CHICKEN SALAD SANDWICHES

prep/total time: 10 min.

1	cup cubed cooked chicken breast	1/4	teaspoon salt
1/3	cup chopped seeded peeled cucumber	1/8	teaspoon dill weed
1/4	cup fat-free mayonnaise	2	lettuce leaves
		4	slices tomato
		2	sandwich buns, split

In a small bowl, combine the first five ingredients. Place lettuce and tomato on bun bottoms; top with chicken salad. Replace bun tops. **YIELD: 2 SERVINGS.**

**EVA WRIGHT
GRANT, ALABAMA**

I dress up chicken salad with crunchy cucumber and dill for this summery sandwich that's ready in just 10 minutes. If you're watching salt, omit it from the recipe.

TUNA MELT ON CORN BREAD

prep/total time: 30 min.

1	package (8-1/2 ounces) corn bread/muffin mix	1	hard-cooked egg, chopped
2	cans (6 ounces *each*) light water-packed tuna, drained and flaked	1	teaspoon dill weed
		1/4	teaspoon salt
		1/8	teaspoon pepper
1/3	cup mayonnaise	6	slices cheddar cheese
1/3	cup chopped celery	1	medium tomato, sliced
2	tablespoons finely chopped onion	1	medium ripe avocado, peeled and sliced

Prepare and bake corn bread according to package directions, using a greased 8-in. square baking pan. Cool on a wire rack.

In a small bowl, combine the tuna, mayonnaise, celery, onion, egg, dill, salt and pepper. Cut the corn bread into six pieces; place on an ungreased baking sheet. Top each with 1/4 cup tuna mixture and a slice of cheese.

Broil 4-6 in. from the heat for 2-3 minutes or until cheese is melted. Top with tomato and avocado. **YIELD: 6 SERVINGS.**

**TASTE OF HOME
TEST KITCHEN**

Try this new twist on a tuna melt that uses corn bread, Cheddar cheese and avocado. Yum!

ELIZABETH HINER CHICO, CALIFORNIA

My sister and I found this recipe 15 years ago, changed a few ingredients and made it our own. It's a quick crowd-pleaser that goes great with summer.

FLANK STEAK SANDWICHES

prep: 25 min. + marinating | grill: 25 min.

1	cup chopped onion		1	medium sweet red pepper, cut into 1-inch strips
1	cup dry red wine *or* beef broth		1	medium sweet yellow pepper, cut into 1-inch strips
3/4	cup soy sauce		1	medium red onion, thickly sliced
1/2	cup olive oil, *divided*		1/4	teaspoon pepper
4-1/2	teaspoons minced garlic, *divided*		6	French rolls, split
1-1/2	teaspoons ground mustard			
1-1/2	teaspoons ground ginger			
1	beef flank steak (1-1/2 pounds)			

In a small bowl, combine the onion, wine or broth, soy sauce, 1/4 cup olive oil, 2-1/2 teaspoons garlic, mustard and ginger. Pour 1-3/4 cups into a large resealable plastic bag; add steak. Pour the remaining marinade into another resealable plastic bag; add the peppers and onion. Seal bags and turn to coat; refrigerate for 3 hours or overnight, turning occasionally.

Drain and discard marinade from steak. Grill, covered, over medium heat for 6-7 minutes on each side or until meat reaches desired doneness (for medium-rare, a meat thermometer should read 145°; medium, 160°; well-done, 170°).

Drain and discard marinade from vegetables. Place in a grill basket. Grill, uncovered, over medium-hot heat for 9-11 minutes or until tender, stirring frequently.

In a small bowl, combine the pepper and remaining oil and garlic; brush over cut sides of rolls. Place cut side down on grill for 2-3 minutes or until golden brown.

Thinly slice steak across the grain; place on bun bottoms. Top with the vegetables and bun tops. **YIELD: 6 SERVINGS.**

EDITOR'S NOTE: If you do not have a grill wok or basket, use a disposable foil pan. Poke holes in the bottom of the pan with a meat fork to allow liquid to drain.

FRESH VEGGIE POCKETS

prep/total time: 15 min.

1	carton (8 ounces) spreadable cream cheese	1	medium tomato, thinly sliced
1/4	cup sunflower kernels	1	medium cucumber, thinly sliced
1	teaspoon seasoned salt *or* salt-free seasoning blend	1	cup sliced fresh mushrooms
4	wheat pita breads, halved	1	ripe avocado, peeled and sliced

In a large bowl, combine the cream cheese, sunflower kernels and seasoned salt; spread about 2 tablespoons on the inside of each pita half. Layer with the tomato, cucumber, mushrooms and avocado. **YIELD: 4 SERVINGS.**

LINDA REEVES
CLOVERDALE, INDIANA

One summer I worked at a health food store that sold sandwiches. We were close to a college campus, so I made lots of these fresh-filled pitas for the students. Crunchy with crisp vegetables and sunflower kernels, the pockets are a fast-to-fix lunch when you're on the go.

GRILLED TOMATO SANDWICHES

prep/total time: 30 min.

8	slices tomato (3/4 inch thick)	1	tablespoon balsamic vinegar
1/2	teaspoon salt, *divided*	1/4	teaspoon pepper
6	tablespoons mayonnaise	1	cup chopped water-packed artichoke hearts, rinsed and drained
1	teaspoon lemon juice		
1	garlic clove, minced	3	cups torn romaine *or* spinach
1	round cheese focaccia bread *or* focaccia bread of your choice (12 inches), halved lengthwise		

Sprinkle one side of tomato slices with 1/8 teaspoon salt. Place salt side down on paper towels for 10 minutes. Repeat with second side. Combine mayonnaise, lemon juice and garlic; set aside.

Moisten a paper towel with cooking oil and with long-handled tongs, lightly coat the grill rack. Place bread cut side down on grill. Place tomatoes on grill. Grill, covered, over medium heat for 2 minutes or until bread is golden brown.

Sprinkle tomatoes with vinegar, pepper and remaining salt. Spread mayonnaise mixture over bread. On the bottom half, layer tomatoes, artichokes and romaine; replace bread top. Cut into wedges; serve immediately. **YIELD: 4 SERVINGS.**

WENDY STENMAN
GERMANTOWN, WISCONSIN

These sandwiches can be assembled in a snap. Be sure the tomatoes are sliced thick and that they are not grilled for longer than 2 minutes.

TEXAS TOAST STEAK SANDWICHES
prep/total time: 30 min.

1/3	cup mayonnaise	2	cups fresh baby spinach
2	teaspoons minced chipotle pepper in adobo sauce	6	Muenster cheese slices (1/2 ounce *each*)
6	slices Texas toast	6	tomato slices
6	beef cubed steaks (4 ounces *each*)		

In a small bowl, combine the mayonnaise and chipotle pepper. Heat Texas toast on a foil-lined baking sheet according to the package directions.

Meanwhile, in a large skillet coated with cooking spray, cook beef in batches over medium heat until no longer pink.

Layer warmed Texas toast with spinach, steaks, mayonnaise mixture, cheese and tomato. Broil 3-4 in. from the heat for 1-2 minutes or until cheese is melted. **YIELD: 6 SERVINGS.**

TARYN KUEBELBECK
PLYMOUTH, MINNESOTA

These hearty open-faced sandwiches are layered with fresh spinach, cheese, tomato and beef. Serve them with ice-cold lemonade for a knockout lunch!

SPINACH FETA BURGERS
prep/total time: 20 min.

1	cup torn fresh spinach	1-1/2	teaspoons dill weed
1/2	cup crumbled feta cheese	1	teaspoon salt
1/2	cup chopped seeded plum tomatoes	1	teaspoon pepper
		2	pounds ground beef
2	green onions, chopped	8	hamburger buns, split

In a large bowl, combine the first seven ingredients. Crumble beef over mixture and mix well. Shape into eight 4-in. patties.

Grill, covered, over medium heat or broil 4 in. from the heat for 4-5 minutes on each side or until a meat thermometer reads 160° and juices run clear. Serve on buns. **YIELD: 8 SERVINGS.**

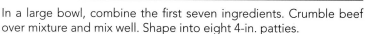

SUZANNE KERN
LOUISVILLE, KENTUCKY

My husband is Greek, therefore this is a great compliment to his heritage. We often serve them with a tomato and cucumber salad.

OPEN-FACED VEGGIE SANDWICHES

prep/total time: 15 min.

4 teaspoons spicy brown *or* horseradish mustard	1 cup (4 ounces) shredded cheddar cheese
4 English muffins, split	
1/2 cup *each* chopped fresh broccoli, cauliflower and sweet red pepper	

Spread mustard on cut sides of muffins. Top each with vegetables and cheese. Broil 4-6 in. from the heat for 3 minutes or until the cheese is melted. **YIELD: 4 SERVINGS.**

**KAREN MELLO
FAIRHAVEN,
MASSACHUSETTS**

Since I'm a vegetarian, I love these broiled sandwiches. Even nonvegetarians like their fresh taste. The veggie-topped muffin halves make a great snack or quick lunch and are very affordable!

ASPARAGUS BRUNCH POCKETS

prep: 20 min. | bake: 15 min.

1 pound fresh asparagus, trimmed and cut into 1-inch pieces	1/8 teaspoon salt
	Pinch pepper
4 ounces cream cheese, softened	1 tube (8 ounces) refrigerated crescent rolls
1 tablespoon 2% milk	2 teaspoons butter, melted
1 tablespoon mayonnaise	
1 tablespoon diced pimientos	1 tablespoon seasoned bread crumbs
1 tablespoon finely chopped onion	

In a large saucepan, bring 1/2 in. of water to a boil. Add asparagus; cover and boil for 3 minutes. Drain and set aside.

In a small bowl, beat the cream cheese, milk and mayonnaise until smooth. Stir in the pimientos, onion, salt and pepper.

Unroll the crescent dough and separate into triangles; place on an ungreased baking sheet.

Spoon 1 teaspoon of cream cheese mixture into the center of each triangle; top with asparagus. Top each with another teaspoonful of cream cheese mixture. Bring three corners of dough together and twist; pinch edges to seal.

Brush with the butter; sprinkle with bread crumbs. Bake at 375° for 15-18 minutes or until golden brown. **YIELD: 8 SERVINGS.**

**CYNTHIA LINTHICUM
TOWSON, MARYLAND**

These cute bundles are stuffed with a savory asparagus-cream cheese mixture. They're wonderful during a brunch or even as a fun side dish.

SHREDDED BEEF 'N' SLAW SANDWICHES

prep: 20 min. | cook: 2-3/4 hours

4	pounds beef stew meat, cut into 1-inch cubes	2	tablespoons prepared horseradish
2	cups water	1	tablespoon prepared mustard
2	cups ketchup	2	teaspoons salt
1/2	to 3/4 cup Worcestershire sauce	8	cups shredded cabbage
2	tablespoons lemon juice	30	sandwich buns, split

In a Dutch oven, bring beef and water to a boil. Reduce heat; cover and simmer for 2 hours or until tender.

Remove beef with a slotted spoon; shred with two forks and set aside. Skim fat from cooking liquid. Stir in the ketchup, Worcestershire sauce, lemon juice, horseradish, mustard and salt. Add the shredded beef and cabbage. Bring to a boil. Reduce heat; cover and simmer for 45 minutes or until cabbage is tender.

Spoon 1/3 cup onto each sandwich bun. **YIELD: 30 SANDWICHES.**

MARY JOHNSON
WHITEHOUSE, OHIO

I have served these tangy, hearty sandwiches for family gatherings and to many work crews. They have always gone over quite well.

SOURDOUGH VEGGIE SANDWICHES

prep/total time: 20 min.

2	tablespoons mayonnaise	1	large tomato, thinly sliced
4	slices sourdough bread	1/4	cup shredded carrot
1	cup (4 ounces) shredded cheddar cheese	1	to 2 tablespoons salted sunflower kernels
2	small zucchini, halved lengthwise	2	tablespoons butter, softened

Spread mayonnaise on one side of each slice of bread. On two slices, layer with cheese, zucchini, tomato, carrot and sunflower kernels. Top with remaining bread, mayonnaise side down. Spread butter over the outside of bread.

In a large skillet, cook over medium heat until bread is lightly toasted and cheese is melted. **YIELD: 2 SERVINGS.**

BILLIE MOSS
WALNUT CREEK, CALIFORNIA

This appealing sandwich is easy to assemble. My husband and I enjoy them on Sunday after church.

**SUZETTE GESSEL
ALBUQUERQUE,
NEW MEXICO**

*Peppers and onions add a fresh
taste to this zippy sausage filling
for sandwiches. My mother gave
me the recipe. It's simple to make
and gets gobbled up quickly.*

SAUSAGE PEPPER SANDWICHES

prep: 5 min. | cook: 7 hours

6	Italian sausage links (4 ounces *each*)	1	can (8 ounces) tomato sauce
1	medium green pepper, cut into 1-inch pieces	1/8	teaspoon pepper
1	large onion, cut into 1-inch pieces	6	hoagie *or* submarine sandwich buns, split

In a large skillet, brown sausage links over medium heat. Cut into 1/2-in. slices; place in a 3-qt. slow cooker. Stir in the green pepper, onion, tomato sauce and pepper.

Cover and cook on low for 7-8 hours or until sausage is no longer pink and vegetables are tender. Use a slotted spoon to serve on buns. **YIELD: 6 SERVINGS.**

**CHUCK HINZ
PARMA, OHIO**

*These tasty little sandwiches do not
get soggy and are refreshing and
light. My wife and I made them for
a Queen's birthday tea we hosted.*

TEA PARTY CUCUMBER SANDWICHES

prep: 20 min. + standing

1	English cucumber, thinly sliced		Dash pepper
1	tablespoon lemon juice	10	thin slices whole wheat sandwich bread, crusts removed
1	tablespoon olive oil		
1/2	teaspoon salt	5	teaspoons butter, softened
1/8	teaspoon sugar		Watercress sprigs

In a small bowl, combine the cucumber, lemon juice, oil, salt, sugar and pepper. Let stand at room temperature for at least 2 hours.

Spread one side of each slice of bread with butter; cut each into four squares. Drain cucumber and pat dry; place two cucumber slices on each square. Garnish with watercress. **YIELD: 40 SANDWICHES.**

BASIL-TOMATO GRILLED CHEESE

prep/total time: 20 min.

8 slices Italian bread (3/4 inch thick)

8 slices part-skim mozzarella cheese

2 large plum tomatoes, sliced

2 tablespoons minced fresh basil

2 teaspoons balsamic vinegar

Salt and pepper to taste

1/4 cup olive oil

3 tablespoons grated Parmesan cheese

1/4 teaspoon garlic powder

On four slices of bread, layer cheese and tomatoes; sprinkle with the basil, vinegar, salt and pepper. Top with remaining bread.

In a small bowl, combine the oil, cheese and garlic powder; brush over the outsides of each sandwich.

In a small skillet over medium heat, toast sandwiches until golden brown on both sides and cheese is melted. **YIELD: 4 SERVINGS.**

**SYLVIA SCHMITT
SUN CITY, ARIZONA**

The tastes of summer abound in these easy Italian-style grilled cheese sandwiches. Not only are they delicious, they're super-fast, too. I am always busy, especially around lunchtime, so I need something that is very quick and easy to prepare, but it also has to be satisfying as well. These sandwiches do the job.

BEEF SANDWICHES WITH BEET SPREAD

prep/total time: 25 min.

4 ounces cream cheese, softened

1 whole fresh beet, cooked, peeled and mashed (about 1/2 cup)

1/4 cup prepared horseradish

2 tablespoons lemon juice

1 tablespoon white vinegar

1-1/2 teaspoons sugar

Dash cayenne pepper

8 hard rolls, split and toasted

8 teaspoons butter, softened

1 pound thinly sliced deli roast beef

8 lettuce leaves

8 slices tomato

8 slices onion

In a small bowl, beat cream cheese and beet until blended. Beat in the horseradish, lemon juice, vinegar, sugar and cayenne.

Spread rolls with butter and beet spread. Layer with beef, lettuce, tomato and onion. **YIELD: 8 SERVINGS.**

**DAWN SCHUMILAS
WHITE FOX, SASKATCHEWAN**

Stack it up! This old-fashioned beef sandwich has a zesty horseradish spread that really comes alive in your mouth. Topped with fresh onion, lettuce and tomato, it's unbeatable.

**TASTE OF HOME
TEST KITCHEN**

Need a tasty and fast sandwich for your next get-together? Try this one and your guests will be asking for the recipe!

BRICKYARD BISTRO SANDWICH
prep/total time: 15 min.

1	loaf (1 pound) focaccia bread		2	ounces sliced deli smoked turkey
2	tablespoons olive oil		2	ounces thinly sliced hard salami
1	tablespoon balsamic vinegar		2	ounces sliced deli roast beef
2	teaspoons minced fresh oregano		2	ounces sliced provolone cheese
1	teaspoon minced fresh rosemary		1	plum tomato, sliced
2	slices red onion, separated into rings		2	lettuce leaves

Cut the focaccia in half horizontally. In a small bowl, combine the oil, vinegar, oregano and rosemary; brush over cut sides of bread.

On bread bottom, layer the onion, turkey, salami, roast beef, cheese, tomato and lettuce; replace the bread top. Cut into four wedges. **YIELD: 4 SERVINGS.**

**LEE BREMSON
KANSAS CITY, MISSOURI**

This grilled sandwich combines chicken with provolone cheese, spinach and red onion.

CHICKEN FLORENTINE PANINI
prep/total time: 25 min.

1	package (6 ounces) fresh baby spinach		8	slices provolone cheese
2	teaspoons olive oil		1/2	pound shaved deli chicken
1/4	cup butter, softened		2	slices red onion, separated into rings
8	slices sourdough bread			
1/4	cup creamy Italian salad dressing			

In a large skillet, saute the spinach in olive oil for 2 minutes or until wilted; drain.

Spread four bread slices with salad dressing. Layer with a cheese slice, chicken, spinach, onion and another cheese slice. Top with the remaining bread. Butter outsides of sandwiches.

Cook on a panini maker or indoor grill until bread is browned and cheese is melted. **YIELD: 4 SERVINGS.**

CAROLYN PHENICIE TITUSVILLE, PENNSYLVANIA

I tried this sandwich while vacationing in Sedona, Arizona and fell in love with it. When I returned home, I developed this one that tastes just like the original.

Fresh & Easy Tip

Select eggplant with smooth skin and avoid those with soft or brown spots. Store in a cool dry place for 1 to 2 days or place in a plastic bag and refrigerate up to 5 days. You don't need to peel an eggplant before using it.

GRILLED VEGGIE SANDWICHES WITH CILANTRO PESTO

prep: 20 min. + standing | grill: 10 min.

2/3 cup packed fresh cilantro sprigs	2 large sweet red peppers
1/4 cup packed fresh parsley sprigs	4 slices eggplant (1/2 inch thick)
2 tablespoons grated Parmesan cheese	1/2 teaspoon salt
2 garlic cloves, peeled	1/4 teaspoon pepper
2 tablespoons water	1/2 cup shredded part-skim mozzarella cheese
1 tablespoon pine nuts	
1 tablespoon olive oil	4 hard rolls, split
Cooking spray	

For pesto, place the cilantro, parsley, Parmesan cheese and garlic in a small food processor; cover and pulse until chopped. Add the water and pine nuts; cover and process until blended. While processing, gradually add oil in a steady stream. Set aside.

Using long-handled tongs, moisten a paper towel with cooking oil and lightly coat the grill rack. Grill peppers over medium heat for 10-15 minutes or until the skins blister, turning frequently. Immediately place the peppers in a large bowl; cover and let stand for 15-20 minutes. Peel off and discard charred skin. Halve and seed peppers; set aside.

Lightly coat eggplant on both sides with cooking spray; sprinkle with salt and pepper. Grill, covered, over medium heat for 3-5 minutes on each side or until tender.

Top each eggplant slice with a pepper half; sprinkle with the mozzarella cheese. Grill, covered, for 2-3 minutes or until cheese is melted. Spread each roll with 1 tablespoon reserved pesto; top each with an eggplant stack. Replace roll tops. **YIELD: 4 SERVINGS.**

MAIN DISHES

Here, beef, pork, chicken and seafood are paired with fresh vegetables, savory herbs and delicious fruits for no-fuss entrees bursting with goodness. You'll also find meatless dinners that make it a snap to fit an extra serving of produce into your day!

EASY GRILLED FLANK STEAK | PAGE 107

VEGGIE-TOPPED TILAPIA | PAGE 132

CHICKEN BREASTS WITH MELON RELISH
prep/total time: 30 min.

1/4	teaspoon salt	1/4	cup finely chopped celery
1/4	teaspoon ground ginger	1	green onion, chopped
1/4	teaspoon ground nutmeg	2	tablespoons minced fresh mint
1/4	teaspoon pepper	1	tablespoon chopped crystallized ginger
4	boneless skinless chicken breast halves (6 ounces *each*)	1	tablespoon lime juice
1	tablespoon canola oil	1	tablespoon honey
RELISH:		1/2	teaspoon grated lime peel
1	cup diced cantaloupe		

In a small bowl, combine the salt, ginger, nutmeg and pepper. Rub over both sides of the chicken. In a large skillet, cook the chicken in oil over medium heat for 8-10 minutes on each side or until a meat thermometer reads 170°. Meanwhile, in a small bowl, combine the relish ingredients. Serve with chicken. **YIELD: 4 SERVINGS.**

ROXANNE CHAN
ALBANY, CALIFORNIA

The topping is sweet and tasty in this tropical-tasting melon relish recipe. It goes well with the tender chicken breasts to finish a wonderful summery dish.

BISCUIT MUSHROOM BAKE
prep: 20 min. | bake: 15 min.

1	pound sliced fresh mushrooms	1	teaspoon onion powder
2	tablespoons butter	1	teaspoon garlic powder
3	tablespoons all-purpose flour	1/4	teaspoon salt
1	cup chicken broth	1/4	teaspoon pepper
1/2	cup whole milk	1/4	teaspoon paprika
1	tablespoon lemon juice	1	tube (12 ounces) refrigerated biscuits

In a large skillet, saute the mushrooms in butter. Stir in the flour until blended. Gradually add broth and milk. Bring to a boil; cook and stir for 2 minutes or until thickened. Remove from the heat. Stir in the lemon juice, onion powder, garlic powder, salt, pepper and paprika.

Pour into a greased 11-in. x 7-in. baking dish. Arrange the biscuits over the top. Bake, uncovered, at 375° for 15-20 minutes or until the biscuits are golden brown. Let stand for 5 minutes before serving. **YIELD: 5 SERVINGS.**

DAWN ESTERLY
MEADVILLE, PENNSYLVANIA

Mushroom lovers will adore this home-style recipe. Golden biscuits rest atop loads of sliced mushrooms and a flavorful gravy. It's always been a hit in my family.

MARGARET MCCULLY ST. JOHN, NEW BRUNSWICK

Wine lends a warm touch to this satisfying take on a traditional French stew. Serve with garlic bread and a green salad and dinner's done!

SAVORY BEEF STEW
prep: 25 min. | cook: 1-1/2 hours

1/4 cup all-purpose flour	1 teaspoon dried parsley flakes
1 pound beef stew meat, cut into 1-inch cubes	1/4 teaspoon salt
1 small onion, chopped	1/4 teaspoon garlic powder
1 tablespoon canola oil	1/8 teaspoon pepper
1-1/2 cups water	2 medium carrots, chopped
1 can (10-1/2 ounces) condensed beef consomme, undiluted	2 medium parsnips, peeled and chopped
1/2 cup sherry *or* reduced-sodium beef broth	1 large potato, peeled and chopped
1 teaspoon Worcestershire sauce	1 medium turnip, peeled and chopped

Place the flour in a large resealable plastic bag; add the beef, a few pieces at a time, and shake to coat.

In a large saucepan coated with cooking spray, cook beef and onion in oil over medium-high heat until browned on all sides. Stir in water, consomme, sherry or broth, Worcestershire sauce and seasonings. Bring to a boil. Reduce heat; cover and simmer for 1 hour.

Stir in the carrots, parsnips, potato and turnip. Bring to a boil. Reduce heat; cover and simmer for 30-45 minutes or until meat and vegetables are tender. **YIELD: 4 SERVINGS.**

BLACKBERRY-SAUCED PORK CHOPS
prep/total time: 30 min.

1/2 cup seedless blackberry spreadable fruit	Dash ground cinnamon
1 tablespoon lemon juice	4 boneless pork loin chops (5 ounces *each*)
1 tablespoon reduced-sodium soy sauce	2 teaspoons steak seasoning
	2 teaspoons olive oil
	1 cup fresh blackberries

In a small saucepan, combine the spreadable fruit, lemon juice, soy sauce and cinnamon. Cook and stir over low heat until spreadable fruit is melted. Remove from the heat; set aside.

Sprinkle both sides of the pork chops with steak seasoning. In a large nonstick skillet coated with cooking spray, cook the chops in oil over medium-high heat for 5-7 minutes on each side or until a meat thermometer reads 160°. Serve with the sauce and the blackberries. **YIELD: 4 SERVINGS.**

EDITOR'S NOTE: This recipe was tested with McCormick's Montreal Steak Seasoning. Look for it in the spice aisle.

PRISCILLA GILBERT
INDIAN HARBOUR BEACH,
FLORIDA

My family loved these chops the first time I fixed them. As tasty in a skillet as they are grilled, you can enjoy them all year long. The sauce is also great with chicken!

ROASTED CHICKEN WITH VEGGIES
prep: 20 min. | bake: 1-1/2 hours

1 broiler/fryer chicken (3 to 3-1/2 pounds)	3 medium baking potatoes, cut into 1-1/2-inch pieces
1 tablespoon canola oil	2 medium onions, cut into wedges
1/8 teaspoon salt	2 tablespoons butter, melted
1/8 teaspoon pepper	4 teaspoons minced fresh thyme *or* 1 teaspoon dried thyme
6 medium carrots, cut into 1-inch pieces	
4 celery ribs, cut into 1-inch pieces	

Place the chicken, breast side up, in a shallow roasting pan. Rub with the oil; sprinkle with the salt and pepper. Bake, uncovered, at 375° for 45 minutes.

Arrange the carrots, celery, potatoes and onions around chicken. Combine butter and thyme; drizzle over chicken and vegetables.

Cover and bake 45-60 minutes longer or until a meat thermometer inserted into the chicken reads 180° and vegetables are tender. **YIELD: 6 SERVINGS.**

MARY BETH HANSEN
COLUMBIA, TENNESSEE

Thyme flavors this moist, golden brown chicken surrounded by bright, tender vegetables.

CAJUN PEPPER STEAK

prep: 20 min. | cook: 1-1/4 hours

1-1/2	pounds beef top round steak, cubed	1	tablespoon chili powder
2	tablespoons butter	1	tablespoon soy sauce
2	medium onions, halved and sliced	1/2	to 1 teaspoon Cajun seasoning
2	medium green peppers, julienned	1/4	teaspoon hot pepper sauce, optional
1	medium sweet red pepper, julienned	2	tablespoons cornstarch
1	celery rib, sliced	2	tablespoons cold water
1-1/2	cups water		Hot cooked egg noodles or rice
4	teaspoons Worcestershire sauce		

In a large skillet, brown beef in butter over medium heat; drain. Stir in the onions, peppers and celery; cook and stir for 2 minutes.

Add the water, Worcestershire sauce, chili powder, soy sauce, Cajun seasoning and pepper sauce if desired. Bring to a boil. Reduce heat; cover and simmer for 1 to 1-1/2 hours or until meat is tender.

Combine the cornstarch and cold water until smooth; stir into meat mixture. Bring to a boil; cook and stir for 2 minutes or until thickened. Serve with noodles or rice. **YIELD: 4 SERVINGS.**

RONALD TREADWAY ACWORTH, GEORGIA

The seasonings in this recipe turn beef into a zesty dish you'll want to serve again and again.

BROILED PORK CHOPS WITH MANGO SAUCE

prep/total time: 30 min.

3	medium mangoes, peeled, pitted and cut into chunks	1/2	teaspoon ground coriander
1/4	cup chicken broth	4	boneless butterflied pork chops (8 ounces each)
2	tablespoons apricot preserves	2	teaspoons lemon-pepper seasoning

In a blender, combine mangoes and broth; cover and process until smooth. In a small saucepan, combine the mango puree, preserves and coriander. Bring to a boil; cook and stir for 2 minutes. Reduce heat; simmer, uncovered, for 10 minutes.

Meanwhile, sprinkle the pork chops with lemon-pepper. Broil chops 3-4 in. from the heat for 5-6 minutes on each side or until a meat thermometer reads 160°. Serve with mango sauce. **YIELD: 4 SERVINGS.**

TASTE OF HOME TEST KITCHEN

Surprise your gang tonight with this unique pork chop dinner. You won't believe how much flavor you get from just a handful of items.

KAREN MERGENER
ST. CROIX,
MINNESOTA

You'll make any get-together special with these attractive kabobs. Cubes of marinated steak are skewered with shrimp, mushrooms, tomatoes, green peppers and onions, then grilled. For picnics, I like to assemble the kabobs at home.

STEAK AND SHRIMP KABOBS

prep: 20 min. + marinating | grill: 15 min.

1 cup teriyaki sauce	1 pound uncooked large shrimp, peeled and deveined
1 can (6 ounces) pineapple juice	1 pound whole fresh mushrooms
1/2 cup packed brown sugar	2 large green peppers, cut into 1-inch pieces
6 garlic cloves, minced	
1/4 teaspoon Worcestershire sauce	2 medium onions, halved and quartered
1/8 teaspoon pepper	1 pint cherry tomatoes
1 pound beef top sirloin steak, cut into 1-inch cubes	1-1/2 teaspoons cornstarch

In a large bowl, combine the first six ingredients. Pour half of the marinade into a large resealable plastic bag; add the beef. Seal bag and turn to coat; refrigerate for 8 hours or overnight, turning occasionally. Cover and refrigerate remaining marinade.

Drain and discard marinade. On metal or soaked wooden skewers, alternately thread the beef, shrimp, mushrooms, green peppers, onions and tomatoes; set aside. In a small saucepan, combine the cornstarch and reserved marinade until smooth. Bring to a boil; cook and stir for 1-2 minutes or until sauce is thickened.

Using long-handled tongs, dip a paper towel in cooking oil and lightly coat the grill rack. Prepare grill for indirect heat, using a drip pan. Place kabobs over drip pan and grill, covered, over indirect medium heat for 6 minutes, turning once. Baste with the sauce. Continue turning and basting for 8-10 minutes or until shrimp turn pink and beef reaches desired doneness. **YIELD: 6-8 SERVINGS.**

EASY GRILLED FLANK STEAK

prep: 20 min. + marinating | grill: 15 min.

1	small onion, chopped	2	fresh sage leaves, thinly sliced *or* 3/4 teaspoon dried sage leaves
1/2	cup dry red wine *or* reduced-sodium beef broth		
2	tablespoons olive oil	1/2	teaspoon salt
2	garlic cloves, minced	1/2	teaspoon minced fresh gingerroot
1	teaspoon brown sugar		
1/4	teaspoon pepper	1	beef flank steak (1 pound)

In a large resealable plastic bag, combine first nine ingredients. Score the surface of the beef, making diamond shapes 1/4 in. deep; place in bag. Seal bag and turn to coat; refrigerate for 8 hours or overnight.

Drain and discard marinade. Using long-handled tongs, moisten a paper towel with cooking oil and lightly coat the grill rack. Grill the steak, covered, over medium heat or broil 4 in. from the heat for 6-8 minutes on each side or until meat reaches desired doneness (for medium-rare, a meat thermometer should read 145°; medium, 160°; well-done, 170°). Let stand for 5 minutes; thinly slice across grain. **YIELD: 4 SERVINGS.**

VALERIE CHIPMAN LISBON, MAINE

We have made this over an open fire pit, which is really yummy, and also on a gas grill. Try serving it with onions, peppers and potatoes grilled in a foil pack.

SPIRAL HAM WITH CRANBERRY GLAZE

prep: 15 min. | bake: 3 hours

1	bone-in fully cooked spiral-sliced ham (8 pounds)	1	jar (12 ounces) red currant jelly
		1	cup light corn syrup
1	can (14 ounces) whole-berry cranberry sauce	1/2	teaspoon ground ginger
1	package (12 ounces) fresh *or* frozen cranberries		

Place ham on a rack in a shallow roasting pan. Cover and bake at 325° for 2-1/2 hours.

Meanwhile, for glaze, combine remaining ingredients in a saucepan. Bring to a boil. Reduce heat; simmer, uncovered, until cranberries pop, stirring occasionally. Remove from the heat; set aside.

Uncover ham; bake 30 minutes longer or until a meat thermometer reads 140°, basting twice with 1-1/2 cups glaze. Serve remaining glaze with ham. **YIELD: 12-16 SERVINGS.**

PATRICIA PRESCOTT MANCHESTER, NEW HAMPSHIRE

A sweet, tangy glaze complements this ham and looks so pretty. The cranberry flavor pairs well with the meat. It's been a tradition in my home for many years.

PESTO RICE-STUFFED PORK CHOPS

prep: 20 min. | bake: 30 min.

1/2	cup fresh basil leaves	1	tablespoon olive oil
1/2	cup fresh parsley sprigs	1	teaspoon chili sauce
1/2	cup chopped pecans	4	bone-in pork loin chops (8 ounces *each*)
3	garlic cloves, peeled	1/2	teaspoon lemon-pepper seasoning
2/3	cup cooked wild rice		
2	tablespoons grated Parmesan cheese	1	tablespoon butter
2	tablespoons cream cheese, softened		

In a food processor, combine the basil, parsley, pecans and garlic; cover and process until blended. Transfer to a small bowl; add the rice, cheeses, oil and chili sauce.

Cut a pocket in each pork chop by slicing almost to bone. Sprinkle chops with lemon-pepper.

In a large skillet, brown chops in butter; cool for 5 minutes. Fill with rice mixture; secure with toothpicks if necessary. Place in a 13-in. x 9-in. baking dish coated with cooking spray.

Bake the chops, uncovered, at 350° for 28-32 minutes or until a meat thermometer reads 160°. Discard toothpicks. **YIELD: 4 SERVINGS.**

CAROLYN POPWELL
LACEY, WASHINGTON

My family loves pork chops so I experimented stuffing them. I used some of our favorite items, such as pesto, and it was a huge hit!

SWEET 'N' SAVORY PEACH CHICKEN

prep: 25 min. | bake: 45 min.

3	tablespoons all-purpose flour	1	cup orange juice
1	teaspoon salt	2	tablespoons cider vinegar
1/2	teaspoon pepper	2	tablespoons honey
1	broiler/fryer chicken (3-1/2 to 4 pounds), cut up	1	tablespoon minced fresh parsley
2	to 3 tablespoons canola oil	3	medium peaches, peeled and sliced

In a large resealable plastic bag, combine the flour, salt and pepper. Add chicken, a few pieces at a time, and shake to coat.

In a large skillet, fry chicken in oil until browned on all sides. Transfer to a greased 13-in. x 9-in. baking dish.

In a small bowl, combine orange juice, vinegar, honey and parsley; pour over chicken. Cover and bake at 350° for 40 minutes.

Uncover; add the peaches. Bake 5-10 minutes longer or until chicken juices run clear and peaches are heated through. **YIELD: 4 SERVINGS.**

REGENA HOFER
MEADOWS, MANITOBA

This recipe features the sweet flavor of peaches and the savory flavor of roast chicken. They blend perfectly to create a wonderful main dish.

FENNEL STUFFED COD

prep: 20 min. + chilling | bake: 30 min.

1 cup (8 ounces) plain yogurt	1/4 cup chopped onion
2-1/4 cups finely chopped fennel fronds, *divided*	2 to 4 tablespoons canola oil
1 teaspoon lemon juice	4 cups unseasoned stuffing cubes
1 teaspoon minced chives	1 cup chicken broth
1/8 teaspoon salt, optional	2 eggs, lightly beaten
1/8 teaspoon pepper	4 cod *or* flounder fillets (1-1/2 pounds)
2 celery ribs, chopped	1 medium lemon, sliced

For sauce, combine the yogurt, 1/4 cup of fennel, lemon juice, chives, salt if desired and pepper in a bowl. Cover and refrigerate for 2 hours or overnight.

In a large skillet, saute celery and onion in oil until tender. Remove from heat. Stir in the croutons, broth, eggs and remaining fennel.

Spoon about 1 cup stuffing mixture onto each fillet; roll fish around stuffing. Transfer to a greased 2-qt. baking dish. Top each with a lemon slice.

Bake at 350° for 30-35 minutes or until fish flakes easily with a fork and a thermometer inserted in the dressing reads 165°. Serve with fennel sauce. **YIELD: 4 SERVINGS.**

MARY ELLEN WILCOX
BRANT LAKE, NEW YORK

Moist fish, a super stuffing and a creamy sauce always make for a memorable meal.

SHRIMP IN HERBS

prep: 25 min. | cook: 10 min.

2 pounds uncooked medium shrimp, peeled and deveined	1 tablespoon minced fresh tarragon *or* 1 teaspoon dried tarragon
2 tablespoons olive oil	1 teaspoon dried chervil
3 garlic cloves, minced	3/4 teaspoon salt
1-1/2 cups chopped fresh tomatoes	1/4 teaspoon pepper
1 tablespoon minced chives	2 tablespoons butter, cubed
1 tablespoon minced fresh flat-leaf parsley	

In a large nonstick skillet coated with cooking spray, cook shrimp in oil for 2 minutes. Add garlic; cook 1 minute longer. Stir in tomatoes and seasonings. Cook 3-5 minutes longer or until shrimp turn pink. Stir in butter until melted. **YIELD: 4 SERVINGS.**

IOLA EGLE
BELLA VISTA, ARKANSAS

Dressed up with two types of parsley and other herbs, this rich and elegant shrimp entree makes a special weeknight supper.

SUMMER SAUSAGE HOBO PACKETS
prep: 25 min. | grill: 20 min.

1	pound summer sausage, cut into 1-inch pieces	1	small zucchini, sliced
4	medium potatoes, peeled and cut into 1/2-inch cubes	1	small yellow summer squash, sliced
3	cups shredded cabbage	1	pound chicken tenderloins, cut into 1-inch pieces
1	large sweet onion, halved and sliced	2	medium tomatoes, cut into wedges
1	medium green pepper, cut into strips	1/2	cup butter, cut into eight cubes
1	medium sweet red pepper, cut into strips	1/4	cup Italian salad dressing

In a large bowl, combine first eight ingredients. Gently stir in chicken and tomatoes. Divide mixture among eight double thicknesses of heavy-duty foil (about 12 in. square). Top each with a butter cube.

Fold foil around mixture and seal tightly. Grill, covered, over medium heat for 20-25 minutes or until the chicken is no longer pink and vegetables are tender. Carefully open foil to allow steam to escape; drizzle with dressing. **YIELD: 8 SERVINGS.**

**TONIA ANNE CARRIER
ELIZABETHTON, TENNESSEE**

We love to grill, especially when we go camping in our RV. This is a favorite of our family and the foil packet makes for fast clean up.

TURKEY DIVAN PIZZA
prep: 20 min. | bake: 15 min.

1	prebaked 12-inch thin pizza crust	1	can (10-3/4 ounces) condensed broccoli cheese soup, undiluted
2	teaspoons olive oil		
1/2	to 1 teaspoon garlic salt	1/3	cup whole milk
		1/2	cup shredded cheddar cheese
2	cups fresh broccoli florets	2	tablespoons dry bread crumbs
1-1/2	cups cubed cooked turkey	1	tablespoon butter, melted

Place pizza crust on a baking sheet. Brush with oil; sprinkle with garlic salt. Top with broccoli and turkey.

In a small bowl, combine soup and milk; spread over broccoli and turkey. Sprinkle with cheese. Toss bread crumbs and butter; sprinkle over the top.

Bake at 400° for 13-15 minutes or until cheese is melted and broccoli is crisp-tender. **YIELD: 6-8 SERVINGS.**

**CHARLOTTE SMITH
PITTSBURGH,
PENNSYLVANIA**

Kids who are typically picky eaters will gobble up slice after slice of this savory pizza. I often have frozen cubed cooked turkey on hand to make this meal in a moment's notice.

SOUTHWEST STUFFED PEPPERS

prep/total time: 25 min.

1 pound lean ground beef (90% lean)	1/2 teaspoon dried oregano
2/3 cup chopped sweet red pepper	1/4 teaspoon cayenne pepper
1/2 cup chopped onion	1-1/2 cups water, *divided*
2 garlic cloves, minced	4 medium green peppers
1-3/4 cups chopped seeded tomatoes, *divided*	2 tablespoons sour cream
4 teaspoons chili powder	2 tablespoons shredded cheddar cheese
1 teaspoon cornstarch	2 green onions, chopped
1 teaspoon ground cumin	4 grape tomatoes, halved, optional

In a large skillet, cook the beef, red pepper and onion over medium heat until meat is no longer pink. Add garlic; cook 1 minute longer. Drain.

Stir in 1/2 cup tomatoes, chili powder, cornstarch, cumin, oregano and cayenne. Gradually stir in 1/2 cup water. Bring to a boil. Reduce heat; simmer, uncovered, for 15-20 minutes.

Meanwhile, cut the green peppers in half lengthwise; remove seeds. Place in an ungreased shallow 3-qt. microwave-safe dish; add remaining water. Cover and microwave on high for 8-10 minutes or until crisp tender. Drain; fill each pepper half with 1/3 cup beef mixture.

Top with the remaining tomatoes. Garnish with the sour cream, cheese, green onions and grape tomatoes if desired. **YIELD: 4 SERVINGS.**

EDITOR'S NOTE: This recipe was tested in a 1,100-watt microwave.

SAUSAGE VEGETABLE PACKETS
prep: 20 min. | grill: 25 min.

1/2	pound smoked sausage, cut into 1/2-inch pieces	1/4	cup butter, melted
3	medium zucchini, sliced	1	envelope onion soup mix
3	medium tomatoes, sliced	1	tablespoon brown sugar
1	medium green pepper, julienned	1/4	teaspoon salt
		1/4	teaspoon pepper

In a large bowl, combine all the ingredients. Divide between two pieces of double-layered heavy-duty foil (about 12-in. square). Fold foil around sausage mixture and seal tightly.

Grill packets, covered, over medium heat for 25-30 minutes or until the vegetables are tender. Open foil carefully to allow the steam to escape. **YIELD: 4 SERVINGS.**

KAY BISH
THOMPSONVILLE, ILLINOIS

We have so much squash in the summer, but we never tire of this supper. We often leave the sausage out of the foil packets and just serve the veggies as a side dish. Even those who don't usually like zucchini enjoy it.

SWEET-AND-SOUR BEEF WITH BROCCOLI
prep/total time: 30 min.

1	can (20 ounces) unsweetened pineapple tidbits	2	cups fresh broccoli florets
2	tablespoons cornstarch	1/2	pound sliced fresh mushrooms
1	cup reduced-sodium beef broth	1	medium sweet red pepper, julienned
1/4	cup reduced-sodium soy sauce	1	can (8 ounces) sliced water chestnuts, drained
2	teaspoons minced fresh gingerroot	1	tablespoon sesame oil
1	teaspoon minced garlic	1	pound lean ground beef (90% lean)
2-1/2	cups uncooked instant rice		

TASTE OF HOME
TEST KITCHEN

We re-created the classic Chinese beef and broccoli dish using a beautiful variety of colorful vegetables.

Drain pineapple, reserving juice; set pineapple aside. In a small bowl, combine the cornstarch, broth, soy sauce, ginger, garlic and reserved juice until blended; set aside.

Cook the rice according to package directions. Meanwhile, in a large skillet, stir-fry broccoli, mushrooms, red pepper and water chestnuts in oil for 3-5 minutes or until crisp-tender; remove and set aside. In the same pan, cook beef over medium heat until no longer pink; drain.

Stir cornstarch mixture and add to the skillet. Bring to a boil; cook and stir for 1-2 minutes or until thickened. Stir in vegetable mixture and pineapple; heat through. Serve with rice. **YIELD: 6 SERVINGS.**

SWEET POTATO SAUSAGE CASSEROLE
prep: 20 min. | bake: 25 min.

8	ounces uncooked spiral pasta		1	teaspoon minced garlic
8	ounces smoked sausage, cut into 1/4-inch slices		1	can (14-1/2 ounces) diced tomatoes, undrained
2	medium sweet potatoes, peeled and cut into 1/2-inch cubes		1	cup heavy whipping cream
1	cup chopped green pepper		1/4	teaspoon salt
1/2	cup chopped onion		1/4	teaspoon pepper
2	tablespoons olive oil		1	cup (4 ounces) shredded cheddar cheese

Cook pasta according to package directions. Meanwhile, in a large skillet, cook sausage, sweet potatoes, green pepper and onion in oil over medium heat for 5 minutes or until vegetables are tender. Add garlic; cook 1 minute longer. Drain.

Add the tomatoes, cream, salt and pepper. Bring to a boil; remove from the heat. Drain pasta; stir into sausage mixture. Transfer to a greased 13-in. x 9-in. baking dish. Sprinkle with cheese.

Bake, uncovered, at 350° for 25-30 minutes or until bubbly. Let stand for 5 minutes before serving. **YIELD: 8 SERVINGS.**

**RICKEY MADDEN
CLINTON, SOUTH CAROLINA**

Most people never consider combining sweet potatoes with pasta and kielbasa, but I adapted this recipe from several others and I've received several compliments on it. You can add more cheese or sausage to suit your taste.

PORK 'N' POTATO SKILLET
prep/total time: 30 min.

4	boneless pork loin chops (1 inch thick and 4 ounces *each*)		1	medium onion, sliced
			1	teaspoon dried oregano
1/4	teaspoon pepper		1	cup chicken broth
1	tablespoon olive oil		1/2	cup diced roasted sweet red peppers
4	medium red potatoes, thinly sliced			

Sprinkle pork chops with pepper. In a large skillet, brown chops in oil on both sides; drain. Remove and keep warm.

In same skillet, saute potatoes, onion and oregano for 6-8 minutes or until potatoes are almost tender. Stir in broth and red peppers; bring to a boil.

Top with the pork chops. Reduce the heat; cover and simmer for 10-15 minutes or until potatoes are tender and a meat thermometer reads 160°, stirring occasionally. **YIELD: 4 SERVINGS.**

**MARY TALLMAN
ARBOR VITAE, WISCONSIN**

This scrumptious skillet dinner makes the ideal hurry-up entree for a hungry family. Round out the meal with steamed vegetables or a rustic green salad.

*This creamy
dish has lots
of great earthy
flavors. A bit of
rosemary and
mushrooms
make it special,
too. This is sure
to become a
family favorite!*

Fresh & Easy Tip

Steak is easier to slice into thin
strips if it is frozen. Place fresh
steak in the freezer 30 minutes
before slicing. When cutting into
strips, always be sure to slice
across the grain for the most
tender results.

MUSHROOM STEAK 'N' LINGUINE
prep/total time: 30 min.

8 ounces uncooked linguine	1/2 pound sliced fresh mushrooms
1 pound beef top round steak, cut into thin strips	1 cup coarsely chopped fresh spinach
1/4 teaspoon salt	1/2 teaspoon dried rosemary, crushed
1/4 teaspoon pepper	3/4 cup spreadable chive and onion cream cheese
3 teaspoons olive oil, *divided*	1/2 cup sour cream
1 cup chopped sweet red pepper	1 tablespoon whole milk
1/2 cup chopped onion	

Cook linguine according to package directions. Meanwhile, sprinkle beef with salt and pepper. In a large skillet, saute beef in 2 teaspoons oil until tender. Remove and keep warm.

In the same pan, saute red pepper and onion in remaining oil until tender. Add mushrooms; saute 1-2 minutes longer or until tender. Add spinach and rosemary; cook and stir just until spinach is wilted. Stir in the cream cheese, sour cream and milk; heat through (do not boil).

Drain linguine; top with mushroom mixture and beef. **YIELD: 4 SERVINGS.**

OVERNIGHT ASPARAGUS STRATA

prep: 15 min. + chilling | bake: 40 min. + standing

1 pound fresh asparagus, trimmed and cut into 1-inch pieces	1/2 cup chopped sweet red pepper
4 English muffins, split and toasted	8 eggs
2 cups (8 ounces) shredded Colby-Monterey Jack cheese, *divided*	2 cups whole milk
	1 teaspoon salt
	1 teaspoon ground mustard
1 cup cubed fully cooked ham	1/4 teaspoon pepper

In a large saucepan, bring 8 cups water to a boil. Add asparagus; cover and cook for 3 minutes. Drain and immediately place the asparagus in ice water. Drain and pat dry.

Arrange six English muffin halves, cut side up, in a greased 13-in. x 9-in. baking dish. Fill in spaces with remaining muffin halves. Sprinkle with 1 cup cheese, asparagus, ham and red pepper.

In a small bowl, whisk the eggs, milk, salt, mustard and pepper; pour over muffins. Cover and refrigerate overnight.

Remove from the refrigerator 30 minutes before baking. Sprinkle with remaining cheese. Bake, uncovered, at 375° for 40-45 minutes or until a knife inserted near center comes out clean. Let stand for 5 minutes before cutting. **YIELD: 6-8 SERVINGS.**

LYNN LICATA
SYLVANIA, OHIO

I've made this tasty egg dish for breakfast, brunch and even as a Christmas dinner side dish. With its English muffin crust, this is not your run-of-the-mill strata. Friends always ask for the recipe.

MEDITERRANEAN CHICKEN

prep/total time: 25 min.

4 boneless skinless chicken breast halves (6 ounces *each*)	1 pint grape tomatoes
	16 pitted Greek *or* ripe olives, sliced
1/4 teaspoon salt	3 tablespoons capers, drained
1/4 teaspoon pepper	
3 tablespoons olive oil	

Sprinkle chicken with salt and pepper. In a large ovenproof skillet, cook chicken in oil over medium heat for 2-3 minutes on each side or until golden brown. Add the tomatoes, olives and capers. Bake, uncovered, at 475° for 10-14 minutes or until a meat thermometer reads 170°. **YIELD: 4 SERVINGS.**

MARY RELYEA
CANASTOTA, NEW YORK

As special as it is simple to prepare, this moist, flavorful chicken is dressed in tomatoes, olives and capers. It's a knockout entree for your guests.

SNAPPY EGGPLANT SPAGHETTI
prep: 10 min. | cook: 45 min.

1	medium onion, chopped	1/4	cup minced fresh parsley
2	tablespoons olive oil	2	tablespoons minced fresh basil *or* 2 teaspoons dried basil
1	garlic clove, minced		
3-1/2	cups tomato juice	1	teaspoon salt
1	small eggplant, peeled and cubed	1/4	teaspoon crushed red pepper flakes
1	medium green pepper, chopped	1	package (1 pound) spaghetti
16	large pitted ripe olives, finely chopped	1	pound red snapper *or* grouper fillets, cut into 1-inch cubes

BRETT RUSSO
WATERBORO,
SOUTH CAROLINA

This recipe, which I adapted from an old Italian cookbook, offers a flavorful taste of my roots. My gang enjoys it with garlic bread.

In a large saucepan, saute onion in oil until tender. Add garlic; cook 1 minute longer. Stir in tomato juice; bring to a boil. Reduce heat; cover and simmer for 10 minutes. Add the eggplant, green pepper, olives, parsley, basil, salt and red pepper flakes. Cover and simmer for 20 minutes.

Meanwhile, cook spaghetti according to package directions. Add fish to eggplant mixture; cover and simmer 10 minutes longer or until fish flakes easily with a fork. Drain spaghetti; serve with fish mixture. **YIELD: 8 SERVINGS.**

MEXI-MAC SKILLET
prep/total time: 30 min.

1	pound lean ground beef (90% lean)	1/2	cup water
1	large onion, chopped	1-1/4	teaspoons chili powder
1	can (14-1/2 ounces) diced tomatoes, undrained	1	teaspoon dried oregano
		1/2	teaspoon salt
1	can (8 ounces) tomato sauce	2/3	cup uncooked elbow macaroni
1	cup fresh *or* frozen corn	2/3	cup shredded reduced-fat cheddar cheese

MAURANE RAMSEY
FORT WAYNE, INDIANA

This dish really saves time because it eliminates the need to precook the pasta and makes a family-pleasing supper in minutes! It's the tastiest and quickest recipe I have. It's one of my husband's all-time favorites!

In a large nonstick skillet over medium-high heat, cook the beef and onion until meat is no longer pink; drain. Stir in the tomatoes, tomato sauce, corn, water, chili powder, oregano and salt.

Bring to a boil; stir in macaroni. Reduce heat; cover and simmer for 18-22 minutes or until macaroni is tender. Sprinkle with cheese. **YIELD: 5 SERVINGS.**

HERB-CRUSTED PORK ROAST

prep: 25 min. | bake: 2 hours + standing

1 teaspoon ground mustard	1-1/2 cups soft bread crumbs
1 teaspoon lemon-herb seasoning	1/2 cup grated Parmesan cheese
1 teaspoon salt	1/4 cup minced fresh basil *or* 4 teaspoons dried basil
1/2 teaspoon pepper	2 teaspoons minced fresh thyme
1 bone-in pork loin roast (4 pounds)	2 teaspoons minced fresh rosemary
2 tablespoons plus 1/4 cup olive oil, *divided*	2 garlic cloves, minced
1 tablespoon Dijon mustard	1 cup white wine *or* chicken broth

In a small bowl, combine ground mustard, herb seasoning, salt and pepper; rub over roast. In a large skillet, brown roast in 2 tablespoons oil. Place roast fat side up on a rack in a shallow roasting pan. Brush top with Dijon mustard. Combine the bread crumbs, cheese, basil, thyme, rosemary, garlic and remaining oil; press onto roast.

Bake roast, uncovered, at 350° for 2 to 2-1/4 hours or until a meat thermometer reads 160°. Place on a warm serving platter. Let stand for 10-15 minutes before slicing.

Stir wine into roasting pan, scraping to loosen browned bits. Pour into a saucepan. Bring to a boil over medium-high heat; cook until reduced by half. Serve with roast. **YIELD: 12-14 SERVINGS.**

MARY ANN LEE
CLIFTON PARK, NEW YORK

There is nothing like a well-seasoned pork roast, pan-seared and baked to perfection. The tender meat gets a boost from a cheesy herbal crust and reduction sauce.

UNSTUFFED CABBAGE

prep: 20 min. | bake: 45 min.

6 cups chopped cabbage	1/4 teaspoon pepper
1/2 pound lean ground beef (90% lean)	2 cans (10-3/4 ounces *each*) condensed tomato soup, undiluted
1 small onion, chopped	
1 cup uncooked instant rice	1 cup water
1/2 teaspoon salt, optional	1/3 cup shredded cheddar cheese

Place cabbage in a greased 2-1/2-qt. baking dish. In a large skillet, cook beef and onion over medium heat until meat is no longer pink; drain. Stir in rice, salt if desired and pepper; spoon over cabbage.

Combine soup and water; pour over beef mixture. Cover and bake at 350° for 40-50 minutes or until rice and cabbage are tender. Uncover; sprinkle with cheese. Bake 5-10 minutes longer or until the cheese is melted. **YIELD: 4 SERVINGS.**

JUDY THORN
MARS, PENNSYLVANIA

A teacher at the preschool where I work shared the idea for this delicious ground beef and cabbage casserole. It's a nutritious and economical meal for busy families.

**TASTE OF HOME
TEST KITCHEN**

*These crispy pork medallions are
treated to a refreshing strawberry
sauce that's ideal for a
summer meal.*

**KERIN BENJAMIN
CITRUS HEIGHTS,
CALIFORNIA**

*My family (including two small
children), liked this recipe so well,
I made it for a potluck the very
next day. Everyone raved about it
there, too, even people who aren't
particularly fond of fish.*

PORK MEDALLIONS WITH GARLIC-STRAWBERRY SAUCE
prep: 15 min. | cook: 20 min.

1 pork tenderloin (1 pound), cut into 1/2-inch slices	1/2 cup butter, *divided*
1/4 teaspoon salt	2 cups fresh strawberries
1/4 teaspoon pepper	1 teaspoon minced garlic
1/2 cup all-purpose flour	1/4 cup hot water
2 eggs, lightly beaten	1 teaspoon chicken bouillon granules
2/3 cup seasoned bread crumbs	Sliced fresh strawberries, optional

Flatten pork to 1/4-in. thickness; sprinkle with salt and pepper. Place the flour, eggs and bread crumbs in separate shallow bowls. Dip pork in the flour, eggs, then bread crumbs.

In a large skillet over medium heat, cook pork in 1/4 cup butter until juices run clear; remove and keep warm.

Meanwhile, place the strawberries in a food processor. Cover and process until pureed; set aside.

In the same skillet, saute garlic in remaining butter for 1 minute. Add the pureed strawberries, water and bouillon; heat through. Serve the pork with the sauce. Garnish with sliced strawberries if desired. **YIELD: 4 SERVINGS.**

GRILLED SALMON WITH NECTARINES
prep/total time: 30 min.

1 tablespoon honey	1 tablespoon minced fresh basil *or* 1 teaspoon dried basil
1 tablespoon lemon juice	
1 tablespoon olive oil	
1/2 teaspoon salt, *divided*	4 salmon fillets (4 ounces each)
3 medium nectarines, peeled and thinly sliced	1/8 teaspoon pepper

In a small bowl, combine honey, lemon juice, oil and 1/4 teaspoon salt. Stir in nectarines and basil; set aside.

Rinse salmon and pat dry with paper towels. Sprinkle with pepper and remaining salt. Using long-handled tongs, moisten a paper towel with cooking oil and lightly coat the grill rack.

Place salmon, skin side down, on grill. Grill, covered, over medium heat or broil 4 in. from the heat for 15-20 minutes or until fish flakes easily with a fork. Serve with nectarine mixture. **YIELD: 4 SERVINGS.**

TAMMY STRANGE STATHAM, GEORGIA

This elegant meal-in-one features a hearty portion of salmon served on flavorful couscous and topped with an amazing mango sauce.

MANGO COUSCOUS WITH SALMON

prep/total time: 30 min.

1/4 cup canola oil	1 medium mango, peeled and chopped
2-1/2 teaspoons minced garlic	**MANGO SAUCE:**
1/4 teaspoon salt	1 medium mango, peeled and cut into chunks
1/4 teaspoon pepper	2 tablespoons lemon juice
1/4 cup minced fresh parsley, *divided*	2 tablespoons honey
4 salmon fillets (6 ounces *each*)	2 fresh basil leaves
2 cups chicken broth	1 tablespoon minced fresh parsley
1 tablespoon butter	1 tablespoon water
1 package (10 ounces) plain couscous	1 tablespoon Dijon mustard
2 medium tomatoes, chopped	

In a small bowl, combine oil, garlic, salt, pepper and 2 tablespoons parsley. Rub over salmon. Broil 4 in. from the heat for 6-8 minutes on each side or until fish flakes easily with a fork.

Meanwhile, in a large saucepan, bring broth and butter to a boil. Stir in couscous. Cover and remove from heat; let stand 5 minutes. Stir in tomatoes, mango and remaining parsley.

In a blender, combine the sauce ingredients; cover and puree for 1-2 minutes or until smooth. Serve with salmon and couscous. **YIELD: 4 SERVINGS.**

ZUCCHINI LASAGNA
prep: 20 min. | cook: 40 min.

1	pound ground beef	1	teaspoon fennel seed, crushed
1/2	cup chopped onion	1	teaspoon minced garlic
2	jars (one 26 ounces, one 14 ounces) meatless spaghetti sauce	9	no-cook lasagna noodles
1	can (15 ounces) crushed tomatoes	2	cups sliced zucchini
1	teaspoon dried basil	1	cup ricotta cheese
1	teaspoon dried oregano	1	carton (5 ounces) shredded Asiago cheese

In a large skillet, cook beef and onion over medium heat until meat is no longer pink; drain. Stir in the spaghetti sauce, tomatoes, basil, oregano, fennel and garlic. Bring to a boil. Reduce heat; cover and simmer for 10 minutes.

Spread 1-1/2 cups meat sauce in a greased 13-in. x 9-in. baking dish. Top with three noodles. Spread 1-1/2 cups sauce to edges of the noodles. Top with half of the zucchini, 1/2 cup ricotta cheese and 1/2 cup Asiago cheese. Repeat layers. Top with remaining noodles, sauce and Asiago cheese.

Cover and bake at 375° for 30 minutes. Uncover; bake 10-15 minutes more or until bubbly. Let stand for 5 minutes before cutting. **YIELD: 6 SERVINGS.**

TASTE OF HOME TEST KITCHEN

No-cook noodles save prep time for this lasagna recipe. Since these lasagna noodles will expand during baking, avoid overlapping them. The noodles will touch the sides of the dish upon baking.

CHICKEN-STUFFED CUBANELLE PEPPERS
prep: 20 min. | bake: 55 min.

6	Cubanelle peppers *or* mild banana peppers	3/4	cup soft bread crumbs
2	eggs	1/2	cup cooked long grain rice
1	cup salsa	2	cups meatless spaghetti sauce, *divided*
3	cups shredded cooked chicken breast		

Cut tops off peppers and remove seeds. In a large bowl, combine the eggs, salsa, chicken, bread crumbs and rice. Spoon into peppers.

Coat a 13-in. x 9-in. baking dish and an 8-in. square baking dish with cooking spray. Spread 1 cup spaghetti sauce in larger pan and 1/2 cup sauce in smaller pan. Place the peppers over sauce. Spoon the remaining spaghetti sauce over peppers.

Cover and bake at 350° for 55-60 minutes or until peppers are tender. **YIELD: 6 SERVINGS.**

BEV BURLINGAME CANTON, OHIO

Here's a new take on traditional stuffed peppers. I substituted the chicken for the beef and used Cubanelle peppers in place of the usual green peppers.

OREGANO OLIVE CHICKEN

prep: 15 min. | cook: 30 min.

1	broiler/fryer chicken (4 pounds), cut up and skin removed	1/4	cup capers, drained
1/4	teaspoon pepper	2	tablespoons minced fresh oregano
2	tablespoons olive oil	1	tablespoon minced fresh mint
1/2	cup white wine *or* reduced-sodium chicken broth	1	tablespoon cider vinegar
1/2	cup chopped pimiento-stuffed olives	2	garlic cloves, minced
		1	teaspoon minced fresh thyme

Sprinkle chicken with pepper. In a large nonstick skillet coated with cooking spray, brown chicken on all sides in oil. Remove and keep warm. Drain drippings from skillet.

Combine remaining ingredients; pour into skillet, stirring to loosen browned bits. Bring to a boil. Carefully return the chicken to the pan. Reduce heat; cover and simmer for 20-25 minutes or until chicken juices run clear. **YIELD: 8 SERVINGS.**

CONSUELO LEWTER
MURFREESBORO, TENNESSEE

Folks won't believe a recipe that tastes so savory and special could be so light! Full of fresh-herb flavor, this chicken boasts a wonderful fragrance as it cooks.

CHICKEN ENCHILADAS

prep: 20 min. | bake: 35 min.

1	envelope enchilada sauce mix	1-1/3	cups chopped fresh tomatoes, *divided*
2	cups cubed cooked chicken	1/4	cup chopped green pepper
2	cups (8 ounces) shredded Monterey Jack cheese, *divided*	2	tablespoons chopped green onion
1/3	cup sliced ripe olives	10	flour tortillas (6 inches)
		2	cups shredded lettuce

Prepare enchilada sauce according to package directions. In a large bowl, combine 1/2 cup prepared sauce, chicken, 1 cup of cheese, olives, 1/3 cup of tomatoes, green pepper and onion.

Place a rounded 1/4 cupful of chicken mixture down the center of each tortilla. Roll up and place seam side down in a greased 13-in. x 9-in. baking dish. Pour remaining enchilada sauce over top.

Cover and bake at 350° for 30 minutes. Uncover; sprinkle with the remaining cheese. Bake 5-10 minutes longer or until cheese is melted. Top with lettuce and remaining tomatoes. **YIELD: 5 SERVINGS.**

ELAINE ANDERSON
NEW GALILEE, PENNSYLVANIA

These are great for a family dinner or party. I've also cut the baked enchiladas into three sections and served them as appetizers with chips and salsa.

CHICKEN ROLLS WITH RASPBERRY SAUCE

prep: 25 min. | bake: 35 min.

4	boneless skinless chicken breast halves (6 ounces *each*)	2	cups fresh raspberries
1/2	cup crumbled blue cheese	1/4	cup chicken broth
4	strips ready-to-serve fully cooked bacon, crumbled	4	teaspoons brown sugar
2	tablespoons butter, melted, *divided*	1	tablespoon balsamic vinegar
		1/2	teaspoon minced garlic
		1/4	teaspoon dried oregano

Salt and pepper to taste

Flatten chicken to 1/4-in. thickness; sprinkle with blue cheese and bacon to within 1/2 in. of edges. Roll up each jelly-roll style, starting with a short side; secure with toothpicks.

Place in a greased 8-in. square baking dish. Brush with 1 tablespoon butter; sprinkle with salt and pepper. Bake, uncovered, at 375° for 35-40 minutes or until meat is no longer pink.

Meanwhile, in a small saucepan, combine the raspberries, broth, brown sugar, vinegar, garlic and oregano. Bring to a boil. Reduce heat; simmer, uncovered, for 5 minutes or until thickened.

Press through a sieve; discard seeds. Stir in remaining butter until smooth. Discard toothpicks. Serve with raspberry sauce. **YIELD: 4 SERVINGS.**

ASPARAGUS-STUFFED PORK TENDERLOIN

prep: 20 min. | grill: 20 min.

1/4 teaspoon *each* onion powder, garlic powder, chili powder, salt, seasoned salt and poultry seasoning	1 pork tenderloin (1 pound)
1/8 teaspoon cayenne pepper	1 cup water
	7 to 10 fresh asparagus spears, trimmed

In a small bowl, combine the seasonings; set aside. Cut a lengthwise slit down center of the pork tenderloin to within 1/2 in. of bottom. Open so the meat lies flat; cover with plastic wrap. Flatten to 1/4-in. thickness. Remove the plastic; rub 1/2 teaspoon seasoning mix over inside of tenderloin.

In a large nonstick skillet, bring water to a boil. Add asparagus; cover and cook for 2 minutes. Drain asparagus and immediately place in ice water; drain and pat dry. Place asparagus lengthwise over tenderloin.

Fold the meat over asparagus, starting with a long side, and secure with kitchen string. Rub the remaining seasoning over meat. Grill, covered, over indirect medium heat for 20-25 minutes or until a meat thermometer reads 160°, turning occasionally. Let stand for 5 minutes before slicing. **YIELD: 4 SERVINGS.**

TONYA FARMER
IOWA CITY, IOWA

Asparagus looks lovely tucked inside this juicy pork tenderloin. The robust seasoning rub dresses up an eye-catching entree you'll be proud to serve for special occasions.

CRANBERRY SHORT RIBS

prep: 20 min. | bake: 1-1/2 hours

1-1/2 pounds bone-in beef short ribs	1/8 teaspoon ground mustard
1/2 teaspoon salt, *divided*	Dash ground cloves
1/4 teaspoon pepper	3/4 cup water
1 tablespoon all-purpose flour	2 teaspoons cider vinegar
1 tablespoon brown sugar	1-1/2 to 2 teaspoons grated lemon peel
	1/2 cup fresh cranberries

Sprinkle ribs with 1/4 teaspoon salt and pepper. Place in a greased 8-in. square baking dish. Cover and bake at 350° for 1-1/4 hours.

In a small saucepan, combine the flour, brown sugar, mustard, cloves and remaining salt. Stir in the water, vinegar and lemon peel until smooth. Add cranberries. Bring to a boil; cook and stir for 2 minutes or until thickened.

Drain ribs; top with cranberry mixture. Bake 15-25 minutes longer or until meat is tender. **YIELD: 2 SERVINGS.**

CATHY WYLIE
DAWSON CITY, YUKON

This recipe originally came from my mother-in-law. I prepare this comfort food often during the long winter months which pleases my family.

BAKED SEAFOOD AVOCADOS

prep: 15 min. | bake: 25 min.

1	cup mayonnaise	1	can (4 ounces) medium shrimp, rinsed and drained
3/4	cup chopped celery		
1/2	cup thinly sliced green onions	4	large ripe avocados, halved and pitted
1/8	teaspoon salt, optional	1	to 2 tablespoons lemon juice
1/8	teaspoon pepper		
1	can (4-1/2 ounces) crabmeat, drained, flaked and cartilage removed	1/4	cup crushed potato chips, optional

In a large bowl, combine mayonnaise, celery, onions, salt if desired and pepper. Add crab and shrimp; mix well. Peel avocados if desired. Sprinkle avocados with lemon juice; fill with seafood mixture. Sprinkle with potato chips if desired.

Place in an ungreased 13-in. x 9-in. baking dish. Bake, uncovered, at 350° for 25-30 minutes or until bubbly. **YIELD: 8 SERVINGS.**

MARIAN PLATT
SEQUIM, WASHINGTON

Everyone who tastes this wonderful luncheon dish is surprised that the avocados are baked.

BRUSCHETTA PIZZA

prep: 25 min. | bake: 10 min.

1/2	pound reduced-fat bulk pork sausage	1/2	cup fresh basil leaves, thinly sliced
1	prebaked 12-inch pizza crust	1	tablespoon olive oil
1	package (6 ounces) sliced turkey pepperoni	2	garlic cloves, minced
		1/2	teaspoon minced fresh thyme or 1/8 teaspoon dried thyme
2	cups (8 ounces) shredded part-skim mozzarella cheese	1/2	teaspoon balsamic vinegar
		1/4	teaspoon salt
1-1/2	cups chopped plum tomatoes	1/8	teaspoon pepper
			Additional fresh basil leaves, optional

In a small skillet, cook sausage over medium heat until no longer pink; drain. Place the crust on an ungreased baking sheet. Top with pepperoni, sausage and cheese. Bake at 450° for 10-12 minutes or until cheese is melted.

In a small bowl, combine the tomatoes, sliced basil, oil, garlic, thyme, vinegar, salt and pepper. Spoon over the pizza. Garnish with the additional basil if desired. **YIELD: 8 SLICES.**

DEBRA KEIL
OWASSO, OKLAHOMA

Loaded with Italian flavor and plenty of fresh tomatoes, this is bound to become a family favorite. It's even better with a homemade, whole wheat crust.

ASIAN NOODLE TOSS
prep/total time: 20 min.

8 ounces uncooked thin spaghetti	2 cups cubed cooked chicken
1 package (10 ounces) julienned carrots	1 can (11 ounces) mandarin oranges, undrained
1 package (8 ounces) sugar snap peas	1/2 cup stir-fry sauce

Cook spaghetti according to package directions. Stir in carrots and peas; cook 1 minute longer. Drain; place in a bowl. Add the chicken, oranges and stir-fry sauce; toss to coat. **YIELD: 5 SERVINGS.**

CLARA COULSTON WASHINGTON COURT HOUSE, OHIO

I combine leftover chicken with mandarin oranges, colorful veggies and spaghetti to make this quick meal. For a change of pace, I like to use a citrus-flavored stir-fry sauce.

SPAGHETTI SQUASH PRIMAVERA
prep: 25 min. | cook: 20 min.

1 large spaghetti squash (3-1/2 pounds)	1 garlic clove, minced
1/4 cup sliced carrot	1 can (14-1/2 ounces) Italian stewed tomatoes
1/4 cup chopped red onion	
1/4 cup chopped sweet red pepper	1/2 cup frozen corn, thawed
1/4 cup chopped green pepper	1/2 teaspoon salt
2 teaspoons canola oil	1/2 teaspoon dried oregano
1 cup thinly sliced yellow summer squash	1/8 teaspoon dried thyme
1 cup thinly sliced zucchini	4 teaspoons grated Parmesan cheese
	2 tablespoons minced fresh parsley

Cut spaghetti squash in half; discard seeds. Place cut side up on a microwave-safe plate. Microwave, covered, on high for 9 minutes or until tender.

Meanwhile, in a large skillet, saute carrot, onion and peppers in oil for 3 minutes. Add yellow squash and zucchini; saute 2-3 minutes longer or until squash is tender. Add garlic; cook 1 minute longer. Reduce heat; add tomatoes, corn, salt, oregano and thyme. Cook 5 minutes longer or until heated through, stirring occasionally.

Separate the spaghetti squash strands with a fork. Spoon the vegetable mixture into squash; sprinkle with the cheese and parsley. **YIELD: 4 SERVINGS.**

EDITOR'S NOTE: This recipe was tested in a 1,100-watt microwave.

CORALEE COLLIS ANKENY, IOWA

Sunny-colored squash shells make attractive bowls for this satisfying meatless entree. The recipe showcases a medley of vegetables.

PEAR STUFFING FOR TURKEY
prep: 25 min. | bake: 3 hours + standing

1	pound bulk pork sausage	1	cup chicken broth
1	large onion, chopped	1/2	teaspoon salt
3	celery ribs, chopped	1/2	teaspoon pepper
8	cups soft bread crumbs	1/4	teaspoon rubbed sage
2	cups diced peeled ripe pears (about 2 medium)	1	turkey (10 pounds)

In a large skillet, cook sausage, onion and celery over medium heat until meat is no longer pink and vegetables are tender. Remove from heat. Stir in the bread crumbs, pears, broth, salt, pepper and sage.

Just before baking, loosely stuff turkey with stuffing. Skewer turkey openings; tie drumsticks together. Place breast side up on a rack in a roasting pan.

Bake the turkey, uncovered, at 325° for 3 to 3-1/2 hours or until a meat thermometer reads 180° for the turkey and 165° for the stuffing, basting occasionally with pan drippings. (Cover loosely with foil if turkey browns too quickly.)

Cover turkey and let stand for 20 minutes before removing stuffing and carving turkey. If desired, thicken the pan drippings for gravy. **YIELD: 10 SERVINGS (8 CUPS STUFFING).**

MABEL HAMMOCK
THOMSON, GEORGIA

I find this to be a delicious change from the usual Southern-style dressing. I found the recipe in one of my mother's old cookbooks.

TASTE OF HOME
TEST KITCHEN

A tasty herb and citrus sauce nicely glazes the tender, moist chicken for a speedy skillet supper.

LEMON HERB CHICKEN
prep/total time: 30 min.

2	boneless skinless chicken breast halves (4 ounces *each*)	1/2	teaspoon minced fresh rosemary *or* 1/8 teaspoon dried rosemary, crushed
2	teaspoons olive oil	1/4	teaspoon grated lemon peel
1/2	cup chicken broth		
1	tablespoon minced fresh basil *or* 1 teaspoon dried basil	Dash pepper	
2	garlic cloves, minced	1	teaspoon cornstarch
1	teaspoon lemon juice	2	tablespoons water

In a nonstick skillet, brown chicken in oil on both sides over medium heat. Add broth, basil, garlic, lemon juice, rosemary, lemon peel and pepper. Bring to a boil. Reduce heat; cover and simmer for 10-15 minutes or until a meat thermometer reads 170°. Remove chicken and keep warm.

Combine the cornstarch and water until smooth; stir into the pan juices. Bring to a boil; cook and stir for 1-2 minutes or until slightly thickened. Serve with chicken. **YIELD: 2 SERVINGS.**

Fresh & Easy Tip

When selecting mushrooms, choose those with fresh, firm, smooth caps and closed gills. Avoid mushrooms with brown spots or ones that are shriveled. Before using, gently remove dirt by wiping with a paper towel.

CHICKEN BROCCOLI STIR-FRY

prep: 20 min. + marinating | cook: 15 min.

1/2 cup reduced-sodium chicken broth	2 teaspoons cornstarch
6 tablespoons reduced-sodium soy sauce	4 teaspoons canola oil, *divided*
1/4 cup water	2 cups fresh broccoli florets
1/4 cup rice vinegar	1 cup sliced fresh mushrooms
2 garlic cloves, minced	1/2 cup canned sliced water chestnuts
Dash cayenne pepper	1/2 cup canned bamboo shoots
1 pound boneless skinless chicken breasts, cut into 3/4-inch cubes	2 green onions, thinly sliced
	2 cups hot cooked rice

In a small bowl, combine first six ingredients. Cover and refrigerate 3/4 cup. Pour remaining marinade into a large resealable plastic bag; add the chicken. Seal the bag and turn to coat; refrigerate for 1-2 hours.

Drain and discard marinade from chicken. In a small bowl, combine cornstarch and reserved marinade until smooth; set aside.

In a large skillet or wok, stir-fry chicken in 2 teaspoons oil until no longer pink. Remove and keep warm. Stir-fry broccoli in remaining oil for 2 minutes. Add mushrooms; stir-fry 2 minutes longer. Add the water chestnuts, bamboo shoots and onions; cook 1-2 minutes longer or until vegetables are crisp-tender.

Stir cornstarch mixture and add to the pan. Bring to a boil; cook and stir for 2 minutes or until thickened. Add chicken; heat through. Serve with rice. **YIELD: 4 SERVINGS.**

TARRAGON-LEMON TURKEY BREAST

prep: 10 min. | bake: 1-1/2 hours + standing

1/4 cup minced fresh tarragon	1/2 teaspoon seasoned salt
2 tablespoons olive oil	1 bone-in turkey breast (4 pounds)
1 teaspoon lemon-pepper seasoning	

In a small dish, combine the first four ingredients. With your fingers, carefully loosen the skin from both sides of turkey breast. Spread half of the tarragon mixture over the meat under the skin. Smooth skin over meat and secure to underside of breast with wooden toothpicks. Spread remaining tarragon mixture over turkey skin.

Place the turkey breast on a rack in a shallow roasting pan. Bake, uncovered, at 325° for 1-1/2 to 2 hours or until a meat thermometer reads 170°. Let stand for 10-15 minutes. Discard toothpicks before carving. **YIELD: 11 SERVINGS.**

**TASTE OF HOME
TEST KITCHEN**

If you enjoy the flavors of tarragon and lemon-pepper, consider this wet rub. It's perfect for turkey or even chicken.

TRIPLE-MUSHROOM STROGANOFF

prep: 20 min. | cook: 30 min.

5-1/2 cups uncooked egg noodles	1-1/2 cups vegetable broth, *divided*
1/2 pound fresh button mushrooms, halved	2 teaspoons Dijon mustard
2-2/3 cups sliced baby portobello mushrooms	1/2 teaspoon salt
1 package (3-1/2 ounces) sliced fresh shiitake mushrooms	1/4 teaspoon pepper
	2 tablespoons all-purpose flour
3 shallots, chopped	1 cup (8 ounces) fat-free sour cream
2 tablespoons butter	1 tablespoon minced fresh parsley
3 garlic cloves, minced	

**CHERI NEUSTIFTER
STURTEVANT, WISCONSIN**

Three types of mushrooms lend flavor and texture to the creamy sauce of this rich and rustic entree.

Cook noodles according to package directions. Meanwhile, in a large nonstick skillet over medium heat, cook the mushrooms and shallots in butter for 6-8 minutes or until tender. Add garlic; cook 1 minute longer.

Stir in 1-1/4 cups broth, mustard, salt and pepper. Bring to a boil. Reduce heat; simmer, uncovered, for 10 minutes, stirring occasionally.

Combine flour with remaining broth until smooth; gradually stir into mushroom mixture. Bring to a boil; cook and stir for 2 minutes or until thickened and bubbly. Reduce heat to low; gradually stir in sour cream (do not boil). Drain noodles; serve with mushroom sauce. Sprinkle with parsley. **YIELD: 6 SERVINGS.**

SOUTHWESTERN CHICKEN PACKETS

prep: 10 min. | bake: 25 min.

4	boneless skinless chicken breast halves (4 ounces *each*)	1	can (15 ounces) black beans, rinsed and drained
1/2	teaspoon salt	3/4	cup shredded Mexican cheese blend
1/4	teaspoon pepper	1/4	cup sour cream
3/4	cup salsa		
2	cups fresh *or* frozen corn, thawed		

Place each chicken breast half on a greased double thickness of heavy-duty foil (about 18 in. square). Sprinkle with salt and pepper. Top with salsa, corn, beans and cheese. Fold foil around mixture and seal tightly.

Place on a baking sheet. Bake at 425° for 25-30 minutes or until the chicken juices run clear. Open foil carefully to allow steam to escape. Serve with sour cream. **YIELD: 4 SERVINGS.**

**TONYA VOWELS
VINE GROVE, KENTUCKY**

Black beans, corn, salsa and a sprinkling of Mexican cheese add savory flavor to the juicy chicken in these oven-baked foil packets. So dinner's a snap to make and clean up.

SAUSAGE GARDEN QUICHE

prep: 20 min. | bake: 30 min.

Pastry for single-crust pie (9 inches)		1	tablespoon minced chives
5	eggs	1/8	teaspoon salt
3/4	cup whole milk	1/8	teaspoon garlic powder
1/2	cup chopped fresh spinach *or* Swiss chard	Dash pepper	
1/3	cup shredded cheddar cheese	6	brown-and-serve sausage links
1	tablespoon dried minced onion	3	slices fresh tomato, halved

Line a 9-in. pie plate with pastry. Trim pastry to 1/2 in. beyond edge of pie plate; flute edges. Line unpricked pastry shell with a double thickness of heavy-duty foil. Bake at 450° for 8 minutes. Remove the foil; bake 5 minutes longer. Cool on wire rack.

In a large bowl, whisk eggs and milk. Stir in spinach, cheese, onion, chives, salt, garlic powder and pepper. Carefully pour into crust.

Cook sausage according to package directions. Arrange sausage in a spoke pattern in egg mixture; place tomato slices between links. Bake, uncovered, at 350° for 30-35 minutes or until a knife inserted near center comes out clean. Let stand for 10 minutes before cutting. **YIELD: 6 SERVINGS.**

**JANET JACKSON
BAKERS MILLS, NEW YORK**

This quiche is my favorite! I often omit the sausage and add more garden-fresh ingredients. It reheats nicely in the microwave, which I find especially handy after a busy day.

CHICKEN BREASTS WITH FRUIT SALSA

prep/total time: 30 min.

1	tablespoon canola oil		1/2	cup quartered fresh strawberries
1/4	teaspoon salt		1	kiwifruit, peeled, quartered and sliced
1/4	teaspoon pepper			
1	garlic clove, minced		1/4	cup chopped red onion
4	boneless skinless chicken breast halves (4 ounces *each*)		1	jalapeno pepper, seeded and chopped
2	tablespoons butter		1	teaspoon cornstarch
3/4	cup pineapple tidbits, drained		1/4	cup orange juice

In a small bowl, combine oil, salt, pepper and garlic. Spread over one side of each chicken breast.

In a large skillet, saute the chicken seasoned side down in butter for 4-6 minutes. Turn and cook 4-6 minutes longer or until a meat thermometer reads 170°. Remove the chicken to serving platter; keep warm.

Meanwhile, for salsa, in a small bowl, combine fruit, onion and pepper; set aside. Combine cornstarch and juice until smooth; gradually stir into skillet. Bring to a boil; cook and stir for 1-2 minutes or until thickened. Remove from the heat; pour over fruit mixture and gently toss to coat. Serve with chicken. **YIELD: 4 SERVINGS.**

EDITOR'S NOTE: When cutting hot peppers, disposable gloves are recommended. Avoid touching your face.

ASPARAGUS BEEF STIR-FRY

prep: 20 min. | cook: 25 min.

2	tablespoons cornstarch	2	medium onions, halved and thinly sliced
1	cup beef broth	1	medium sweet red pepper, julienned
3	tablespoons soy sauce		
1/2	teaspoon sugar	1	large carrot, cut into 2-1/2-inch strips
2	tablespoons canola oil		
2	whole garlic cloves	2-1/2	cups sliced cooked roast beef (2-1/2-inch strips)
2	pounds fresh asparagus, trimmed and cut into 2-1/2-inch pieces	1	cup salted cashew halves
			Hot cooked rice

In a small bowl, combine cornstarch and broth until smooth. Stir in soy sauce and sugar; set aside. In a wok or large skillet, heat oil; add garlic. Cook and stir for 1 minute or until lightly browned; discard garlic.

Stir-fry asparagus, onions, red pepper and carrot for 15-20 minutes or until crisp-tender. Add roast beef; heat through. Stir reserved sauce; add to the pan. Bring to a boil; cook and stir for 2 minutes or until thickened. Sprinkle with the cashews. Serve with cooked rice. **YIELD: 4-6 SERVINGS.**

APPLE 'N' ONION CHICKEN

prep: 20 min. | bake: 30 min.

3	medium apples, sliced	3/4	cup shredded reduced-fat Swiss cheese
2	large onions, thinly sliced		
1	tablespoon butter	1/4	cup grated Parmesan cheese
6	boneless skinless chicken breast halves (5 ounces *each*)	1/4	cup seasoned bread crumbs
1/4	teaspoon salt	1/2	teaspoon minced fresh thyme
1/8	teaspoon pepper	2	tablespoons unsweetened apple juice

In a large skillet, saute the apples and onions in butter for 10 minutes or until tender. Transfer to a 13-in. x 9-in. baking dish coated with cooking spray. Top with chicken; sprinkle with salt and pepper.

Combine cheeses, bread crumbs and thyme; sprinkle over chicken. Drizzle with apple juice. Bake, uncovered, at 350° for 30-35 minutes or until a meat thermometer reaches 170°. **YIELD: 6 SERVINGS.**

JOYCE HUEBNER
MARINETTE, WISCONSIN

As appetizing to the eye as it is to the palate, this stovetop specialty features lots of vegetables, beef and crunchy cashews. A restaurant once handed out asparagus recipes, including this one.

SHERYL VANDERWAGEN
COOPERSVILLE, MICHIGAN

When I first discovered this recipe, the unique combination of flavors caught my attention. Since then, I have made this many times for company and family, and it always gets rave reviews.

LISSA HUTSON
PHELAN, CALIFORNIA

*With turkey and broccoli, this
special scalloped potato dish is a
meal in itself. Using a jar of Alfredo
sauce makes the preparation
time minimal.*

CHRISTINE BISSONETTE
SCOTIA, NEW YORK

*I invented this fast weeknight
entree using frozen tilapia fillets.
My entire family loved it! I often
serve it with crusty rolls, salad and
rice, and it always gets raves.*

HEARTY ALFREDO POTATOES
prep: 20 min. | bake: 1-1/4 hours + standing

1	jar (16 ounces) Alfredo sauce		Salt and pepper to taste
1	cup whole milk	2	to 3 cups cubed cooked turkey
1	teaspoon garlic powder	3	cups frozen chopped broccoli, thawed
3	pounds potatoes, peeled and thinly sliced	2	cups (8 ounces) shredded Swiss cheese, *divided*
5	tablespoons grated Parmesan cheese, *divided*		

In a large bowl, combine the Alfredo sauce, milk and garlic powder. Pour a fourth of the mixture into a greased 13-in. x 9-in. baking dish. Layer with a fourth of the potatoes; sprinkle with 1 tablespoon Parmesan cheese, salt and pepper.

In a large bowl, combine the turkey, broccoli and 1-1/2 cups Swiss cheese; spoon a third over potatoes. Repeat layers twice. Top with remaining potatoes. Sprinkle with remaining Swiss and Parmesan cheeses. Spread with remaining Alfredo sauce mixture.

Cover and bake at 400° for 45 minutes. Reduce heat to 350°. Bake, uncovered, 30 minutes longer or until potatoes are tender. Let stand for 15 minutes before serving. **YIELD: 6-8 SERVINGS.**

VEGGIE-TOPPED TILAPIA
prep: 15 min. | bake: 20 min.

4	tilapia fillets (5 ounces *each*)	1	medium green pepper, finely chopped
1/3	cup white wine *or* reduced-sodium chicken broth	1	small tomato, chopped
1/2	teaspoon seafood seasoning	3	tablespoons lemon juice
1	medium onion, finely chopped	1	teaspoon olive oil
		1/4	teaspoon garlic powder
		1/4	cup shredded Parmesan cheese

Place fillets in a 13-in. x 9-in. baking dish coated with cooking spray. Drizzle with the wine; sprinkle with seafood seasoning. Combine the onion, green pepper, tomato, lemon juice, oil and garlic powder; spoon over fillets.

Cover and bake at 425° for 15 minutes. Uncover; sprinkle with cheese. Bake 5-10 minutes longer or until vegetables are tender and fish flakes easily with a fork. **YIELD: 4 SERVINGS.**

CAULIFLOWER HAM CASSEROLE

prep: 20 min. | bake: 40 min.

4 cups chopped fresh cauliflower

1/4 cup butter, cubed

1/3 cup all-purpose flour

2 cups whole milk

1 cup (4 ounces) shredded cheddar cheese

1/2 cup sour cream

2 cups cubed fully cooked ham

1 jar (4-1/2 ounces) sliced mushrooms, drained

TOPPING:

1 cup soft bread crumbs

1 tablespoon butter, melted

Place cauliflower in a large saucepan; cover with 1 in. water. Bring to a boil. Reduce heat; cover and simmer for 5-10 minutes or until tender.

Meanwhile, in another large saucepan, melt butter. Stir in flour until smooth; gradually add the milk. Bring to a boil; cook and stir for 2 minutes or until thickened. Remove from the heat. Stir in the cheese and sour cream until melted.

Drain cauliflower. In a large bowl, combine the cauliflower, ham and mushrooms. Add cheese sauce and toss to coat. Transfer to a greased 2-qt. baking dish.

Combine the topping ingredients; sprinkle over the casserole. Bake, uncovered, at 350° for 40-45 minutes or until heated through. **YIELD: 6 SERVINGS.**

SUE HERLUND
WHITE BEAR LAKE, MINNESOTA

Cauliflower replaces the potatoes in this casserole, which I've been making for 30 years. Whenever we have leftover ham, my husband asks me to make this dish.

GOLDEN CHICKEN AND AUTUMN VEGETABLES

prep: 10 min. | cook: 35 min.

4 bone-in chicken breast halves (8 ounces *each*), skin removed

2 large sweet potatoes, peeled and cut into large chunks

2 cups fresh *or* frozen cut green beans

1 cup chicken broth

1 tablespoon minced fresh parsley

1/2 teaspoon garlic powder

1/2 teaspoon dried rosemary, crushed

1/4 teaspoon dried thyme

In a large nonstick skillet, brown chicken over medium-high heat for 4-6 minutes on each side or until a meat thermometer reads 170°. Add sweet potatoes and beans.

In a small bowl, combine remaining ingredients; pour over chicken and vegetables. Bring to a boil. Reduce heat; cover and cook over low heat for 20 minutes or until heated through. **YIELD: 4 SERVINGS.**

TASTE OF HOME
TEST KITCHEN

This comforting combination is sure to warm you up on a chilly day. Tender chicken breasts, sweet potatoes and green beans are cooked in a simple broth seasoned with rosemary, garlic and thyme.

**TASTE OF HOME
TEST KITCHEN**

*Grilled to tender perfection, the
fillets stay moist with a light
coating of lemon and oil. They're
topped with a fruity salsa of
emerald kiwifruit, golden
mango and red peppers for an
eye-catching presentation.*

**KAY YOUNG
PORT CLINTON, OHIO**

*Round out this pizza with a
salad or vegetable relish tray.
Sometimes, I serve a side of low-fat
ranch dressing to dip the veggies
and pizza crust into.*

HALIBUT WITH KIWI SALSA
prep/total time: 20 min.

2	medium mangoes, peeled and cubed (about 1-1/3 cups)	1	tablespoon lime juice
4	kiwifruit, peeled and cubed (about 1 cup)	2	teaspoons minced fresh mint *or* 3/4 teaspoon dried mint
1/2	cup diced sweet red pepper	1	teaspoon honey
1/2	cup chopped onion	1/2	teaspoon salt, *divided*
1	jalapeno pepper, seeded and minced	1	tablespoon olive oil
2	tablespoons lemon juice, *divided*	4	halibut fillets (4 ounces each)
		1/4	teaspoon chili powder

In a large bowl, combine mangoes, kiwi, red pepper, onion, jalapeno, 1 tablespoon lemon juice, lime juice, mint, honey and 1/4 teaspoon salt. Cover and refrigerate until serving.

In a small bowl, combine oil and remaining lemon juice; drizzle over both sides of fish. Sprinkle with chili powder and remaining salt.

Using long-handled tongs, moisten a paper towel with cooking oil and lightly coat the grill rack. Grill fillets, covered, over medium heat or broil 4 in. from the heat for 5-7 minutes on each side or until fish flakes easily with a fork. Serve with salsa. **YIELD: 4 SERVINGS.**

EDITOR'S NOTE: When cutting hot peppers, disposable gloves are recommended. Avoid touching your face.

GREEK SPINACH PIZZA
prep/total time: 20 min.

2	cups fresh baby spinach	1	cup (4 ounces) crumbled feta cheese
3	tablespoons olive oil	1/4	cup shredded part-skim mozzarella cheese
3	teaspoons Italian seasoning	1/4	cup chopped pitted Greek olives
1	prebaked 12-inch thin pizza crust	2	tablespoons chopped sweet onion
2	plum tomatoes, thinly sliced		

In a small bowl, toss the spinach, oil and Italian seasoning. Place crust on an ungreased 12-in. pizza pan. Arrange spinach mixture over crust to within 1/2 in. of edge. Place tomatoes on top; sprinkle with the cheeses, olives and onion.

Bake at 450° for 10-15 minutes or until cheese is melted and edges are lightly browned. **YIELD: 6-8 SLICES.**

**KATHY JOHNSON
LAKE CITY,
SOUTH DAKOTA**

*I'm a home health
nurse and got this
recipe from one of
my elderly clients,
who had used it
for years. It's one
of our favorites.*

SCALLOPED POTATOES 'N' HAM
prep: 25 min. | bake: 1 hour

3/4 cup powdered nondairy creamer	3/4 teaspoon paprika
1-3/4 cups water	6 large potatoes, peeled and thinly sliced
3 tablespoons butter	
3 tablespoons all-purpose flour	2 cups diced fully cooked ham
2 tablespoons dried minced onion	1 cup (4 ounces) shredded cheddar cheese
1 teaspoon salt	

In a small bowl, combine creamer and water until smooth. In a small saucepan, melt butter. Stir in the flour, onion, salt and paprika until smooth; gradually add creamer mixture. Bring to a boil; cook and stir for 1-2 minutes or until thickened.

In a greased shallow 2-1/2-qt. baking dish, combine the potatoes and ham. Pour sauce over the top.

Cover and bake at 350° for 15 minutes. Uncover; bake 40-50 minutes longer or until potatoes are tender. Sprinkle with cheese; bake for 5-10 minutes or until edges are bubbly and cheese is melted. **YIELD: 6 SERVINGS.**

CABBAGE KIELBASA SKILLET
prep/total time: 25 min.

1	large red onion, sliced	1	package (16 ounces) coleslaw mix
1	large green pepper, julienned	1/2	cup reduced-sodium chicken broth
1	large sweet red pepper, julienned	1	teaspoon garlic powder
2	tablespoons butter	1/2	teaspoon pepper
1	pound smoked kielbasa *or* Polish sausage, cut into 1-inch slices		

In a large skillet, saute onion and peppers in butter until tender. Add remaining ingredients. Cook and stir for 6-8 minutes or until heated through. **YIELD: 4 SERVINGS.**

**SHONA GERMINO
CASA GRANDE, ARIZONA**

This colorful medley comes together in no time with sausage and a packaged coleslaw mix. It makes a lot and is very filling.

COQ AU VIN
prep: 20 min. | bake: 50 min.

6	medium red potatoes, quartered	1/2	teaspoon dried parsley flakes
1/2	cup water	1/4	teaspoon dried thyme
2	medium carrots, sliced	1/4	teaspoon pepper
1	can (10-3/4 ounces) condensed cream of mushroom soup, undiluted	4	boneless skinless chicken breast halves (6 ounces *each*)
1/2	cup white wine *or* chicken broth	1/2	pound sliced fresh mushrooms
1-1/2	teaspoons chicken bouillon granules	4	bacon strips, cooked and crumbled
1	teaspoon minced garlic	1/3	cup chopped green onions

Place the potatoes and water in a microwave-safe dish; cover and microwave on high for 3 minutes. Add carrots; cook 4 minutes longer or until vegetables are tender. Drain.

In a large bowl, combine the soup, wine or broth, bouillon, garlic, parsley, thyme and pepper. Cut each chicken breast half into three pieces. Add chicken, potato mixture, mushrooms, bacon and onions to soup mixture; stir to coat.

Transfer to a greased 13-in. x 9-in. baking dish. Cover and bake at 350° for 50-55 minutes or until the chicken is no longer pink. **YIELD: 6 SERVINGS.**

EDITOR'S NOTE: This recipe was tested in a 1,100-watt microwave.

**LINDA CLARK
STONEY CREEK, ONTARIO**

Don't let the name fool you, this upscale classic is deliciously home-style. It has potatoes, chicken, carrots and a ton of flavor in every bite.

DIJON CHICKEN WITH GRAPES
prep/total time: 20 min.

4	boneless skinless chicken breast halves (4 ounces *each*)	2	tablespoons Dijon mustard
1	teaspoon olive oil	3/4	cup seedless red grapes, halved
1/2	cup refrigerated nondairy creamer	3/4	cup seedless green grapes, halved

In a large nonstick skillet coated with cooking spray, cook chicken in oil over medium heat for 4-5 minutes on each side or until a meat thermometer reads 170°. Remove and keep warm.

Add creamer to the skillet; cook over medium-low heat, stirring to loosen browned bits from pan. Whisk in mustard until blended. Add grapes; cook and stir until heated through. Serve with the chicken. **YIELD: 4 SERVINGS.**

**MARGARET WILSON
SUN CITY, CALIFORNIA**

My entree features sweet grapes in a creamy Dijon sauce served atop golden chicken breast halves. It's a quick-to-fix main course.

ZUCCHINI CRESCENT PIE
prep: 25 min. | bake: 20 min.

1	package (8 ounces) refrigerated crescent rolls	1/2	teaspoon pepper
		1/4	teaspoon dried basil
2	medium zucchini, sliced lengthwise and quartered	1/4	teaspoon dried oregano
		2	eggs, lightly beaten
1/2	cup chopped onion	2	cups (8 ounces) shredded part-skim mozzarella cheese
1/4	cup butter, cubed		
2	teaspoons minced fresh parsley	3/4	cup cubed fully cooked ham
1/2	teaspoon salt	1	medium Roma tomato, thinly sliced
1/2	teaspoon garlic powder		

Separate crescent dough into eight triangles; place in a greased 9-in. pie plate with points toward the center. Press onto the bottom and up the sides to form a crust; seal seams and perforations. Bake at 375° for 5-8 minutes or until lightly browned.

Meanwhile, in a large skillet, saute the zucchini and onion in butter until tender; stir in seasonings. Spoon into crust. Combine the eggs, cheese and ham; pour over zucchini mixture. Top with tomato slices.

Bake at 375° for 20-25 minutes or until a knife inserted near the center comes out clean. Let stand for 5 minutes before cutting. **YIELD: 6 SERVINGS.**

**SUSAN DAVIS
ANN ARBOR, MICHIGAN**

This is one of my mother's many recipes designed to take advantage of bountiful zucchini. This pie is inexpensive, nutritious, tasty, filling—and so easy. Refrigerated crescent rolls and cooked ham cut prep time but not taste.

**KIMBERLY WAGNER
CASTLE ROCK,
COLORADO**

*I added shrimp
to a simple, easy
primavera, and
the result was
a timely and
fabulous dinner
bursting with
flavor in every
bite. This recipe
capitalizes on
summer's bounty
with five differ-
ent vegetables in
a dish ideal for
special occasions.*

PASTA PRIMAVERA WITH SHRIMP

prep/total time: 30 min.

- 1 package (16 ounces) linguine
- 1 pound uncooked medium shrimp, peeled and deveined
- 2 cups chopped fresh broccoli
- 1 cup sliced fresh carrots
- 1 cup fresh green beans, cut into 2-inch pieces
- 1 medium zucchini, cut into 1/4-inch slices

- 1 medium sweet red pepper, julienned
- 2 tablespoons all-purpose flour
- 1-1/4 cups heavy whipping cream
- 3/4 cup chicken broth
- 1/4 cup grated Parmesan cheese
- 3/4 teaspoon salt
- 1/2 teaspoon pepper

In a Dutch oven, cook the linguine according to package directions, adding shrimp and vegetables during the last 4 minutes.

Meanwhile, in a small saucepan, combine the flour, cream and broth until smooth. Add the cheese, salt and pepper. Bring to a boil over medium heat; cook and stir for 2 minutes or until thickened.

Drain linguine mixture and return to the pan. Add cream sauce; toss to coat. **YIELD: 6 SERVINGS.**

STRAWBERRY PORK CHOPS

prep/total time: 20 min.

3/4	cup raspberry vinaigrette	2	teaspoons dried rosemary, crushed
2	tablespoons chopped green onion	1/2	to 1 teaspoon pepper
1	tablespoon brown sugar	4	bone-in pork loin chops (1 inch thick and 6 ounces *each*)
1/4	teaspoon paprika	1	tablespoon canola oil
1/4	teaspoon Worcestershire sauce	2	cups sliced fresh strawberries (1/4-inch slices)

In a small bowl, combine the vinaigrette, onion, brown sugar, paprika and Worcestershire sauce; set aside. Combine rosemary and pepper; rub over both sides of pork chops.

In a large skillet, cook the chops in oil over medium-high heat for 5-6 minutes on each side or until a meat thermometer reads 160°. Pour vinaigrette mixture over meat; cook 3-4 minutes longer or until pork juices run clear.

Remove the chops and keep warm. Add strawberries to the cooking juices and toss to coat; serve with pork chops. **YIELD: 4 SERVINGS.**

TASTE OF HOME TEST KITCHEN

Moist, juicy and just right for warm summer evenings, these strawberry-topped pork chops are everyday-easy but special enough to serve guests.

PORK TENDERLOIN WITH PINEAPPLE SALSA

prep: 15 min. | bake: 35 min. + standing

2	pork tenderloins (1 pound *each*)	1/3	cup chopped sweet red pepper
3	tablespoons brown sugar	1	small jalapeno pepper, seeded and chopped
3	tablespoons Dijon mustard	2	green onions, chopped
3/4	teaspoon minced fresh gingerroot	1	tablespoon minced fresh cilantro
SALSA:		1	tablespoon brown sugar
2	cups chopped fresh pineapple		

Place the pork on a greased rack in a foil-lined shallow roasting pan. Combine brown sugar, mustard and ginger; spread over pork. Bake, uncovered, at 425° for 35-40 minutes or until a meat thermometer reads 160°. Let stand for 5-10 minutes before slicing. In a large bowl, combine the salsa ingredients. Serve with pork. **YIELD: 6 SERVINGS.**

EDITOR'S NOTE: When cutting hot peppers, disposable gloves are recommended. Avoid touching your face.

PAT SCHMELING GERMANTOWN, WISCONSIN

The fresh salsa makes this dish perfect for a hot summer night or picnic. It's great the rest of the year, though, too!

TASTE OF HOME TEST KITCHEN

This main dish is a refreshing change of pace. The distinctive sweet-tart sauce complements any grilled fish nicely.

DIANE LOMBARDO NEW CASTLE, PENNSYLVANIA

The meaty texture of portobello mushrooms will make you think you're eating steak. With a cheesy spinach filling, this is a marvelous main dish. Pepper flakes add color and a little kick.

COD WITH RHUBARB SAUCE

prep/total time: 25 min.

1	teaspoon olive oil	3	teaspoons minced fresh parsley
3	cups diced fresh *or* frozen rhubarb, thawed	1	teaspoon minced fresh basil
1/4	cup sugar	1/4	teaspoon lime juice
1/2	cup chopped red onion		Coarsely ground pepper to taste
4-1/2	teaspoons Dijon mustard	4	cod fillets (6 ounces each)

In a large saucepan, heat oil over medium heat. Add rhubarb and sugar; cook for 5-7 minutes or until rhubarb is tender. Remove from heat; stir in the onion, mustard, parsley, basil, lime juice and pepper.

Using long-handled tongs, moisten a paper towel with cooking oil and coat grill rack. Grill the cod, covered, over medium heat for 5-6 minutes on each side or until the fish flakes easily with a fork. Serve with sauce. **YIELD: 4 SERVINGS (2 CUPS SAUCE).**

EDITOR'S NOTE: If using frozen rhubarb, measure rhubarb while still frozen, then thaw completely. Drain in a colander, but do not press liquid out.

SPINACH-STUFFED PORTOBELLOS

prep/total time: 30 min.

4	large portobello mushrooms	3	tablespoons chopped green onions
2	tablespoons olive oil	2	tablespoons grated Romano cheese
1	can (14-1/2 ounces) diced tomatoes, drained	1/4	teaspoon crushed red pepper flakes
1	package (10 ounces) frozen chopped spinach, thawed and squeezed dry	1/8	teaspoon salt
		1/2	cup shredded part-skim mozzarella cheese

Remove and discard the stems and gills from mushrooms. In a large skillet over medium heat, cook mushrooms in oil for 10-15 minutes or just until tender, turning once.

In a small bowl, combine the tomatoes, spinach, onions, Romano cheese, pepper flakes and salt. Spoon into mushroom caps. Sprinkle with mozzarella cheese.

Place on a baking sheet lined with heavy-duty foil. Bake at 375° for 10-15 minutes or until heated through and cheese is melted. **YIELD: 4 SERVINGS.**

BASIL TUNA STEAKS
prep/total time: 20 min.

6	tuna steaks (6 ounces *each*)	3	tablespoons minced fresh basil
4-1/2	teaspoons olive oil	3/4	teaspoon salt
		1/4	teaspoon pepper

Drizzle both sides of tuna steaks with oil. Sprinkle with the basil, salt and pepper.

Using long-handled tongs, moisten a paper towel with cooking oil and coat grill rack. Grill tuna, covered, over medium heat or broil 4 in. from heat for 4-5 minutes on each side for medium-rare or until slightly pink in the center. **YIELD: 6 SERVINGS.**

LINDA MCLYMAN
SYRACUSE, NEW YORK

This five-ingredient recipe is great. Tuna can be grilled in no time.

ROSEMARY-SKEWERED ARTICHOKE CHICKEN
prep: 20 min. + marinating | grill: 20 min.

1/3	cup olive oil	6	fresh rosemary stems (18 inches)
2	tablespoons snipped fresh dill	1	can (14 ounces) water-packed artichoke hearts, rinsed, drained and halved
1	tablespoon minced fresh oregano		
2	teaspoons grated lemon peel	2	medium yellow summer squash, cut into 1-inch slices
2	garlic cloves, minced		
1/2	teaspoon salt	6	cherry tomatoes
1/4	teaspoon pepper		
1-1/2	pounds boneless skinless chicken breasts, cut into 1-inch cubes		

In a large resealable plastic bag, combine oil, dill, oregano, lemon peel, garlic, salt and pepper; add chicken. Seal bag and turn to coat; refrigerate for at least 2 hours.

Using a vegetable peeler, peel bark from bottom half of each rosemary stem and make a point at each end; soak in water until ready to use.

Drain and discard marinade. On soaked rosemary stems, alternately thread the chicken, artichokes, squash and tomatoes. Position the leaf parts of the rosemary stems so they are outside of the grill cover.

Using long-handled tongs, dip a paper towel in cooking oil and lightly coat the grill rack. Grill, covered, over medium heat or broil 4 in. from the heat for 10-15 minutes on each side or until chicken is no longer pink and vegetables are tender. **YIELD: 6 SERVINGS.**

LISA WHITE
SAN DIEGO, CALIFORNIA

The chicken and vegetables in my kabobs have a lovely, fresh herb flavor whether you choose to use the rosemary stems as skewers or not.

ROXANNE LYNNES
GRAND FORKS,
NORTH DAKOTA

I am a big fan of pasta, and this dish is one of my favorite meatless meals. It's very colorful and flavorful.

TRICOLOR PEPPER PASTA
prep/total time: 20 min.

8	ounces uncooked penne pasta	3	tablespoons olive oil
1	*each* large sweet red, yellow and green pepper, cut into 1/2-inch strips	3	tablespoons red wine vinegar
		1	tablespoon sugar
1	large onion, cut into 1/2-inch strips	1-1/2	teaspoons salt
		3/4	teaspoon dried basil
1/2	pound fresh mushrooms, sliced	1/2	teaspoon pepper

Cook pasta according to package directions. Meanwhile, in a large nonstick skillet, saute the peppers, onion and mushrooms in oil until tender. Stir in the vinegar, sugar, salt, basil and pepper. Drain pasta; add to vegetables and toss to coat. **YIELD: 6 SERVINGS.**

TASTE OF HOME
TEST KITCHEN

For an easy grilled salmon, try grilling directly on lemon slices! It leaves the salmon moist, flaky and extremely aromatic.

LEMONY GRILLED SALMON
prep: 10 min. + marinating | grill: 15 min.

1/2	cup honey	1/2	teaspoon minced garlic
1/4	cup lemon juice	1/4	teaspoon crushed red pepper flakes
1/4	cup unsweetened pineapple juice	4	salmon fillets (6 ounces *each*), skin removed
2	teaspoons teriyaki sauce	8	lemon slices (3/4 inch thick)
1	teaspoon grated lemon peel		

In a small bowl, combine the first seven ingredients. Pour 2/3 cup into a large resealable plastic bag; add salmon. Seal bag and turn to coat; refrigerate for at least 2 hours. Cover and refrigerate remaining marinade for basting.

Drain and discard marinade. Using long-handled tongs, moisten a paper towel with cooking oil and lightly coat the grill rack. Arrange lemon slices on rack. Place each salmon fillet over two lemon slices.

Grill the salmon, covered, over medium heat for 5 minutes. Brush with some of the reserved marinade. Grill 10-15 minutes longer or until fish flakes easily with a fork, basting occasionally with remaining marinade. **YIELD: 4 SERVINGS.**

**JULIE STERCHI
HARRISBURG,
ILLINOIS**

*This recipe goes
together in a snap
and is a hit at my
house. If you don't
like your food hot,
just leave out the
red pepper flakes.*

CHICKEN FAJITAS

prep: 20 min. + marinating | cook: 5 min.

4 tablespoons canola oil, *divided*	1-1/2 pounds boneless skinless chicken breasts, cut into thin strips
2 tablespoons lemon juice	1/2 medium sweet red pepper, julienned
1-1/2 teaspoons seasoned salt	1/2 medium green pepper, julienned
1-1/2 teaspoons dried oregano	4 green onions, thinly sliced
1-1/2 teaspoons ground cumin	1/2 cup chopped onion
1 teaspoon garlic powder	6 flour tortillas (8 inches), warmed
1/2 teaspoon chili powder	Shredded cheddar cheese, taco sauce, salsa, guacamole and sour cream
1/2 teaspoon paprika	
1/2 teaspoon crushed red pepper flakes, optional	

In a large resealable plastic bag, combine 2 tablespoons oil, lemon juice and seasonings. Add chicken. Seal and turn to coat; refrigerate for 1-4 hours.

In a large skillet, saute the peppers and onions in remaining oil until crisp-tender. Remove and keep warm.

Drain and discard the marinade. In the same skillet, cook the chicken over medium-high heat for 5-6 minutes or until no longer pink. Return pepper mixture to pan; heat through.

Spoon filling down center of tortillas; fold in half. Serve with the cheese, taco sauce, salsa, guacamole and sour cream. **YIELD: 6 SERVINGS.**

CHRISTINE SHERRILL
HERNDON, VIRGINIA

When I'm in the mood for Chinese food, I turn to this snappy recipe. The colorful nutty dish is sure to stir your creativity...substitute broccoli for the asparagus or add carrots and mushrooms.

KACI KOLTZ
CASSVILLE, WISCONSIN

My mom used to call this Potato Pizza, and it was always a treat to be served this hearty dish. It's still one of my favorites on a cold winter day.

ASPARAGUS CASHEW STIR-FRY
prep/total time: 20 min.

1 pound fresh asparagus, trimmed and cut into 1-inch pieces	3 tablespoons reduced-sodium soy sauce
1/2 cup chopped green onions	1/4 teaspoon ground ginger
1/2 cup chopped sweet red pepper	1/2 cup lightly salted cashews
1 teaspoon canola oil	1 teaspoon sesame oil
1 garlic clove, minced	4 cups hot cooked brown rice
2 tablespoons cornstarch	
1-1/2 cups vegetable broth	

In a large nonstick skillet, saute asparagus, onions and red pepper in oil until tender. Add garlic; cook 1 minute longer. Combine cornstarch, broth, soy sauce and ginger until blended; gradually stir into skillet. Bring to a boil; cook and stir for 2 minutes or until thickened.

Reduce heat; add cashews and sesame oil. Cook 2 minutes longer or until heated through. Serve with rice. **YIELD: 4 SERVINGS.**

ITALIAN MEAT AND POTATOES
prep: 25 min. | bake: 1-1/2 hours

1 pound ground beef	1 teaspoon garlic powder
1 pound bulk pork sausage	1 teaspoon dried oregano
1/2 cup chopped onion	1/2 teaspoon sugar
1/4 teaspoon pepper	6 medium potatoes, peeled and thinly sliced
1/8 teaspoon salt	
1 can (10-3/4 ounces) condensed cheddar cheese soup, undiluted	2 cups (8 ounces) shredded part-skim mozzarella cheese
1-1/4 cups milk	
1 can (8 ounces) tomato sauce	

In a large skillet, cook the beef, sausage, onion, pepper and salt over medium heat until meat is no longer pink. Meanwhile, in a small saucepan, combine the soup, milk, tomato sauce, garlic powder, oregano and sugar. Bring to a boil. Reduce heat; simmer, uncovered, for 5 minutes or until heated through.

Drain meat mixture; spoon half into a greased 13-in. x 9-in. baking dish. Layer half of potatoes. Repeat layers. Top with soup mixture.

Cover and bake at 350° for 1-1/4 hours or until potatoes are tender. Uncover; sprinkle with cheese. Bake 15 minutes longer or until cheese is melted. **YIELD: 10-12 SERVINGS.**

STUFFED ZUCCHINI BOATS

prep: 25 min. | bake: 40 min.

1	pound lean ground beef (90% lean)	1/2	cup tomato sauce
1	large onion, chopped	1/4	cup shredded Parmesan cheese
3	cups cubed French bread	1	egg, lightly beaten
1	package (10 ounces) frozen chopped spinach, thawed and squeezed dry	1	teaspoon salt
		1/2	teaspoon dried thyme
		6	medium zucchini (6 to 8 inches)
1/2	cup minced fresh parsley	1	cup water

In a large skillet, cook beef and onion over medium heat until meat is no longer pink; drain. Stir in bread cubes, spinach, parsley, tomato sauce, Parmesan cheese, egg, salt and thyme; set aside.

Cut each zucchini in half lengthwise. Scoop out the seeds, leaving a 1/4-in. shell. Spoon about 6 tablespoons beef mixture into each zucchini half.

Place in two ungreased 13-in. x 9-in. baking dishes. Pour 1/2 cup water into each dish. Cover and bake at 350° for 30 minutes. Uncover; bake 10 minutes longer or until zucchini is tender. **YIELD: 6 SERVINGS.**

**ISABEL FOWLER
ANCHORAGE, ALASKA**

Here's a great way to put that zucchini crop to good use. I stuff the "boats" with a tasty ground beef filling.

VEGETARIAN TACOS

prep/total time: 20 min.

8	taco shells	1	cup salsa
3	cups shredded cabbage	1	can (4 ounces) chopped green chilies
1	cup sliced onion	1	teaspoon chili powder
1	cup julienned sweet red pepper	1	teaspoon minced garlic
		1/4	teaspoon ground cumin
2	tablespoons canola oil		
2	teaspoons sugar	1/2	cup shredded cheddar cheese
1	can (15 ounces) black beans, rinsed and drained	1	medium ripe avocado, peeled and sliced

Heat the taco shells according to the package directions. Meanwhile, in a large skillet, saute the cabbage, onion and red pepper in oil for 5 minutes or until crisp-tender. Sprinkle with sugar.

Stir in the beans, salsa, chilies, chili powder, garlic and cumin. Bring to a boil. Reduce heat; cover and simmer for 5 minutes or until heated through. Spoon into taco shells. Garnish with cheese and avocado. **YIELD: 4 SERVINGS.**

**TASTE OF HOME
TEST KITCHEN**

With a blend of sauteed cabbage, peppers and black beans these tacos are so, flavorful and filling you won't even miss the meat! Let the kids top their own with avocado, cheese or a dollop of sour cream.

**RUTH KOLARITSCH
TOWACO,
NEW JERSEY**

*When plums
are in season, I
make this every
other week.
I originally
adapted the
recipe for use
with chicken,
but discovered it
was even better
with pork.*

SPICED PORK LOIN WITH PLUMS

prep: 25 min. | cook: 1-1/2 hours

1 tablespoon ground cumin	2 tablespoons olive oil, *divided*
1 teaspoon ground cinnamon	1 large onion, chopped
1/2 teaspoon salt	2 tablespoons sugar
1/2 teaspoon ground allspice	1/2 cup cranberry juice
1/4 teaspoon pepper	1 cup chicken broth
1/4 teaspoon ground cloves	4 medium fresh plums, pitted and sliced
1 boneless whole pork loin roast (3 to 4 pounds)	

In a small bowl, combine the first six ingredients; rub over roast. In a Dutch oven, brown the roast in 1 tablespoon oil on all sides. Remove roast and set aside.

In same pan, cook onion in remaining oil over medium heat until tender. Add sugar; cook, stirring occasionally, 3-4 minutes longer. Add cranberry juice; bring to a boil. Cook until liquid is reduced by half.

Return the roast to the pan; add the broth. Bring to a boil. Reduce the heat; cover and simmer for 1-1/4 hours.

Add the plums; cover and simmer 30-45 minutes longer or until a meat thermometer reads 160°. Thicken the pan juices if desired. **YIELD: 8-10 SERVINGS.**

APPLE TURKEY POTPIE

prep: 10 min. | bake: 25 min.

1/4 cup chopped onion	1 large unpeeled tart apple, cubed
1 tablespoon butter	1/3 cup golden raisins
2 cans (10-3/4 ounces *each*) condensed cream of chicken soup, undiluted	1 teaspoon lemon juice
	1/4 teaspoon ground nutmeg
3 cups cubed cooked turkey	Pastry for a single-crust pie (9 inches)

In a large saucepan, saute the onion in butter until tender. Add the soup, turkey, apple, raisins, lemon juice and nutmeg. Spoon into an ungreased 11-in. x 7-in. baking dish.

On a lightly floured surface, roll out pastry to fit top of dish. Place over filling; flute edges and cut slits in top. Bake at 425° for 25-30 minutes or until the crust is golden brown and the filling is bubbly. **YIELD: 6 SERVINGS.**

GEORGIA MACDONALD
DOVER, NEW HAMPSHIRE

I take leftover holiday turkey and prepare this delicious potpie. Apples and raisins add sweetness.

TUNA-STUFFED POTATOES

prep: 10 min. | cook: 25 min.

4 medium baking potatoes	2 tablespoons reduced-fat mayonnaise
1/2 teaspoon salt	
1/8 teaspoon pepper	1/2 cup shredded reduced-fat cheddar cheese, *divided*
1 can (6 ounces) light water-packed tuna, drained and flaked	
	2 green onions, finely chopped

Scrub and pierce the potatoes; place on a microwave-safe plate. Microwave, uncovered, on high for 18-22 minutes or until tender, turning once. Let stand for 5 minutes. Cut a thin slice off the top of each potato and discard. Scoop out pulp, leaving a thin shell.

In a large bowl, mash the pulp with salt and pepper. Stir in the tuna, mayonnaise, 1/4 cup cheese and onions. Spoon into potato shells. Sprinkle with remaining cheese.

Microwave, uncovered, on high for 3-5 minutes or until heated through. **YIELD: 4 SERVINGS.**

EDITOR'S NOTE: This recipe was tested in a 1,100-watt microwave.

BOBBY TAYLOR
MICHIGAN CITY, INDIANA

Turn a baked potato into a light meal in minutes with my creamy and delicious tuna topping. Serve this tasty twist on twice-baked potatoes with a leafy green salad for a lovely, spur-of-the-minute lunch or late-night supper.

BREADS &
BAKED GOODS

Your family will be delighted with these fresh-from-the-oven muffins, scones, coffee cakes and breads. Their aroma will have your gang wandering into the kitchen looking for samples. Imagine their pleasure as they bite into these homemade goodies studded with fresh herbs, fruits and/or nuts.

TOUCH OF SPRING MUFFINS │ **PAGE 157**

APPLE-TOPPED BISCUITS │ **PAGE 164**

MANGO COLADA SCONES
prep: 20 min. | bake: 15 min.

2-1/2	cups biscuit/baking mix	1	cup chopped peeled mango
2	tablespoons brown sugar	3	tablespoons flaked coconut
3	tablespoons cold butter, *divided*	1/4	cup macadamia nuts, chopped
1/2	cup frozen non-alcoholic pina colada mix, thawed		

In a large bowl, combine the biscuit mix and brown sugar. Cut in 2 tablespoons butter until mixture resembles coarse crumbs. Stir in pina colada mix just until moistened. Fold in mango.

Turn onto a floured surface; knead 10 times. Pat into a 9-in. x 7-in. rectangle. Cut into 10 rectangles; separate rectangles and place on a greased baking sheet. Melt remaining butter; brush over scones.

Bake at 400° for 12 minutes. Sprinkle with the flaked coconut and nuts; bake 2-4 minutes longer or until golden brown. Serve warm. **YIELD: 10 SCONES.**

**CHERYL PERRY
HERTFORD,
NORTH CAROLINA**

The mango adds a great tropical flavor to these scones. I love to serve them with a hot cup of tea for breakfast.

LEMON BLUEBERRY MUFFINS
prep/total time: 30 min.

2	cups biscuit/baking mix	1	cup fresh *or* frozen blueberries
1/2	cup plus 2 tablespoons sugar, *divided*	2	teaspoons grated lemon peel
1	egg		
1	cup (8 ounces) sour cream		

In a large bowl, combine biscuit mix and 1/2 cup sugar. Whisk egg and sour cream; stir into dry ingredients just until moistened. Fold in the blueberries.

Fill greased or paper-lined muffin cups half full. Combine lemon peel and remaining sugar; sprinkle over batter.

Bake at 400° for 20-25 minutes or until a toothpick inserted near the center comes out clean. Cool for 5 minutes before removing from pan to a wire rack. Serve warm. **YIELD: 1 DOZEN.**

EDITOR'S NOTE: If using frozen blueberries, use without thawing to avoid discoloring the batter.

**KRIS MICHELS
WALLED LAKE, MICHIGAN**

When my sister and I spent the night at our grandmother's house, we often requested these muffins. Today, I bake them for my kids. The very aroma is a trip down memory lane.

CHRISTINE BENNER POTTSVILLE, PENNSYLVANIA

I usually pass on desserts because I need to watch my fat intake. However, with reduced-fat cream cheese and egg substitute, I can enjoy this great berry cake!

Fresh & Easy Tip

Purchase raspberries that are brightly colored without the hulls attached. One-half pint equals about 1 cup. When you get home, discard any berries that are soft, shriveled or moldy.

RASPBERRY CREAM CHEESE COFFEE CAKE

prep: 25 min. | bake: 25 min. + cooling

3 tablespoons butter, softened	1-1/4 teaspoons baking powder
3/4 cup sugar, *divided*	1/4 teaspoon baking soda
1/4 cup plus 2 tablespoons egg substitute, *divided*	1/4 teaspoon salt
1 teaspoon grated lemon peel	1/2 cup buttermilk
1 teaspoon vanilla extract	1 cup fresh raspberries
1-1/4 cups all-purpose flour	2 ounces reduced-fat cream cheese
	1 teaspoon confectioners' sugar

In a large bowl, beat butter and 1/2 cup sugar until crumbly, about 2 minutes. Beat in 1/4 cup egg substitute, lemon peel and vanilla. Combine the flour, baking powder, baking soda and salt; add to butter mixture alternately with buttermilk.

Pour into a 9-in. springform pan coated with cooking spray; sprinkle with the berries. In a small bowl, beat the cream cheese and remaining sugar until fluffy. Beat in remaining egg substitute. Pour over berries.

Place pan on a baking sheet. Bake at 375° for 25-30 minutes or until a toothpick inserted near the center comes out clean. Cool on a wire rack for 10 minutes. Carefully run a knife around edge of pan to loosen; remove sides of pan. Sprinkle with confectioners' sugar. Serve warm. Refrigerate leftovers. **YIELD: 8 SERVINGS.**

CABBAGE PATCH BREAD
prep: 25 min. + rising | bake: 25 min.

1	package (1/4 ounce) active dry yeast		1	medium carrot, cut into chunks
1/3	cup warm water (110° to 115°)		1/4	cup sliced celery
1	can (5 ounces) evaporated milk		1/4	cup minced fresh parsley *or* 4 teaspoons dried parsley flakes
1/4	cup canola oil		2	tablespoons honey
1	egg		1	teaspoon salt
3/4	cup coarsely chopped cabbage		3	cups whole wheat flour
			1-1/4	cups all-purpose flour

In a large bowl, dissolve yeast in warm water. In a blender, combine the milk, oil, egg, cabbage, carrot, celery, parsley, honey and salt; cover and process until smooth. Add to yeast mixture. Stir in whole wheat flour and enough all-purpose flour to form a soft dough.

Turn onto a floured surface; knead until smooth and elastic, about 6-8 minutes. Place in a greased bowl, turning once to grease top. Cover and let rise in a warm place until doubled, about 1-1/2 hours.

Punch the dough down. Turn onto a lightly floured surface; divide in half. Cover and let rest for 10 minutes. Shape into round loves. Place on two greased baking sheets. Cover and let rise until doubled, about 1 hour.

Bake at 350° for 25-30 minutes or until golden brown. Cover loosely with foil during the last 10 minutes if top browns too quickly. Remove from pans to wire racks to cool. **YIELD: 2 LOAVES (10 SLICES EACH).**

JEANNE BENNETT MINDEN, LOUISIANA

I make my own bread, but I could never get my children to eat any of the whole-grain breads I considered more nutritious...until I came across this one. The name caught their attention, but the taste got their approval!

POPPY SEED PLUM MUFFINS
prep: 15 min. | bake: 20 min. + cooling

2	cups all-purpose flour		1/2	teaspoon ground cinnamon
2/3	cup sugar		1	egg
1	tablespoon baking powder		3/4	cup whole milk
1	tablespoon poppy seeds		1/4	cup butter, melted
1/2	teaspoon salt		1/2	cup finely chopped peeled fresh plums

In a large bowl, combine the first six ingredients. In another bowl, beat the egg, milk and butter; stir into dry ingredients just until moistened. Fold in plums. Fill greased or paper-lined muffin cups two-thirds full.

Bake at 425° for 18-22 minutes or until a toothpick inserted near the center comes out clean. Cool for 5 minutes before removing from pan to a wire rack. Serve warm. **YIELD: 1 DOZEN.**

CAROL TWARDZIK SPY HILL, SASKATCHEWAN

Bring the harvest-flavor taste of ripe plums to the breakfast table with these change-of-pace muffins. I top them with fruit jam. I don't mind making an extra batch because they freeze so well.

TRIPLE BERRY MUFFINS

prep: 15 min. | bake: 20 min.

3	cups all-purpose flour	2	eggs
1-1/2	cups sugar	1-1/4	cups whole milk
4-1/2	teaspoons ground cinnamon	1	cup butter, melted
3	teaspoons baking powder	1	cup fresh blueberries
1/2	teaspoon salt	1/2	cup fresh raspberries
1/2	teaspoon baking soda	1/2	cup chopped fresh strawberries

In a large bowl, combine the first six ingredients. In another bowl, beat the eggs, milk and butter; stir into dry ingredients just until moistened. Fold in berries.

Fill greased or paper-lined muffin cups three-fourths full. Bake at 375° for 18-20 minutes or until a toothpick inserted near the center comes out clean. Cool for 5 minutes before removing from pans to wire racks. Serve warm. **YIELD: ABOUT 1-1/2 DOZEN.**

**MICHELLE TURNIS
HOPKINTON, IOWA**

Fresh blueberries, raspberries and strawberries lend eye-catching color and fruity flair to these moist muffins that are nicely spiced with cinnamon. They come together in no time and bake up in a snap.

PINEAPPLE NUT BREAD

prep: 15 min. | bake: 50 min.

1-3/4	cups all-purpose flour	2	eggs
3/4	cup packed brown sugar	1	cup finely chopped fresh pineapple
2	teaspoons baking powder	3/4	cup coarsely chopped macadamia nuts
1/2	teaspoon salt	1	tablespoon sugar
1/4	teaspoon baking soda	1/4	teaspoon ground cinnamon
3	tablespoons butter, melted		

In a large bowl, combine the flour, brown sugar, baking powder, salt and baking soda. Set aside half of the flour mixture. In a small bowl, whisk the butter and eggs. Stir into the dry ingredients just until moistened. Fold in the pineapple and nuts. Gradually add the reserved flour mixture.

Pour into a greased 8-in. x 4-in. loaf pan. Combine the sugar and cinnamon; sprinkle over loaf. Bake at 350° for 50-55 minutes or until a toothpick inserted near center comes out clean. Cool on a wire rack. **YIELD: 1 LOAF (16 SLICES).**

**BRITTANY JEWETTE
EWA BEACH, HAWAII**

This lovely loaf is loaded with lots of luscious pineapple and macadamia nuts. Welcome your family and friends with a tempting slice today!

**CHANTELLE ROSS
FOREST GROVE,
BRITISH COLUMBIA**

*This bread has won many ribbons
at our fall fair. The recipe yields
two nicely spiced loaves.*

ZUCCHINI CHIP LOAVES
prep: 20 min. | bake: 1 hour + cooling

3	cups all-purpose flour	3	eggs
2	cups sugar	2	cups grated zucchini
3	teaspoons ground cinnamon	1	cup canola oil
1	teaspoon baking soda	3	teaspoons vanilla extract
1/2	teaspoon salt	1	cup (6 ounces) semisweet chocolate chips
1/2	teaspoon baking powder	1	cup raisins, optional
1/2	teaspoon ground allspice		

In a large bowl, combine the first seven ingredients. In a small bowl, beat the eggs, zucchini, oil and vanilla. Stir into dry ingredients just until moistened. Fold in chocolate chips and raisins if desired.

Pour into two greased 8-in. x 4-in. loaf pans. Bake at 325° for 60-65 minutes or until a toothpick inserted near the center comes out clean. Cool for 10 minutes before removing from pans to wire racks. **YIELD: 2 LOAVES (12 SLICES EACH).**

**JULIE WALLBERG
CARSON CITY, NEVADA**

*No one can resist these buttery
muffins bursting with juicy
blackberries. They make a great
addition to any breakfast table.*

BLACKBERRY MUFFINS
prep: 15 min. | bake: 20 min.

1/2	cup butter, softened	2	teaspoons baking powder
1-1/4	cups plus 1 tablespoon sugar, *divided*	1/2	teaspoon salt
2	eggs	1/2	cup whole milk
2	cups all-purpose flour	2	cups fresh *or* frozen blackberries

In a large bowl, cream butter and 1-1/4 cups sugar. Add eggs, one at a time, beating well after each addition. Combine the flour, baking powder and salt; gradually stir into creamed mixture alternately with milk, beating well after each addition. Fold in blackberries.

Fill greased or paper-lined muffins cups two-thirds full. Sprinkle with remaining sugar. Bake at 375° for 20-25 minutes or until a toothpick inserted near the center comes out clean. Cool for 5 minutes before removing from pans to wire racks. Serve warm. **YIELD: 1-1/2 DOZEN.**

STRAWBERRIES 'N' CREAM SCONES
prep/total time: 30 min.

2	cups all-purpose flour	1/4	teaspoon ground cinnamon
1/3	cup plus 2 teaspoons sugar, *divided*	1/4	cup cold butter, cubed
2-1/4	teaspoons baking powder	2/3	cup half-and-half cream
1	teaspoon grated lemon peel	1/2	cup coarsely chopped fresh strawberries
3/4	teaspoon salt	1	egg, lightly beaten

In a large bowl, combine the flour, 1/3 cup sugar, baking powder, lemon peel, salt and cinnamon. Cut in butter until mixture resembles coarse crumbs. Stir in cream just until moistened.

Turn onto a lightly floured surface; knead five times. Gently knead in strawberries, about five times. Pat into an 8-in. circle; brush with egg and sprinkle with remaining sugar. Cut into eight wedges.

Separate wedges and place 2 in. apart on a greased baking sheet. Bake at 425° for 9-12 minutes or until golden brown. Serve warm. **YIELD: 8 SCONES.**

AGNES WARD
STRATFORD, ONTARIO

If you are like me, you won't be able to eat just one of these warm scones rich with cream and packed with berry goodness.

ZUCCHINI CHEDDAR BISCUITS
prep/total time: 25 min.

1	large onion, chopped	1/2	teaspoon dried thyme
1/4	cup butter, cubed	3	eggs, lightly beaten
2-1/2	cups biscuit/baking mix	1/4	cup whole milk
1	tablespoon minced fresh parsley	1-1/2	cups shredded zucchini
1/2	teaspoon dried basil	1	cup (4 ounces) shredded cheddar cheese

In a large skillet, saute onion in butter until tender. In a large bowl, combine the biscuit mix, parsley, basil, thyme and onion mixture. In another bowl, combine eggs and milk. Stir into biscuit mixture just until combined. Fold in zucchini and cheese.

Drop by 1/4 cupfuls 2 in. apart onto greased baking sheets. Bake at 400° for 10-14 minutes or until biscuits are golden brown. Serve warm. Refrigerate leftovers. **YIELD: 16 BISCUITS.**

JEAN MOORE
PLINY, WEST VIRGINIA

My husband grows a big garden, and our squash crop always seems to multiply! We give squash to everyone but still have plenty left over for making jelly, relish, pickles, cakes and these biscuits.

**MARY ANN
LUDWIG
EDWARDSVILLE,
ILLINOIS**

*Frozen bread
dough is the
convenient base
for this herb-
flavored flat
Italian bread.
These savory
slices are a
super appetizer
at a summer
gathering. It's a
good way to use
up abundant
garden bounty.*

Fresh & Easy Tip

Dried herbs don't spoil, but they
do lose flavor over time. You may
want to replace herbs that are
over a year old. Store dried herbs
in airtight containers and keep
them away from heat and light.

GARDEN FOCACCIA

prep: 15 min. + rising | bake: 25 min.

1	loaf (1 pound) frozen bread dough, thawed		1/4	cup finely chopped onion
1	tablespoon olive oil		1	garlic clove, minced
1	tablespoon minced fresh rosemary *or* 1 teaspoon dried rosemary, crushed		4	large fresh mushrooms, sliced
1	tablespoon minced fresh thyme *or* 1 teaspoon dried thyme		3	medium tomatoes, sliced
1	package (8 ounces) cream cheese, softened		1	small zucchini, thinly sliced
			1/4	cup grated Parmesan cheese

On a lightly floured surface, roll dough into a 15-in. x 10-in. rectangle. Place in a greased 15-in. x 10-in. x 1-in. baking pan. Cover and let rise for 30 minutes.

Using your fingertips, press indentations in the dough. Brush with oil; sprinkle with rosemary and thyme. Bake at 400° for 12-15 minutes or until golden brown. Cool slightly.

In a large bowl, combine the cream cheese, onion and garlic. Spread over the crust. Top with the mushrooms, tomatoes and zucchini; sprinkle with Parmesan cheese.

Bake for 12-15 minutes or until lightly browned. Cool for 5 minutes before cutting. **YIELD: 20 SLICES.**

TOUCH OF SPRING MUFFINS

prep: 10 min. | bake: 25 min.

2	cups all-purpose flour	1/2	cup sliced fresh strawberries
1/2	cup sugar	1/2	cup sliced fresh rhubarb
1	tablespoon baking powder		

TOPPING:

1/2	teaspoon salt	6	small fresh strawberries, halved
1	egg	2	teaspoons sugar
3/4	cup whole milk		
1/3	cup canola oil		

In a large bowl, combine the flour, sugar, baking powder and salt. In a small bowl, beat the egg, milk and oil until smooth. Stir into dry ingredients just until moistened. Fold in strawberries and rhubarb.

Fill greased or paper-lined muffin cups three-fourths full. Place a strawberry half, cut side down, on each. Sprinkle with sugar.

Bake at 375° for 22-25 minutes or until a toothpick inserted near the center comes out clean. Cool for 5 minutes before removing from pan to a wire rack. Serve warm. **YIELD: 1 DOZEN.**

**GAIL SYKORA
MENOMONEE FALLS,
WISCONSIN**

Strawberries and rhubarb are a winning combination, and their sweet-tart pairing makes these lovely muffins delightful as part of a meal or as a snack.

PEACH PRALINE MUFFINS

prep/total time: 30 min.

1-2/3	cups all-purpose flour	1	cup chopped fresh *or* frozen peaches, thawed and drained
1/2	cup packed brown sugar		
2	teaspoons baking powder	1/2	cup chopped pecans

TOPPING:

1/4	teaspoon salt	1/4	cup packed brown sugar
1/2	cup whole milk		
1/3	cup canola oil	1/4	cup chopped pecans
1	egg	1	tablespoon cold butter
1	teaspoon vanilla extract		

In a large bowl, combine the flour, brown sugar, baking powder and salt. In another bowl, combine the milk, oil, egg and vanilla. Stir into dry ingredients just until moistened. Fold in peaches and pecans.

Fill greased or paper-lined muffin cups two-thirds full. Combine the topping ingredients until crumbly; sprinkle over batter.

Bake at 400° for 15-18 minutes or until a toothpick inserted near the center comes out clean. Cool for 5 minutes before removing from pan to a wire rack. **YIELD: 1 DOZEN.**

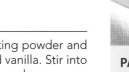

**PAULA WIERSMA
EASTAMPTON, NEW JERSEY**

We eat a lot of muffins around our house. The kids love to nibble on them around the clock. This recipe is a family favorite.

POTATO PAN ROLLS

prep: 15 min. + rising | bake: 20 min.

4-1/2	to 5 cups all-purpose flour	1-1/4	cups water
3	tablespoons sugar	3	tablespoons butter
2	packages (1/4 ounce *each*) quick-rise yeast	1/2	cup mashed potatoes (without added milk and butter)
1-1/2	teaspoons salt		Additional all-purpose flour

In a large bowl, combine 2 cups flour, sugar, yeast and salt. In a small saucepan, heat the water and butter to 120°-130°. Add to the dry ingredients; beat until smooth. Stir in mashed potatoes and enough remaining flour to form a soft dough.

Turn onto a floured surface and knead until smooth and elastic, about 6-8 minutes. Cover and let rest for 10 minutes. Divide into 16 pieces. Shape each into a ball. Place in two greased 8-in. or 9-in. round baking pans. Cover and let rise in a warm place until doubled, about 30 minutes.

Sprinkle with the additional flour. Bake at 400° for 18-22 minutes or until golden brown. Remove from the pans to wire racks to cool. **YIELD: 16 ROLLS.**

**CONNIE STORCKMAN
EVANSTON, WYOMING**

My family loves these rolls, which is why they're requested often. They don't take long to make because quick-rise yeast is used.

CANTALOUPE NUT BREAD

prep: 10 min. | bake: 55 min. + cooling

1/3	cup shortening	1/4	teaspoon baking soda
2/3	cup sugar	1/4	teaspoon salt
1	egg	1	cup mashed ripe cantaloupe, drained
1-3/4	cups all-purpose flour	1/2	cup chopped nuts
2	teaspoons baking powder		

In a large bowl, cream shortening and sugar until light and fluffy. Beat in egg. Combine flour, baking powder, baking soda and salt; add to creamed mixture alternately with cantaloupe until blended (mixture will appear curdled). Fold in nuts. Transfer to a greased 8-in. x 4-in. loaf pan.

Bake at 350° for 55-60 minutes or until a toothpick inserted near the center comes out clean. Cool for 10 minutes before removing from pan to a wire rack. **YIELD: 1 LOAF (16 SLICES).**

**LORIE MCGUIRE
ST. PAUL, KANSAS**

Slices of this unusual melon-flavored loaf are good plain, served with cantaloupe wedges or garnished with whipped cream for dessert. While it looks like ordinary bread, its terrific taste sets it apart.

BASIL-CHEESE BREAD STRIPS

prep: 15 min. + standing | bake: 15 min.

2-1/2	cups all-purpose flour	1/2	teaspoon salt
1/4	cup toasted wheat germ	2	garlic cloves, minced
1	package (1/4 ounce) active dry yeast	1/4	cup shredded part-skim mozzarella cheese
1	cup warm water (120° to 130°)	2	tablespoons grated Parmesan cheese
2	tablespoons olive oil, *divided*	2	tablespoons minced fresh parsley
1	tablespoon honey	10	fresh basil leaves, coarsely chopped

In a large bowl, combine 1-1/2 cups flour, wheat germ, yeast, warm water, 1 tablespoon oil, honey and salt; beat for 2 minutes. Stir in enough remaining flour to make a soft dough.

Turn onto a floured surface; knead for 5-6 minutes. Cover and let rest for 10 minutes. Coat a 15-in. x 10-in. x 1-in. baking pan with cooking spray. Pat the dough into pan. Bake at 425° for 10 minutes or until golden brown.

In a small bowl, combine garlic and remaining oil; brush over bread. Sprinkle with cheeses, parsley and basil. Bake 5 minutes longer or until cheese is melted. Cut into strips. Refrigerate the leftovers. **YIELD: 2 DOZEN.**

MELINDA RHOADS SLIPPERY ROCK, PENNSYLVANIA

Tender and chewy, these bread sticks always go fast. My daughters could eat every last one.

ORANGE CARROT MUFFINS

prep: 20 min. | bake: 20 min.

1/3	cup butter-flavored shortening	1	teaspoon baking soda
1/2	cup sugar	1	teaspoon baking powder
2	eggs	1/8	teaspoon ground nutmeg
1/2	cup orange juice	1/8	teaspoon ground cloves
1-3/4	cups all-purpose flour	2	cups shredded carrots
3	teaspoons grated orange peel		

In a large bowl, cream shortening and sugar until light and fluffy. Beat in the eggs and orange juice. Combine the flour, orange peel, baking soda, baking powder, nutmeg and cloves; add to creamed mixture just until combined. Fold in carrots. Fill greased or paper-lined muffin cups three-fourths full.

Bake at 350° for 18-22 minutes or until a toothpick inserted near the center comes out clean. Cool for 5 minutes before removing from pan to a wire rack. Serve warm. **YIELD: 1 DOZEN.**

ARLYN GAGNON ROCHESTER, MINNESOTA

Nutmeg, cloves and orange peel make these carrot muffins a special anytime treat.

DOROTHY SMITH
EL DORADO, ARKANSAS

This quick Italian flat bread is a delicious savory snack and is also good with soup or a salad.

ANN NIEMELA
ELY, MINNESOTA

These light pleasant-tasting rolls complement almost any entree. With the chive filling swirled through the golden bread, they're attractive enough for special occasions.

TOMATO ROSEMARY FOCACCIA
prep/total time: 25 min.

1	tube (13.8 ounces) refrigerated pizza crust	1	tablespoon minced fresh rosemary *or* 1 teaspoon dried rosemary, crushed, *divided*
2	tablespoons olive oil		
2	garlic cloves, minced		
1/4	teaspoon salt	2	to 3 plum tomatoes, thinly sliced
		1	small red onion, thinly sliced

Unroll pizza crust onto a greased baking sheet. Combine the oil, garlic, salt and half of the rosemary; spread over crust. Top with tomatoes and onion; sprinkle with remaining rosemary. Bake at 425° for 12-15 minutes or until golden. Cut into rectangles. **YIELD: 6 SERVINGS.**

CHIVE PINWHEEL ROLLS
prep: 25 min. + rising | bake: 30 min.

3-1/2	cups all-purpose flour	1/4	cup mashed potatoes (without added milk and butter)
3	tablespoons sugar		
1	package (1/4 ounce) active dry yeast	1	egg
1-1/2	teaspoons salt	**CHIVE FILLING:**	
1	cup milk	1	cup (8 ounces) sour cream
1/3	cup canola oil	1	cup minced chives
1/4	cup water	1	egg yolk
		Butter, melted	

In a large bowl, combine 2-1/2 cups flour, sugar, yeast and salt. In a small saucepan, heat milk, oil, water and mashed potatoes to 120°-130°. Add to dry ingredients; beat just until moistened. Add egg; beat until smooth. Stir in enough remaining flour to form a soft dough.

Turn onto a floured surface; knead until smooth and elastic, about 6-8 minutes. Place in a greased bowl; turn once to grease top. Cover and let rise in a warm place until doubled, about 1 hour.

Turn dough onto a floured surface. Roll into a 15-in. x 10-in. rectangle. In a bowl, combine sour cream, chives and egg yolk. Spread over dough to within 1/2 in. of edges.

Roll up jelly-roll style, starting with a long side; pinch seam to seal. Cut into 1-in. slices. Place cut side down in a 13-in. x 9-in. baking pan. Cover and let rise until doubled, about 1 hour.

Bake at 350° for 30-35 minutes or until golden brown. Brush with the butter. Cool on a wire rack. Refrigerate leftovers. **YIELD: 15 ROLLS.**

KENNETH JACQUES HEMET, CALIFORNIA

I'm retired now, but when I was working I made this coffee cake for coworkers and also a men's Bible study class. I changed the recipe from strawberry to cherry, which gives the cake a richer flavor.

CHERRY RHUBARB COFFEE CAKE
prep: 25 min. | bake: 40 min.

4	cups chopped fresh *or* frozen rhubarb		1	teaspoon baking soda
2	tablespoons lemon juice		1/2	teaspoon salt
1	cup sugar		1	cup cold butter, cubed
1/3	cup cornstarch		1	cup buttermilk
1	can (20 ounces) cherry pie filling		2	eggs, lightly beaten
CAKE:			1	teaspoon vanilla extract
3	cups all-purpose flour		**CRUMB TOPPING:**	
1	cup sugar		1-1/2	cups sugar
1	teaspoon baking powder		1	cup all-purpose flour
			1/2	cup cold butter, cubed

In a large saucepan, cook rhubarb and lemon juice over medium-low heat for 5 minutes, stirring often to prevent burning. Combine sugar and cornstarch; add to rhubarb mixture. Cook and stir 5 minutes more or until thickened and bubbly. Stir in pie filling; set aside to cool.

For cake, combine the flour, sugar, baking powder, baking soda and salt in a large bowl. Cut in the butter until mixture resembles fine crumbs. In a small bowl, beat the buttermilk, eggs and vanilla. Add to flour mixture; stir just until moistened.

Spread a little more than half of the batter into a greased 13-in. x 9-in. baking pan. Spread cooled filling over batter. Drop remaining batter by teaspoonfuls onto filling.

For topping, combine the sugar and flour. Cut in butter until mixture resembles coarse crumbs. Sprinkle over batter. Bake at 350° for 40-45 minutes or until a toothpick inserted near center comes out clean. **YIELD: 16-20 SERVINGS.**

EDITOR'S NOTE: If using frozen rhubarb, measure rhubarb while still frozen, then thaw completely. Drain in a colander, but do not press liquid out.

**JEANNE ALEXANDER
QUALICUM BEACH,
BRITISH COLUMBIA**

*I serve these golden scones for
brunch. Add a scoop of ice cream
and they make a great dessert, too!*

APPLE CHEDDAR SCONES
prep/total time: 30 min.

1-3/4	cups all-purpose flour		1/3	cup cold butter, cubed
2	tablespoons sugar		1	cup buttermilk
1-1/2	teaspoons baking powder		1	cup (4 ounces) shredded cheddar cheese
1/2	teaspoon salt		1	cup diced peeled apples
1/4	teaspoon baking soda			

In a large bowl, combine the first five ingredients. Cut in butter until mixture resembles coarse crumbs. Stir in the buttermilk just until moistened. Gently fold in the cheese and apples. Turn onto a floured surface; knead 10 times.

Pat into a 9-in. circle. Cut into eight wedges. Separate wedges and place on a greased baking sheet. Bake the scones at 450° for 12-15 minutes or until golden brown. **YIELD: 8 SCONES.**

**MARLENE HUFFSTETLER
CHAPIN, SOUTH CAROLINA**

*Enjoy the fresh flavor of summer
squash with this moist and hearty
cornbread. This is good enough to
eat by itself.*

SQUASH CORN BREAD
prep: 15 min. | bake: 20 min.

5	medium yellow summer squash (about 2 pounds), chopped		2/3	cup 4% cottage cheese
2	packages (8-1/2 ounces *each*) corn bread/muffin mix		1/2	cup shredded cheddar cheese
4	eggs, lightly beaten		1/2	cup chopped onion
			1/4	teaspoon salt
			1/4	teaspoon pepper

Place the squash in a steamer basket; place in a large saucepan over 1 in. of water. Bring to a boil; cover and steam for 3-5 minutes or until tender. Drain and squeeze dry.

In a large bowl, combine corn bread mixes and eggs. Fold in the squash, cheeses, onion, salt and pepper.

Pour into two 8-in. square baking pans coated with cooking spray. Bake at 400° for 20-25 minutes or until a toothpick inserted near the center comes out clean. Cut into 24 squares. **YIELD: 2 DOZEN.**

FOUR-HERB BREAD

prep: 10 min. | bake: 3-4 hours

1-1/4	cups water (70° to 80°)	1	tablespoon minced fresh thyme *or* 1 teaspoon dried thyme
2	tablespoons butter, softened	2	teaspoons minced fresh basil *or* 1/2 teaspoon dried basil
3	cups bread flour		
2	tablespoons nonfat dry milk powder	1	teaspoon salt
2	tablespoons sugar	3	teaspoons active dry yeast
1	tablespoon minced chives		
1	tablespoon minced fresh marjoram *or* 1 teaspoon dried marjoram		

In bread machine pan, place all ingredients in order suggested by manufacturer. Select basic bread setting. Choose crust color and loaf size if available. Bake according to bread machine directions (check dough after 5 minutes of mixing; add 1 to 2 tablespoons of water or flour if needed). **YIELD: 1 LOAF (1-1/2 POUNDS, 16 SLICES).**

KIWIFRUIT MUFFINS

prep: 20 min. | bake: 15 min.

1	cup all-purpose flour	1	egg
1/2	cup sugar	1/2	cup whole milk
1/2	teaspoon baking soda	2	tablespoons butter, melted
1/2	teaspoon ground cinnamon	2	kiwifruit, peeled and chopped
1/4	teaspoon ground allspice	1/2	cup raisins

Dash salt

In a large bowl, combine the dry ingredients. In a small bowl, whisk the egg, milk and butter. Stir into dry ingredients just until moistened. Fold in kiwi and raisins.

Fill paper-lined muffin cups three-fourths full. Bake at 425° for 15-18 minutes or until a toothpick inserted near the center comes out clean. Cool for 5 minutes before removing from pan to a wire rack. Serve warm. **YIELD: 10 MUFFINS.**

SUE MURPHY
GREENWOOD, MICHIGAN

Marjoram, thyme, basil and chives season this moist loaf. A friend gave me the recipe. The aroma while it's baking will make you think of a stuffed turkey roasting in the oven.

TIM FINK
STEAMBOAT SPRINGS,
COLORADO

I received this recipe while living in New Zealand with a friend. His wife prepared a batch of these moist muffins for him. I "sampled" so many that the next time, she doubled the recipe so there were plenty for both of us.

SHARON ROSE RISTICH
ROCHESTER, NEW YORK

Everyone raves about the tasty fruit topping I created for refrigerated biscuits. I usually double this recipe and put it in two pie plates to serve a crowd. It really isn't hard to make the topping.

APPLE-TOPPED BISCUITS
prep: 15 min. + standing | bake: 20 min.

3	cups sliced peeled tart apples		1/8	teaspoon salt
1/3	cup sugar		1/8	teaspoon ground nutmeg
1	tablespoon quick-cooking tapioca		1	tube (16.3 ounces) large refrigerated buttermilk biscuits
1-1/2	teaspoons lemon juice			
1/2	teaspoon ground cinnamon			

In a large saucepan, combine the apples, sugar, tapioca, lemon juice, cinnamon, salt and nutmeg. Let stand for 15 minutes. Cook over medium heat for 8-10 minutes or until apples are tender.

Transfer apple mixture to a greased 9-in. pie plate. Place biscuits over apples. Bake at 375° for 18-20 minutes or until biscuits are browned. Immediately invert onto a serving plate. **YIELD: 8 SERVINGS.**

SANDRA FISH
NEWBERG, OREGON

As a former home economics teacher, I enjoy experimenting with recipes. One day I decided to add poppy seeds to my family's favorite cranberry bread. They loved it!

CRANBERRY-NUT POPPY SEED BREAD
prep: 20 min. | bake: 1 hour + cooling

4	cups all-purpose flour		1/2	cup canola oil
2	cups sugar		3	tablespoons poppy seeds
2	teaspoons salt		2	tablespoons grated orange peel
1	teaspoon baking soda		2	cups chopped fresh *or* frozen cranberries
1/2	teaspoon baking powder		1-1/2	cups chopped nuts
2	eggs			
1-1/2	cups orange juice			

In a large bowl, combine flour, sugar, salt, baking soda and baking powder. In another bowl, whisk the eggs, orange juice, oil, poppy seeds and orange peel. Stir into dry ingredients just until moistened. Fold in cranberries and nuts.

Spoon into two greased 8-in. x 4-in. loaf pans. Bake at 350° for 60-65 minutes or until a toothpick inserted near the center comes out clean (cover loosely with foil if tops brown too quickly). Cool for 10 minutes before removing from the pans to wire racks to cool completely. **YIELD: 2 LOAVES (12 SLICES EACH).**

TARRAGON CHEESE LOAF

prep: 10 min. | bake: 25 min.

1	unsliced round bread (1 pound)	1	cup (4 ounces) shredded Monterey Jack cheese
1/4	cup butter, softened		
2	tablespoons minced fresh tarragon	2	cups shredded Parmesan cheese

Slice bread horizontally into thirds; remove top section and set aside. Spread butter over the bottom and middle sections; sprinkle with tarragon and cheeses.

Reassemble loaf; tightly wrap in foil. Bake at 350° for 25 minutes or until cheese begins to melt. Let stand for 5 minutes. Cut into wedges. **YIELD: 8-10 SERVINGS.**

SHERYL HURD-HOUSE
FENTON, MICHIGAN

The distinctive taste of tarragon seasons this savory layered bread. I use a round loaf of sourdough. Warm wedges are especially good with spaghetti or lasagna.

NUT-TOPPED STRAWBERRY RHUBARB MUFFINS

prep: 25 min. | bake: 20 min. + cooling

2-3/4	cups all-purpose flour	2	teaspoons vanilla extract
1-1/3	cups packed brown sugar		
2-1/2	teaspoons baking powder	1	cup chopped fresh strawberries
1/2	teaspoon baking soda	3/4	cup diced fresh *or* frozen rhubarb
1/2	teaspoon ground cinnamon		**TOPPING:**
1/4	teaspoon salt	1/2	cup chopped pecans
1	egg	1/3	cup packed brown sugar
1	cup buttermilk		
1/2	cup canola oil	1/2	teaspoon ground cinnamon
		1	tablespoon cold butter

In a large bowl, combine the first six ingredients. In another bowl, whisk the egg, buttermilk, oil and vanilla. Stir into dry ingredients just until moistened. Fold in strawberries and rhubarb. Fill greased or paper-lined muffin cups two-thirds full.

In a small bowl, combine pecans, brown sugar and cinnamon. Cut in butter until mixture resembles coarse crumbs. Sprinkle over batter.

Bake at 400° for 20-25 minutes or until a toothpick inserted near the center comes out clean. Cool for 5 minutes before removing from pans to wire racks. Serve warm. **YIELD: 1-1/2 DOZEN.**

EDITOR'S NOTE: If using frozen rhubarb, measure rhubarb while still frozen, then thaw completely. Drain in a colander, but do not press liquid out.

AUDREY STALLSMITH
HADLEY, PENNSYLVANIA

A sweet, crispy topping highlights these tender muffins that are filled with two favorite spring foods, rhubarb and strawberries. They're perfect for a brunch or a grab-and-go breakfast.

EVA RIDER MONTGOMERY, ALABAMA

Studded with cranberries and nuts, these moist golden loaves make wonderful breakfast treats and gifts for grateful friends. I experimented for years, and this recipe is now near perfection!

CRANBERRY BANANA BREAD

prep: 25 min. | bake: 50 min. + cooling

1/3 cup shortening	1-1/2 teaspoons baking powder
2/3 cup sugar	1/2 teaspoon baking soda
2 eggs	1/2 teaspoon salt
1 cup mashed ripe bananas (about 2 medium)	1/2 cup chopped walnuts *or* pecans
1-1/2 cups all-purpose flour	1/2 cup dried cranberries
1/3 cup cinnamon graham cracker crumbs (about 2 whole crackers)	

In a large bowl, cream shortening and sugar until light and fluffy. Add eggs, one at a time, beating well after each addition. Stir in bananas. Combine the flour, cracker crumbs, baking powder, baking soda and salt; gradually add to creamed mixture and mix well. Fold in walnuts and cranberries. Pour into a greased 8-in. x 4-in. loaf pan.

Bake at 350° for 50-55 minutes or until a toothpick inserted near the center comes out clean. Cool for 10 minutes before removing from pan to a wire rack. **YIELD: 1 LOAF (12 SLICES).**

GREEN ONION DROP BISCUITS
prep/total time: 30 min.

2	cups all-purpose flour	1/2	teaspoon salt
1/2	cup thinly sliced green onions	1/4	teaspoon baking soda
2	teaspoons sugar	6	tablespoons cold butter, cubed
2	teaspoons baking powder	1	egg
		3/4	cup buttermilk

In a small bowl, combine the flour, onions, sugar, baking powder, salt and baking soda. Cut in butter until mixture resembles coarse crumbs. Combine the egg and buttermilk; stir into crumb mixture just until moistened.

Drop the dough by 1/4 cupfuls 2 in. apart onto a greased baking sheet. Bake at 400° for 12-15 minutes or until golden brown. Serve warm. **YIELD: 10 SERVINGS.**

**TASTE OF HOME
TEST KITCHEN**

These golden gems are beyond scrumptious!

RHUBARB STICKY BUNS
prep: 25 min. + rising | bake: 20 min.

1	package (16 ounces) hot roll mix	2	cups sliced fresh *or* frozen rhubarb
4	tablespoons sugar, *divided*	1/2	cup packed brown sugar
1	cup warm water (120° to 130°)	1/2	cup light corn syrup
1	egg, lightly beaten	2	teaspoons ground cinnamon
2	tablespoons plus 1/2 cup butter, softened, *divided*		

In a large bowl, combine contents of the roll mix and yeast packets with 2 tablespoons sugar. Stir in the water, egg and 2 tablespoons butter to form a soft dough. Turn onto a floured surface. Knead until smooth, about 5 minutes. Cover and let rest for 5 minutes.

Meanwhile, in a large saucepan, combine the rhubarb, brown sugar, corn syrup and the remaining butter. Bring to a boil; cook and stir for 3 minutes. Pour into an ungreased 13-in. x 9-in. baking dish.

On a lightly floured surface, roll dough into a 15-in. x 10-in. rectangle. Combine cinnamon and remaining sugar; sprinkle over dough.

Roll-up jelly-roll style, starting with a long side; pinch seam to seal. Cut into 12 slices. Place cut side down over rhubarb sauce. Cover and let rise in a warm place until doubled, about 30 minutes.

Bake at 375° for 20-25 minutes or until golden brown. Immediately invert onto a serving platter. Serve warm. **YIELD: 1 DOZEN.**

**KATHY KITTELL
LENEXA, KANSAS**

These simple cinnamon buns don't last long at my house. Warm and gooey, these morning starters have the added flavor of rhubarb.

SIDE DISHES & MORE

Discover fresh new treatments for nature's bounty in the simple-to-make dishes on the pages that follow. The pleasing pairing of vegetables, seasonings and sauces will tickle your family's taste buds and have them asking for seconds.

ORANGE RHUBARB SPREAD | **PAGE 172**

FETTUCCINE WITH GREEN VEGETABLES | **PAG**

KATRINA STITT
ZEPHYRHILLS, FLORIDA

The mild taste of Vidalias makes my casserole appealing to everyone, whether they like onions or not. It's an excellent accompaniment to beef, pork or chicken.

VIDALIA ONION BAKE

prep: 25 min. | bake: 20 min.

6	large sweet onions, sliced (about 12 cups)	1	cup shredded Parmesan cheese
1/2	cup butter, cubed	1/2	cup shredded cheddar cheese
2	cups crushed butter-flavored crackers	1/4	cup shredded Romano cheese

In a large skillet, saute onions in butter until tender and liquid has evaporated. Place half of the onions in a greased 2-qt. baking dish; sprinkle with half of the cracker crumbs and cheeses. Repeat layers.

Bake, uncovered, at 325° for 20-25 minutes or until golden brown. **YIELD: 8 SERVINGS.**

LORRAINE FOSS
PUYALLUP, WASHINGTON

This might look like potato salad, but it's actually kohlrabi cubes covered in a white, velvety sauce and accented with chives. Kohlrabi is a favorite vegetable of mine.

CREAMED KOHLRABI

prep/total time: 30 min.

4	cups cubed peeled kohlrabies (about 6 medium)	1/2	teaspoon salt
		1/4	teaspoon pepper
2	tablespoons butter		Dash paprika
2	tablespoons all-purpose flour	1	egg yolk, lightly beaten
2	cups whole milk		Minced chives and additional paprika

Place the kohlrabies in a large saucepan; add 1 in. of water. Bring to a boil. Reduce the heat; cover and simmer for 6-8 minutes or until crisp-tender.

Meanwhile, in a small saucepan, melt butter. Stir in flour until smooth; gradually add the milk. Bring to a boil. Stir in the salt, pepper and paprika. Gradually stir a small amount of hot mixture into egg yolk; return all to the pan, stirring constantly. Bring to a gentle boil; cook and stir for 2 minutes.

Drain the kohlrabies; place in a serving bowl. Add sauce; stir to coat. Sprinkle with chives and additional paprika. **YIELD: 6 SERVINGS.**

AMY SAUSER OMAHA, NEBRASKA

This beautiful pasta is well coated with a delicious garlic-cream sauce. It's a versatile dish that can be served as a side or even as a meat-free entree.

Fresh & Easy Tip

Store garlic in a cool, dark place in an open container. It keeps about 8 weeks. If it has sprouted green shoots but is firm, you may still use it. Split the garlic in half; remove and discard the green portion before mincing.

PASTA WITH CREAM SAUCE
prep: 15 min. | cook: 25 min.

1	package (16 ounces) bow tie pasta	1-1/2	teaspoons minced fresh basil
1	small red onion, chopped	1-1/2	teaspoons minced fresh oregano
3	tablespoons olive oil	1/4	teaspoon salt
4	large garlic cloves, minced	1/4	teaspoon pepper
3/4	cup chicken broth	1	cup heavy whipping cream

Cook pasta according to package directions. Meanwhile, in a large skillet, saute the onion in oil until tender. Add garlic; cook 1 minute longer. Stir in the broth, basil, oregano, salt and pepper. Bring to a boil; cook for 8 minutes or until reduced by about half. Stir in cream.

Cook, uncovered, 8-10 minutes longer or until sauce is reduced to 1-1/4 cups. Drain pasta; toss with sauce. **YIELD: 8 SERVINGS.**

BETTY NYENHUIS
OOSTBURG, WISCONSIN

This tangy spread is easy to make and tastes especially good on hot buttered cinnamon toast. The recipe makes enough to keep the spread on hand well beyond rhubarb season.

TASTE OF HOME
TEST KITCHEN

Our home economists came up with this slightly sweet compote. It's wonderful alongside spicy main courses.

ORANGE RHUBARB SPREAD
prep: 5 min. | cook: 20 min. + standing

4 cups diced fresh or frozen rhubarb	1 package (1-3/4 ounces) powdered fruit pectin
2 cups water	4 cups sugar
1 can (6 ounces) frozen orange juice concentrate, thawed	

In a large saucepan, bring the rhubarb and water to a boil. Reduce heat; simmer, uncovered, for 7-8 minutes or until rhubarb is tender. Drain and reserve the cooking liquid. Cool rhubarb and liquid to room temperature.

Place rhubarb in a blender; cover and process until pureed. Transfer to a 4-cup measuring cup; add enough reserved cooking liquid to measure 2-1/3 cups. Return to the saucepan.

Add orange juice concentrate and pectin; bring to a full rolling boil, stirring constantly. Stir in sugar. Return to a full rolling boil; boil and stir for 1 minute. Remove from the heat; skim off foam.

Pour into jars or freezer containers; cool to room temperature, about 1 hour. Cover and let stand overnight or until set, but not longer than 24 hours. Refrigerate or freeze. Refrigerate for up to 3 weeks and freeze for up to 12 months. **YIELD: 5 HALF-PINTS.**

PINEAPPLE COMPOTE
prep/total time: 20 min.

6 cups cubed fresh pineapple	1/3 cup packed brown sugar
2/3 cup pear nectar or unsweetened pineapple juice	1/3 cup raspberry vinegar
	1/2 teaspoon ground allspice

In a large saucepan, combine all the ingredients. Bring to a boil over medium-low heat. Reduce heat; simmer, uncovered, for 10 minutes or until slightly thickened, stirring frequently. Transfer to a serving bowl. Serve warm or chilled. **YIELD: 4 CUPS.**

ALMOND PEAR CHUTNEY
prep: 15 min. | cook: 30 min.

4 cups chopped peeled ripe pears	1/4 teaspoon ground cinnamon
1 small unpeeled navel orange, halved and thinly sliced	1/3 cup coarsely chopped unblanched almonds, toasted
1/2 cup water	2 tablespoons chopped crystallized ginger
2 teaspoons lemon juice	
1-1/2 cups sugar	

In a large saucepan, combine the pears, orange, water and lemon juice. Bring to a boil, stirring constantly. Reduce the heat; simmer, uncovered, for 10 minutes. Stir in sugar and cinnamon. Bring to a boil. Reduce heat; simmer, uncovered, for 15-20 minutes or until thickened, stirring occasionally.

Remove from the heat; stir in almonds and ginger. Serve warm or cold. May be refrigerated for up to 1 week. **YIELD: 3 CUPS.**

MICHAELA ROSENTHAL WOODLAND HILLS, CALIFORNIA

My deliciously chunky chutney—flavored with orange, almond and ginger—is fabulous with chicken, turkey or pork. You can prepare it a couple of days in advance and use it to dress up a plain weekday supper.

CRAN-ORANGE SWISS CHARD
prep/total time: 25 min.

1 medium onion, sliced	2 tablespoons dried cranberries
1 tablespoon olive oil	Dash salt and pepper
10 cups chopped Swiss chard	2 tablespoons coarsely chopped walnuts, toasted
1/4 cup orange juice	

In a large skillet, saute onion in oil until tender. Add chard; saute for 3-5 minutes or just until wilted.

Stir in the orange juice, cranberries, salt and pepper; cook for 1-2 minutes or until cranberries are softened. Sprinkle with walnuts. **YIELD: 4 SERVINGS.**

JOAN JACKAMAN NOBLETON, ONTARIO

The flavors of this side dish will keep your guests wanting seconds.

ANGELA LIVELY BAXTER, TENNESSEE

This is one of my all-time favorite recipes because it uses items from the garden. Milk and Parmesan cheese give this side dish a creaminess everyone's sure to enjoy.

Fresh & Easy Tip

To remove kernels from ears of corn, stand one end of the cob on a cutting board. Starting at the top, run a sharp knife down the cob, cutting deeply. One medium cob yields 1/3 to 1/2 cup kernels.

TOMATO 'N' CORN RISOTTO

prep: 15 min. | cook: 35 min.

2-1/2	cups water
2	cups whole milk
3	tablespoons chicken broth
1	large onion, finely chopped
2	tablespoons butter
1	garlic clove, minced
3/4	cup uncooked arborio rice
1-1/3	cups fresh corn (about 5 ears of corn)
1	medium tomato, peeled, seeded and chopped
1/2	cup grated Parmesan cheese
1/2	cup fresh basil leaves, thinly sliced
1/2	teaspoon salt
	Pepper to taste

In a large saucepan, heat the water, milk and broth; keep warm.

In a large skillet, saute onion in butter until tender. Add garlic; cook 1 minute longer. Add rice; cook and stir for 2-3 minutes. Stir in 1 cup hot water mixture. Cook and stir until all liquid is absorbed.

Add the remaining water mixture, 1/2 cup at a time, stirring constantly. Allow the liquid to absorb between additions. Cook until the risotto is creamy and rice is almost tender. (Cooking time is about 20 minutes.) Stir in the remaining ingredients; heat through. **YIELD: 5 SERVINGS.**

SPROUTS WITH WATER CHESTNUTS

prep/total time: 30 min.

2	pounds fresh brussels sprouts, trimmed and halved		1/4	teaspoon salt
			1/4	teaspoon pepper
2	tablespoons butter		1	cup chicken broth
2	tablespoons all-purpose flour		1	can (8 ounces) sliced water chestnuts, drained

Place the sprouts in a steamer basket; place in a large saucepan over 1 in. of water. Bring to a boil; cover and steam for 9-11 minutes or until crisp-tender.

Meanwhile, in a small saucepan, melt the butter; stir in flour, salt and pepper until smooth. Gradually stir in broth. Bring to a boil; cook and stir for 2 minutes or until thickened. Stir in water chestnuts. Transfer brussels sprouts to a serving dish; serve with water chestnut mixture. **YIELD: 9 SERVINGS.**

**GENELLE SMITH
HANOVER, PENNSYLVANIA**

This tasty side dish has become a family tradition at Thanksgiving, as well as throughout the year. A creamy sauce and water chestnuts give the sprouts a nice lift.

BASIL BUTTER

prep/total time: 10 min.

1-1/2	cups loosely packed fresh basil leaves		1	teaspoon seasoned pepper
1	cup butter, softened		1/2	teaspoon garlic salt
1	teaspoon lemon juice			Hot cooked corn on the cob

Place basil in a food processor; cover and process until coarsely chopped. Add the butter, lemon juice, seasoned pepper and garlic salt; cover and process until blended. Serve with corn. Refrigerate leftovers. **YIELD: 1-1/2 CUPS.**

**EMILY CHANEY
PENOBSCOT, MAINE**

Add a wonderful basil flavor to your corn on the cob with this delicious butter spread. It is so easy and will taste great.

ROASTED RADISHES

prep: 10 min. | bake: 30 min.

2-1/4 pounds radishes, trimmed and quartered	1/4 teaspoon salt
3 tablespoons olive oil	1/8 teaspoon pepper
1 tablespoon minced fresh oregano *or* 1 teaspoon dried oregano	

In a large bowl, combine all ingredients. Transfer to a greased 15-in. x 10-in. x 1-in. baking pan. Bake, uncovered, at 425° for 30 minutes or until crisp-tender, stirring once. **YIELD: 5 SERVINGS.**

RAINBOW VEGETABLE SKILLET

prep/total time: 30 min.

1 medium butternut squash (about 2 pounds)	1/2 teaspoon pepper
1/4 cup reduced-fat butter, melted	1/4 teaspoon ground cinnamon
2 tablespoons brown sugar	1 medium green pepper, cut into 1-inch pieces
1 tablespoon chili powder	1 medium sweet yellow pepper, cut into 1-inch pieces
1 tablespoon minced fresh cilantro	1 medium red onion, cut into wedges
1 teaspoon salt	1 tablespoon olive oil
	2 cups grape tomatoes

Cut the squash in half; discard the seeds. Place the cut side down in a microwave-safe dish; add 1/2 in. of water. Microwave, uncovered, on high for 10-12 minutes or until almost tender.

Meanwhile, in a small bowl, combine the butter, brown sugar, chili powder, cilantro, salt, pepper and cinnamon; set aside. When squash is cool enough to handle, peel and discard the rind. Cut pulp into 1/2-in. pieces.

In a large skillet, saute peppers and onion in oil until tender. Add tomatoes and squash; heat through. Transfer to a large bowl; add butter mixture and toss to coat. **YIELD: 9 SERVINGS.**

EDITOR'S NOTE: This recipe was tested with Land O'Lakes light stick butter and used a 1,100-watt microwave.

SEASONED YUKON GOLD WEDGES
prep: 10 min. | bake: 40 min.

1-1/2	pounds Yukon Gold potatoes (about 3 medium), cut into wedges	1/4	teaspoon dried oregano
1	tablespoon olive oil	1/4	teaspoon dried thyme
1/4	cup dry bread crumbs	1/4	teaspoon ground cumin
1-1/2	teaspoons paprika	1/8	teaspoon pepper
3/4	teaspoon salt	1/8	teaspoon cayenne pepper

In a large bowl, toss the potatoes with oil. Combine the remaining ingredients; sprinkle over potatoes and toss to coat.

Arrange potatoes in a single layer in a 15-in. x 10-in. x 1-in. baking pan coated with cooking spray. Bake, uncovered, at 425° for 40-45 minutes or until tender, stirring once. **YIELD: 6 SERVINGS.**

EGGPLANT WITH TOMATO SAUCE
prep/total time: 20 min.

1	medium eggplant	1/4	teaspoon garlic powder
2	tablespoons butter, melted	1/4	cup grated Parmesan cheese, optional
Salt and pepper to taste			
1	can (8 ounces) tomato sauce		

Cut eggplant lengthwise into 1/2-in.-thick slices. Place on a broiler pan. Brush with butter; sprinkle with salt and pepper. Broil 4 in. from the heat for 3-4 minutes on each side or until tender.

Meanwhile, heat the tomato sauce and garlic powder. Drizzle over eggplant. Sprinkle with cheese if desired. **YIELD: 6-8 SERVINGS.**

**JANE LYNCH
SCARBOROUGH, ONTARIO**

These zesty potatoes are a snap to make. My two boys and husband just love them. They're good with roast or chops, but can also be served as an appetizer with a dip.

**EDNA HOFFMAN
HEBRON, INDIANA**

Things don't get much quicker than this tasty dish. I broil sliced eggplant before topping it with a speedy garlic-seasoned tomato sauce and a little Parmesan cheese.

**MARIE HATTRUP
THE DALLES, OREGON**

Artichokes are fun to prepare and eat as an appetizer or side dish. Serve each person a small bowl of herb butter to dip the leaves in.

ARTICHOKES WITH TARRAGON BUTTER
prep/total time: 20 min.

2	medium artichokes	1/4	teaspoon dried oregano
4	teaspoons lemon juice, *divided*	1/4	teaspoon dried tarragon
1/4	cup butter, melted		
1/4	teaspoon dill weed		

Using a sharp knife, level bottom of each artichoke and cut 1 in. from the top. Using kitchen scissors, snip off tips of outer leaves. Brush cut edges with 1 teaspoon lemon juice.

Place the artichokes in a deep 8-in. microwave-safe dish; add 1 in. of water. Cover and microwave on high for 10-12 minutes or until leaves near the center pull out easily. Let stand for 5 minutes.

Meanwhile, in a small bowl, combine butter, dill, oregano, tarragon and the remaining lemon juice. Serve with the artichokes. **YIELD: 2 SERVINGS.**

EDITOR'S NOTE: This recipe was tested in a 1,100-watt microwave.

**JACQUELYNNE STINE
LAS VEGAS, NEVADA**

Panko bread crumbs have a coarser texture than ordinary bread crumbs, which you can also use to coat the tomatoes. However, the panko crumbs will give them a uniquely light and crispy texture.

FRIED GREEN TOMATOES
prep: 20 min. | cook: 25 min.

3/4	cup all-purpose flour	5	medium green tomatoes, cut into 1/4-inch slices
3	eggs, lightly beaten		
2	cups panko (Japanese) bread crumbs		Oil for deep-fat frying
			Salt

In three separate shallow bowls, place the flour, eggs and bread crumbs. Dip tomatoes in flour, then in eggs; coat with bread crumbs.

In an electric skillet or deep-fat fryer, heat oil to 375°. Fry tomatoes, a few at a time, for 2-3 minutes on each side or until golden brown. Drain on paper towels. Sprinkle with the salt. Serve immediately. **YIELD: 10 SERVINGS.**

SUGAR SNAP PEA STIR-FRY

prep/total time: 20 min.

1 pound fresh sugar snap peas	1-1/2 teaspoons reduced-sodium soy sauce
2 teaspoons canola oil	1 teaspoon sesame oil
1 garlic clove, minced	Dash cayenne pepper
2 teaspoons minced fresh gingerroot	1 tablespoon minced fresh basil *or* 1 teaspoon dried basil
1-1/2 teaspoons balsamic vinegar	2 teaspoons sesame seeds, toasted

In a large nonstick skillet or wok, saute the peas in canola oil until crisp-tender. Add the garlic, ginger, vinegar, soy sauce, sesame oil and cayenne; saute 1 minute longer. Add basil; toss to combine. Sprinkle with sesame seeds. **YIELD: 6 SERVINGS.**

GINGERED ORANGE BEETS
prep: 10 min. | bake: 70 min.

1-1/2	pounds whole fresh beets (about 4 medium), trimmed and cleaned	1-1/2	teaspoons grated orange peel, *divided*
6	tablespoons olive oil, *divided*	1/2	teaspoon minced fresh gingerroot
1/4	teaspoon salt	1	medium navel orange, peeled, sectioned and chopped
1/4	teaspoon white pepper	1/3	cup pecan halves, toasted
1	tablespoon rice vinegar		
1	tablespoon thawed orange juice concentrate		

Brush beets with 4 tablespoons oil; sprinkle with salt and pepper. Wrap loosely in foil; place on a baking sheet. Bake at 425° for 70-75 minutes or until fork-tender. Cool slightly.

In a small bowl, whisk vinegar, orange juice concentrate, 1 teaspoon orange peel, ginger and remaining oil; set aside.

Peel beets and cut into wedges; place in a serving bowl. Add the orange sections and pecans. Drizzle with orange sauce and toss to coat. Sprinkle with remaining orange peel. **YIELD: 4 SERVINGS.**

WALNUT CRANBERRY BUTTER
prep: 20 min. + chilling

3/4	cup butter, softened	1	cup chopped fresh cranberries
2	tablespoons brown sugar	2	tablespoons chopped walnuts, toasted
2	tablespoons honey		

In a small bowl, beat the butter, brown sugar and honey until fluffy, about 5 minutes. Add cranberries and walnuts; beat 5 minutes longer or until butter turns pink.

Transfer butter to a sheet of plastic wrap; roll into a log. Refrigerate until chilled. Unwrap the butter and slice or place it on a butter dish. **YIELD: 1-1/3 CUPS.**

SWEET PICKLED ASPARAGUS
prep: 15 min. | process: 20 min. + standing

10	pounds fresh asparagus	2	quarts water
5	tablespoons dill seed	3	cups cider vinegar
5	teaspoons mixed pickling spices	2/3	cup sugar
		1/4	cup canning salt

Wash, drain and trim asparagus; cut into 5-3/4-in. spears (discard ends or save for another use). Pack asparagus into five 1-qt. jars to within 1/2 in. of top. Place 1 tablespoon dill seed and 1 teaspoon pickling spices in each jar.

In a Dutch oven, bring the water, vinegar, sugar and salt to a boil. Carefully ladle hot liquid over asparagus mixture, leaving 1/2-in. headspace. Remove air bubbles; wipe rims and adjust lids. Process for 15 minutes in a boiling-water canner. **YIELD: 5 QUARTS.**

VALERIE GIESBRECHT OTHELLO, WASHINGTON

Here in Washington, we enjoy lots of fresh asparagus in the spring. This is how my grandmother used to pickle it.

ORANGE BLUEBERRY FREEZER JAM
prep: 25 min. + standing

2-1/2	cups sugar	1	pouch liquid fruit pectin
1	medium orange		
1-1/2	cups fresh blueberries, mashed		

Place sugar in a shallow baking dish. Bake at 250° for 15 minutes. Meanwhile, grate 1 tablespoon peel from orange. Peel, segment and chop orange.

In a large bowl combine peel, chopped orange, blueberries and sugar; let stand for 10 minutes stirring occasionally. Stir in pectin. Stir constantly for 3 minutes.

Ladle into jars or freezer containers. Cover and let stand overnight or until set, but not longer than 24 hours. Refrigerate for up to 3 weeks and freeze for up to 12 months. **YIELD: 4 CUPS.**

EDITOR'S NOTE: When grating citrus fruits, be sure to grate only the outside of the peel; the white pith makes the peel bitter.

MARK MORGAN WATERFORD, WISCONSIN

I buy blueberries by the flat from a local produce supplier who trucks berries from Michigan the day they are picked. While my children can eat them by the pint, this quick jam allows me to savor the berries year round.

MEREDITH HOLMAN SILVER SPRING, MARYLAND

Even those who do not like to eat veggies enjoy this pretty, medley. Cheese adds extra flavor that everyone just loves.

CHEESE-TOPPED ROASTED VEGETABLES
prep: 15 min. | bake: 45 min.

3 small red potatoes, quartered	6 large fresh mushrooms, quartered
2 medium carrots, cut into 1/2-inch slices	2 garlic cloves, minced
1 small onion, cut into wedges	1/2 cup shredded cheddar cheese
3 teaspoons olive oil, *divided*	1/2 cup shredded part-skim mozzarella cheese
1/4 teaspoon salt, *divided*	1 tablespoon grated Parmesan cheese
1/4 teaspoon pepper, *divided*	1 teaspoon minced fresh basil
1 large zucchini, cut into 1/2-inch pieces	1 teaspoon minced fresh oregano
1 large sweet red pepper, cut into 1-inch pieces	

Place the potatoes, carrots and onion in a large resealable plastic bag. Add 1-1/2 teaspoons oil, 1/8 teaspoon salt and 1/8 teaspoon pepper; turn to coat. Place mixture in a single layer in a greased 15-in. x 10-in. x 1-in. baking pan (set bag aside). Bake at 425° for 20 minutes.

Add the zucchini, red pepper, mushrooms and garlic to the reserved bag. Add the remaining oil, salt and pepper; turn to coat. Stir into potato mixture.

Bake 25-30 minutes longer or until vegetables are tender. Transfer to a large serving bowl. Sprinkle with cheeses and herbs. **YIELD: 8 SERVINGS.**

SWEET 'N' SOUR ONIONS
prep/total time: 25 min.

3 cups water	1/4 cup white wine vinegar
2-2/3 cups green onions (white portion only)	4 teaspoons honey
1/4 cup butter, cubed	1/2 teaspoon salt
1/4 cup minced fresh parsley	1/4 teaspoon pepper

In a large saucepan, bring water to a boil. Add onions; cover and boil for 3 minutes. Drain and immediately place onions in ice water. Drain and pat dry.

In a large skillet, saute onions in butter until tender. Stir in the parsley, vinegar, honey, salt and pepper; heat through. **YIELD: 4 SERVINGS.**

**PENNY VANDERHOFF
ELLIJAY, GEORGIA**

If you like onions and want to try something new, give this easy recipe a shot. It's a great side dish for any meal.

MASHED POTATO SPINACH BAKE
prep: 25 min. | bake: 20 min.

6 medium potatoes, peeled and quartered	1-1/2 teaspoons salt
1 package (10 ounces) fresh spinach, torn	1 teaspoon sugar
3/4 cup sour cream	1/4 teaspoon pepper
1/4 cup butter, cubed	1/4 teaspoon dill weed
2 teaspoons minced chives	1 cup (4 ounces) shredded cheddar cheese

Place the potatoes in a large saucepan and cover with water. Bring to a boil. Reduce the heat; cover and cook for 15-20 minutes or until tender. Meanwhile, cook spinach in a small amount of water until wilted; drain well.

Drain potatoes; place in a large bowl and mash. Stir in the spinach, sour cream, butter, chives and seasonings.

Transfer to a greased 2-1/2-qt. baking dish. Sprinkle with cheese. Bake, uncovered, at 400° for 20-25 minutes or until heated through. **YIELD: 8 SERVINGS.**

**FAUNEIL BENNETT
WAYNE, NEBRASKA**

This potato casserole can be made ahead. So when company rings the bell, all I have to do is place it in the oven.

AMY SHORT
LESAGE, WEST VIRGINIA

Golden brown sweet potatoes make these cakes pretty to look at and even better to eat. The green onions and thyme add an extra boost of flavor.

PARSNIP SWEET POTATO PANCAKES
prep: 20 min. | cook: 30 min.

1	cup all-purpose flour	1	pound parsnips, peeled and grated
3	tablespoons minced fresh thyme	12	green onions, sliced diagonally
2	teaspoons salt	1/2	cup vegetable oil
1/4	teaspoon pepper		
4	eggs, lightly beaten		
2	pounds sweet potatoes, peeled and grated		

In a large bowl, combine the flour, thyme, salt and pepper. Stir in eggs until blended. Add the sweet potatoes, parsnips and onions; toss to coat.

In an electric skillet or deep-fat fryer, heat oil to 375°. Drop batter by 1/4 cupfuls, a few at a time, into hot oil; press lightly to flatten. Fry for 3-4 minutes on each side or until golden brown. Drain on paper towels. Serve warm. **YIELD: 2 DOZEN.**

MELANIE KNOLL
MARSHALLTOWN, IOWA

Mushrooms cooked over hot coals always taste good, but this easy recipe makes them simply fantastic.

GRILLED MUSHROOMS
prep/total time: 15 min.

1/2	pound whole fresh medium mushrooms	1/2	teaspoon dill weed
1/4	cup butter, melted	1/2	teaspoon garlic salt

Thread mushrooms on skewers. Combine butter, dill and garlic salt; brush over mushrooms.

Using long-handled tongs, moisten a paper towel with cooking oil and lightly coat the grill rack. Grill over hot heat or broil 3-4 in. from the heat for 10-15 minutes, basting and turning every 5 minutes. **YIELD: 4 SERVINGS.**

CREAMY BROCCOLI WITH CASHEWS
prep/total time: 20 min.

9	cups fresh broccoli florets	2	teaspoons honey
1/4	cup chopped onion	1	teaspoon cider vinegar
2	tablespoons butter	1/2	teaspoon salt
1	cup (8 ounces) sour cream	1/2	teaspoon paprika
		1/2	cup coarsely chopped cashews

Place the broccoli in a steamer basket; place in a large saucepan over 1 in. of water. Bring to a boil; cover and steam for 3-4 minutes or until crisp-tender.

Meanwhile, in a small skillet, saute the onion in butter until tender. Remove from heat; stir in sour cream, honey, vinegar, salt and paprika.

Transfer broccoli to a serving bowl. Add sour cream mixture and toss to coat. Sprinkle with cashews. **YIELD: 6 SERVINGS.**

**KAREN ANN BLAND
GOVE, KANSAS**

Looking for a holiday side dish that's something special? The sour cream sauce in this broccoli casserole is a little different from the usual, and the cashews lend a nice crunch. It's great with a variety of entrees.

SLOW-ROASTED TOMATOES
prep: 10 min. | bake: 2 hours

16	plum tomatoes, halved lengthwise and seeded	1	teaspoon sugar
1/4	cup grated Parmesan cheese	1	teaspoon salt
1	tablespoon dried oregano	1/2	teaspoon pepper
		2	tablespoons olive oil

Place tomatoes, cut side up, on baking sheets coated with cooking spray. Sprinkle with cheese, oregano, sugar, salt and pepper; drizzle with oil. Bake at 250° for 2 hours. **YIELD: 8 SERVINGS.**

**MARTHA CHAYET
MANCHESTER,
MASSACHUSETTS**

Seasoned with oregano and cheese, these tomatoes take on an Italian flair. We like them in the summer alongside grilled chicken, but they're good year-round.

RUBY HUBBARD
CLEVELAND, OKLAHOMA

This is my very favorite rice dish. I've served it many times and it's always received rave reviews. I hope you enjoy it as much as I do.

HEATHER RATIGAN
KAUFMAN, TEXAS

I don't usually create my own recipes, but this one passed my palate test. It offers a buttery flavor that those of us who are watching our weight sometimes miss.

OKRA PILAF
prep/total time: 25 min.

4 bacon strips, cut into 1/2-inch pieces	2 medium tomatoes, peeled, seeded and chopped
1 medium onion, chopped	1/2 teaspoon salt, optional
1/2 cup chopped green pepper	1/4 teaspoon pepper
1 cup sliced fresh *or* frozen okra, thawed	3 cups cooked rice

In a large skillet, cook the bacon over medium heat until crisp; remove with a slotted spoon to paper towel to drain. Saute onion and green pepper in drippings for 6-8 minutes or until tender.

Stir in okra, tomatoes, salt if desired and pepper; cook over medium heat for 5 minutes. Add rice; cook for 10-15 minutes or until okra is tender and liquid is absorbed. Crumble bacon; stir into rice mixture. **YIELD: 8 SERVINGS.**

RICE WITH SUMMER SQUASH
prep: 15 min. | cook: 25 min.

1 cup chopped carrots	1/4 teaspoon salt
1/2 cup chopped onion	1/4 teaspoon pepper
1 tablespoon butter	1 medium yellow summer squash, chopped
1 cup reduced-sodium chicken broth *or* vegetable broth	1 medium zucchini, chopped
1/3 cup uncooked long grain rice	

In a large saucepan coated with cooking spray, cook the carrots and onion in butter until tender. Stir in the broth, rice, salt and pepper. Bring to a boil. Reduce heat; cover and simmer for 13 minutes.

Stir in yellow squash and zucchini. Cover and simmer 6-10 minutes longer or until rice and vegetables are tender. **YIELD: 4 SERVINGS.**

APPLE STUFFING
prep/total time: 15 min.

1	medium tart apple, chopped	1	tablespoon butter
1/2	cup chopped onion	1	package (6 ounces) stuffing mix
1/4	cup chopped celery		

In a large skillet, saute the apple, onion and celery in butter until tender. Prepare stuffing mix according to package directions. Stir in apple mixture. **YIELD: 5 SERVINGS.**

TERRI MCKITRICK
DELAFIELD, WISCONSIN

Common fruit and veggies give store-bought stuffing mix a taste that's anything but ordinary. It's an easy alternative to from-scratch stuffings that can take over an hour to make.

FESTIVE BEAN 'N' PEPPER BUNDLES
prep: 25 min. | bake: 15 min.

1	pound fresh green beans, trimmed	1/2	teaspoon garlic powder
1	pound fresh wax beans, trimmed	3	medium zucchini
2	tablespoons chicken bouillon granules	2	medium sweet red peppers, julienned
		1/4	cup butter, melted

In a large saucepan, combine the beans, bouillon and garlic powder; cover with water. Bring to a boil. Cook, uncovered, for 8-10 minutes or until crisp-tender; drain.

Cut the zucchini into 1/2-in. slices. Hollow out centers, leaving 1/4-in. rings; discard the centers. Thread the beans and peppers through squash rings.

Place in a greased 15-in. x 10-in. x 1-in. baking pan; drizzle with the butter. Cover and bake at 350° for 15-20 minutes or until zucchini is crisp-tender. **YIELD: 12-15 SERVINGS.**

JUDITH KRUCKI
LAKE ORION, MICHIGAN

This is a beautiful way to prepare vegetables for dinner or even brunch. The flavor pairs well with a variety of entrees.

VALERIE BELLEY
ST. LOUIS, MISSOURI

This is my favorite way to prepare potatoes. A handful of ingredients, a pot and a bowl are all you need to quickly make a great side that goes with any meal.

MITZI SENTIFF
ANNAPOLIS, MARYLAND

This is the best grilled corn I have ever tasted! The butter, garlic and cheese make it hard to resist. Consider it for your next cookout.

MASHED POTATOES WITH A KICK

prep/total time: 30 min.

10	medium potatoes (3 pounds), peeled and cubed	1/4	cup butter, cubed
1	cup heavy whipping cream	2	tablespoons prepared horseradish
		1	teaspoon salt
		1	teaspoon pepper

Place the potatoes in a Dutch oven and cover with water. Bring to a boil. Reduce the heat; cover and cook for 10-15 minutes or until tender. Drain. In a large bowl, mash the potatoes with remaining ingredients. **YIELD: 8 SERVINGS.**

GARLIC-BUTTER PARMESAN CORN

prep: 15 min. + soaking | grill: 25 min.

8	medium ears sweet corn in husks	1/4	teaspoon salt
1/3	cup butter, cubed	1/4	cup grated Parmesan cheese
1/2	teaspoon minced garlic		

Soak the corn in cold water for 20 minutes. Meanwhile, in a small saucepan, combine the butter, garlic and salt. Cook and stir over medium heat until butter is melted; set aside 2 tablespoons.

Carefully peel back corn husks to within 1 in. of bottoms; remove silk. Brush with remaining butter mixture. Rewrap corn in husks and secure with kitchen string.

Grill the corn, covered, over medium heat for 25-30 minutes or until tender, turning occasionally. Cut the string and peel back the husks. Drizzle corn with the reserved butter mixture; sprinkle with the cheese. **YIELD: 8 SERVINGS.**

FRUIT-STUFFED ACORN SQUASH

prep: 15 min. | bake: 70 min.

2	medium acorn squash	2	tablespoons butter, melted
1/4	teaspoon salt		
2	cups chopped unpeeled tart apples	1/4	teaspoon ground cinnamon
3/4	cup fresh or frozen cranberries	1/8	teaspoon ground nutmeg
1/4	cup packed brown sugar		

Cut squash in half; discard seeds. Place squash cut side down in an ungreased 13-in. x 9-in. baking dish. Add 1 in. of hot water to the pan. Bake, uncovered, at 350° for 30 minutes.

Drain water from pan; turn squash cut side up. Sprinkle with salt. Combine the remaining ingredients; spoon into squash. Bake 40-50 minutes longer or until squash is tender. **YIELD: 4 SERVINGS.**

**PEGGY WEST
GEORGETOWN, DELAWARE**

Holiday meals are even more fun when I serve colorful acorn squash with a fruity medley spooned inside each half. It makes a festive addition to winter menus.

CRAN-ORANGE RELISH

prep/total time: 25 min.

8	packages (12 ounces each) fresh cranberries	6	large unpeeled navel oranges, cut into wedges
		4	cups sugar

In a food processor, process the cranberries and oranges in batches until finely chopped. Place in a large container; stir in sugar. Cover and refrigerate until serving. **YIELD: 4-1/2 QUARTS.**

**CLARA HONEYAGER
NORTH PRAIRIE, WISCONSIN**

With its vibrant color and citrus-cranberry flavor, this lovely relish works well at seasonal gatherings. It's also convenient because you can make it in advance.

CARROTS AND SNOW PEAS

prep/total time: 25 min.

1-3/4	cups sliced fresh carrots	1	shallot, minced
2	tablespoons butter	1/4	teaspoon salt
2-3/4	cups fresh snow peas	1	tablespoon sherry or chicken broth

In a large skillet or wok, stir-fry the carrots in butter for 3 minutes. Add the snow peas, shallot and salt; stir-fry 2 minutes longer or until the vegetables are crisp-tender. Stir in the sherry; heat through. **YIELD: 4 SERVINGS.**

CHERYL DONNELLY
ARVADA, COLORADO

This is without question my best side dish, both for flavor and ease of preparation. Sherry adds a unique twist to the vegetables.

KOHLRABI 'N' CARROT BAKE

prep: 35 min. | bake: 20 min.

3	medium kohlrabies, peeled and sliced	1/2	teaspoon salt
			Dash pepper
4	medium carrots, sliced	1-1/2	cups whole milk
1/4	cup chopped onion	1/4	cup minced fresh parsley
3	tablespoons butter, *divided*	1	tablespoon lemon juice
2	tablespoons all-purpose flour	3/4	cup soft bread crumbs

Place the kohlrabies and carrots in a large saucepan and cover with water. Bring to a boil. Reduce heat; cover and cook for 15-20 minutes or until tender. Drain well; set aside.

In a large skillet, saute onion in 2 tablespoons butter until tender. Stir in the flour, salt and pepper until blended. Gradually whisk in milk. Bring to a boil; cook and stir for 2 minutes or until thickened.

Remove from heat. Stir in vegetable mixture, parsley and lemon juice. Transfer to a shallow 2-qt. baking dish coated with cooking spray.

In a small skillet, melt the remaining butter over medium heat. Add bread crumbs; cook and stir for 2-3 minutes or until lightly browned. Sprinkle over vegetable mixture.

Bake, uncovered, at 350° for 20-25 minutes or until heated through. **YIELD: 6 SERVINGS.**

DIANNE BETTIN
TRUMAN, MINNESOTA

We love kohlrabi from our garden, but there doesn't seem to be many recipes that use this sensational vegetable. This one is wonderful!

SUSAN MCCARTNEY ONALASKA, WISCONSIN

I like to serve this rich side with different entrees. It makes any meal seem special, and I'm always asked for the recipe.

Fresh & Easy Tip

To prepare asparagus, rinse it in cold water and snap off the stalk ends where they easily break when gently bent. Peel the ends of large stalks to remove tough areas. Scrape off large scales with a knife.

FETTUCCINE WITH GREEN VEGETABLES

prep: 15 min. | cook: 20 min.

4 ounces uncooked fettuccine	1/4 teaspoon salt
1/4 pound fresh asparagus, trimmed and cut into 1-inch pieces	1/8 teaspoon pepper
1 medium zucchini, chopped	1/4 cup shredded Romano cheese
1 tablespoon canola oil	2 tablespoons minced fresh parsley
1 green onion, thinly sliced	4 teaspoons minced chives
1 garlic clove, minced	Additional shredded Romano cheese, optional
1/4 cup frozen peas, thawed	

Cook the fettuccine according to package directions. Meanwhile, in a small saucepan, bring 1/2 in. of water to a boil. Add asparagus; cover and boil for 3 minutes. Drain and immediately place asparagus in ice water. Drain and pat dry.

In a large nonstick skillet, saute the zucchini in oil for 3 minutes. Add the onion and garlic; saute 1 minute longer. Add the peas, salt, pepper and asparagus; saute until vegetables are crisp-tender.

Drain fettuccine; add to vegetable mixture. Stir in the cheese, parsley and chives. Garnish with additional cheese if desired. **YIELD: 4 SERVINGS.**

MARI ANNE WARREN
MILTON, WISCONSIN

Seasoned with lemon and butter, these red potatoes are a perfect addition to weekend meals. Mom often made them for us to enjoy with our Sunday pork roast.

LEMON PARSLEY POTATOES
prep/total time: 25 min.

3	pounds small red potatoes	1/3	cup minced fresh parsley
1/2	cup butter	1	tablespoon lemon juice

With a vegetable peeler, remove a strip of peel around the middle of each potato. Place potatoes in a large saucepan and cover with water. Bring to a boil. Reduce heat; cover and cook for 15-20 minutes or until tender. Drain.

Meanwhile, in a small saucepan, melt the butter; stir in parsley and lemon juice. Pour over potatoes; toss to coat. **YIELD: 8 SERVINGS.**

SANDRA COREY
CALDWELL, IDAHO

The herb butter in this recipe can be used for everything from carrots to game hens.

HERB-BUTTERED BABY CARROTS
prep: 10 min. | bake: 50 min.

1/2	cup butter, melted	1/4	teaspoon *each* dried oregano, marjoram and thyme
1	garlic clove, minced		
1	teaspoon dried parsley flakes	1/4	teaspoon dried rosemary, crushed
1/2	teaspoon dried basil	1	pound fresh baby carrots, trimmed

In a large bowl, combine the butter, garlic and herbs. Add carrots and stir until coated. Transfer to a greased 1-1/2-qt. baking dish.

Cover and bake at 375° for 50-60 minutes or until tender, stirring once. **YIELD: 6 SERVINGS.**

GINGERED PEACH CHUTNEY

prep: 20 min. | cook: 50 min.

4	cups chopped peeled fresh peaches	1/3	cup chopped crystallized ginger
1-1/2	cups cider vinegar	1	tablespoon mustard seed
1	cup plus 2 tablespoons packed brown sugar	1	tablespoon chili powder
1	small onion, finely chopped	1	teaspoon salt
1/2	cup raisins	1	small garlic clove, minced

In a Dutch oven, combine all the ingredients. Bring to a boil over medium heat. Reduce heat; simmer, uncovered, for 45-50 minutes or until thickened and reduced to about 3-1/2 cups, stirring occasionally.

Serve chutney warm or at room temperature. Refrigerate leftovers. **YIELD: 3-1/2 CUPS.**

MARLENE WICZEK LITTLE FALLS, MINNESOTA

This chutney showcases peaches... some of the best fruit of the summer. I love to spoon it over pork chops.

GARLICKY KALE

prep: 20 min. | cook: 15 min.

3	cups water	1/4	cup pitted ripe olives, sliced
2	bunches kale, trimmed and coarsely chopped	1/4	teaspoon salt
4	garlic cloves, minced	1/4	teaspoon crushed red pepper flakes
1	teaspoon olive oil		
1/2	cup golden raisins		

In a large saucepan, bring water to a boil. Stir in kale. Cover and cook for 6-8 minutes or until almost tender; drain and set aside.

In a large nonstick skillet coated with cooking spray, cook garlic in oil for 1 minute. Stir in the raisins, olives, salt and pepper flakes; cook 1 minute longer. Stir in the kale; cook for 3-4 minutes or until tender. **YIELD: 6 SERVINGS.**

CLARA COULSTON WASHINGTON COURT HOUSE, OHIO

This warm and zippy side features fresh kale and sweet raisins. It tastes wonderful served hot or cold.

**KRISTIN ARNETT
ELKHORN,
WISCONSIN**

*This broccoli
dish features a
piquant lemon
sauce, making it
a quaint part of
any dinner.*

BROCCOLI TIMBALES WITH LEMON SAUCE
prep: 20 min. + standing | bake: 25 min.

1-1/2 cups heavy whipping cream, *divided*
  2 tablespoons lemon juice
  3 eggs
  3 egg yolks
  2 packages (3 ounces *each*) cream cheese, softened
  5 tablespoons butter, softened, *divided*
  2 to 3 tablespoons grated Parmesan cheese

  4 cups chopped fresh broccoli (about 1-1/4 pounds)
1/2 teaspoon salt, *divided*
1/4 teaspoon white pepper, *divided*
  1 tablespoon all-purpose flour
  1 teaspoon chicken bouillon granules
  3 tablespoons snipped fresh dill
Fresh dill sprigs, optional

In a small bowl, combine 1 cup cream and lemon juice; let stand for 1 hour at room temperature. Place the remaining cream in a blender. Add the eggs, egg yolks, cream cheese, 4 tablespoons butter and cheese; cover and process until blended. Transfer mixture to a large bowl; fold in the broccoli, 1/4 teaspoon salt and 1/8 teaspoon pepper.

Spoon 1 cup broccoli mixture into six 6-oz. ramekins. Place cups in a baking pan. Fill the pan with boiling water to a depth of 1 in. Bake, uncovered, at 350° for 25-30 minutes or until a knife inserted near the center comes out clean.

For sauce, combine flour and remaining butter to form a paste. In a large, heavy saucepan, combine the lemon-cream mixture, bouillon and remaining salt and pepper. Bring to boil. Whisk butter mixture into cream mixture until smooth and mixture is thickened. Add snipped dill. Remove from the heat and set aside.

Carefully run a knife around the edge of each custard cup to loosen. Arrange on individual serving plates top side up. Spoon the sauce around each timbale and garnish with dill sprigs if desired.
YIELD: 6 SERVINGS.

EDITOR'S NOTE: Muffin cups may be substituted for the ramekins.

GLAZED CARROTS AND GREEN BEANS

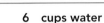

prep/total time: 20 min.

6	cups water	1/2	cup chicken broth
1/2	pound fresh baby carrots	1	tablespoon butter
1/2	pound fresh green beans, trimmed	1	teaspoon sugar
		Salt and pepper to taste	

In a large saucepan, bring water to a boil. Add carrots; cover and cook for 1 minute. Add beans; cover and cook 2 minutes longer. Drain and immediately place vegetables in ice water. Drain and pat dry.

Place the vegetables in a large skillet; add broth and butter. Bring to a boil; cook, uncovered, for 2-3 minutes or until liquid is reduced to about 2 teaspoons. Add the sugar, salt and pepper; cook and stir for 1 minute. **YIELD: 6 SERVINGS.**

**SUSAN KAKUK
PLYMOUTH, MINNESOTA**

This simple dish is always a big hit, even with nonvegetable lovers. I've substituted frozen green beans for fresh, omitting the blanching process, and it still tastes great.

CHUNKY APPLESAUCE

prep: 10 min. | cook: 30 min.

3	cups chopped peeled tart apples (about 1 pound)	3/4	teaspoon vanilla extract
3	tablespoons brown sugar	1/4	teaspoon ground cinnamon

In a small saucepan, combine all of the ingredients. Cover and cook over medium-low heat for 30-40 minutes or until apples are tender, stirring occasionally.

Remove from the heat; mash until sauce reaches desired consistency. Serve warm or chilled. **YIELD: 2 SERVINGS.**

**DEBORAH AMRINE
GRAND HAVEN, MICHIGAN**

Applesauce is easy to make—so forget buying it in the grocery store. This one has such delicious flavor and is sure to be a favorite with your children.

ONION TOPPING FOR SAUSAGES

 prep/total time: 15 min.

2	cups thinly sliced onions	1-1/2	teaspoons sugar
1	tablespoon butter	1	teaspoon white vinegar
1	tablespoon canola oil	1/2	teaspoon salt
4-1/2	teaspoons ketchup	1/4	teaspoon ground turmeric

In a large skillet over medium heat, cook onions in butter and oil until tender. Stir in the remaining ingredients. Cook until liquid is absorbed, stirring occasionally. Serve warm. **YIELD: 2/3 CUP.**

BETTY CLAYCOMB
ALVERTON, PENNSYLVANIA

Here's a great onion recipe I've been making for many years. It's a hit served over hot dogs or any kind of sausage. My mouth waters just thinking about it!

VENETIAN RICE

prep: 10 min. | cook: 25 min.

1	medium onion, chopped	1	teaspoon dried basil
3	tablespoons butter	1/2	teaspoon seasoned salt
1	cup uncooked long grain rice		Dash pepper
1	can (14-1/2 ounces) chicken broth	2/3	pound fresh *or* frozen peas, thawed
1	cup water	2	tablespoons grated Parmesan cheese

In a large saucepan, saute onion in butter until tender. Add the rice; saute until golden brown, about 5 minutes.

Stir in the broth, water, basil, seasoned salt and pepper. Bring to a boil. Reduce heat; cover and simmer for 15-18 minutes or until rice is tender (some liquid will remain).

Stir in peas. Remove from the heat; cover and let stand for 5 minutes. Stir in cheese. **YIELD: 6 SERVINGS.**

NITA CINQUINA
SURPRISE, ARIZONA

When I want a change from potatoes, this is the dish I reach for. It is one of my gang's favorites.

MUSHROOM RICE MEDLEY

prep: 10 min. | cook: 1 hour

3	cups water	1/2	pound sliced bacon, diced
1/2	cup uncooked brown rice	1/2	pound sliced fresh mushrooms
1/2	cup uncooked wild rice	1	small onion, chopped
1	teaspoon chicken bouillon granules	1/4	teaspoon salt, optional
1	teaspoon dried oregano		

In a large saucepan, combine water, brown rice, wild rice, bouillon and oregano. Bring to a boil. Reduce the heat; cover and simmer for 50-60 minutes or until rice is tender.

In a large skillet, cook bacon over medium heat until crisp. Using a slotted spoon, remove to paper towels. Drain, reserving 2 tablespoons drippings. In the drippings, saute the mushrooms and onion until tender. Stir in the rice and bacon; heat through. Season with the salt if desired. **YIELD: 6 SERVINGS.**

SUE MULLIS
SHARON, WISCONSIN

We would never hear the end of it if we failed to have my grandmother's mushroom rice dish on the table for any family gathering. It's the one item my dad requests most often.

ROASTED ASPARAGUS WITH FETA

prep/total time: 25 min.

2	pounds fresh asparagus, trimmed	2	medium tomatoes, seeded and chopped
1	tablespoon olive oil	1/2	cup crumbled feta cheese
Kosher salt to taste			

Arrange asparagus in an ungreased 13-in. x 9-in. baking dish. Drizzle with oil and sprinkle with salt.

Bake, uncovered, at 400° for 15-20 minutes or until tender. Transfer to a serving dish; sprinkle with the tomatoes and feta cheese. Serve immediately. **YIELD: 6 SERVINGS.**

PHYLLIS SCHMALZ
KANSAS CITY, KANSAS

Pretty and festive, these simple asparagus stalks are delicious right out of the oven.

DESSERTS

Plump, juicy, fresh fruits are showcased in these easy-to-make pies, cakes, crisps, cobblers and other treats. These sweet delights make a heavenly ending to any meal and a sensational after-dinner indulgence. What a delicious way to serve up a helping of fruit.

GINGERED CRANBERRY PEAR CRISP | PAGE 219

MOM'S LEMON CUSTARD PIE | PAGE 230

CREAM CHEESE BLUEBERRY PIE

prep: 20 min. + cooling

4	ounces cream cheese, softened	2/3	cup sugar
1/2	cup confectioners' sugar	1/4	cup cornstarch
		1/2	cup water
1/2	cup heavy whipping cream, whipped	1/4	cup lemon juice
1	pastry shell (9 inches), baked	3	cups fresh or frozen blueberries

In a small bowl, beat cream cheese and confectioners' sugar until smooth. Fold in whipped cream. Spread into pastry shell.

In a large saucepan, combine the sugar, cornstarch, water and lemon juice until smooth; stir in blueberries. Bring to a boil over medium heat; cook and stir for 2 minutes or until thickened. Cool. Spread over cream cheese layer. Refrigerate until serving. **YIELD: 6-8 SERVINGS.**

**LISIEUX BAUMAN
CHEEKTOWAGA, NEW YORK**

This pie is sure to have everyone's approval.

MANGO FRUIT CRISP

prep: 20 min. | bake: 30 min.

4	medium peaches, peeled and sliced	1/2	teaspoon salt
		TOPPING:	
3	medium mangoes, peeled and chopped	1/2	cup whole wheat flour
1/3	cup sugar	1/3	cup packed brown sugar
1/4	cup orange juice		
2	tablespoons whole wheat flour	3	tablespoons cold butter
1	tablespoon lemon juice	1/2	cup granola without raisins

In a large bowl, combine the first seven ingredients. Transfer to an 11-in. x 7-in. baking dish coated with cooking spray.

For topping, in a small bowl, combine flour and brown sugar. Cut in butter until crumbly; stir in granola. Sprinkle over fruit mixture.

Bake at 375° for 30-35 minutes or until topping is golden brown and fruit is tender. Serve warm. **YIELD: 8 SERVINGS.**

**JUDY SCHATZBERG
LIVINGSTON, NEW JERSEY**

This is one of my most delicious summer desserts. I use whole wheat flour to make it a bit more healthy.

**BETTIE DE BOEUF
LAWRENCEVILLE,
ILLINOIS**

*Special occasions
call for wonderful
recipes like this.
The simple-to-
make rum sauce
complements the
apple cake well.*

APPLE NUT CAKE WITH RUM SAUCE

prep: 15 min. + standing | bake: 35 min.

4 cups chopped peeled apples	1/2 cup chopped pecans
2 cups sugar	**SAUCE:**
2 eggs	1/2 cup butter, cubed
1/2 cup canola oil	1 cup sugar
1 teaspoon almond extract	2 tablespoons all-purpose flour
2 cups all-purpose flour	1/8 teaspoon salt
2 teaspoons baking powder	1 cup water
1 teaspoon salt	2 teaspoons vanilla extract
1 teaspoon ground cinnamon	1/2 teaspoon rum extract

In a large bowl, combine the apples and sugar. Let stand for 30 minutes. In a small bowl, whisk the eggs, oil and almond extract. Add to apple mixture and toss to coat. Combine the flour, baking powder, salt and cinnamon; stir into apple mixture just until moistened. Stir in pecans.

Transfer to a greased 11-in. x 7-in. baking dish. Bake at 350° for 35-40 minutes or until a toothpick inserted near the center comes out clean.

For sauce, in a small saucepan, melt butter. Stir in the sugar, flour and salt until smooth. Gradually add water. Bring to a boil; cook and stir for 2 minutes. Remove from the heat; stir in extracts. Serve with warm cake. **YIELD: 9 SERVINGS (2 CUPS SAUCE).**

TASTE OF HOME
TEST KITCHEN

These crunchy meringue shells will have guests oohing and aahing. Topped with your favorite fresh fruit, they're pretty served with a spring meal.

MERINGUE NESTS

prep: 25 min. + standing | bake: 45 min. + cooling

3 egg whites	3/4 cup sugar
1/2 teaspoon vanilla extract	Fresh fruit such as sliced fresh strawberries, fresh raspberries, mandarin oranges *or* cubed fresh pineapple
1/4 teaspoon cream of tartar	

Place egg whites in a large bowl; let stand at room temperature for 30 minutes. Beat egg whites, vanilla and cream of tartar on medium speed until soft peaks form. Gradually beat in sugar, 1 tablespoon at a time, on high until stiff peaks form.

Drop the meringue into eight mounds on a parchment paper-lined baking sheet. Shape into 3-in. cups with the back of a spoon. Or, place the meringue mixture in pastry bag fitted with star tip. Pipe meringue onto parchment paper to form eight 3-in. cups.

Bake at 275° for 45-50 minutes or until set and dry. Turn off oven and do not open door; leave meringues in oven for 1 hour. Fill with fruit. **YIELD: 8 SERVINGS.**

TONDA POWELL
MCGEHEE, ARKANSAS

I love this recipe because I'm not super confident about making pies. The cobbler lets me enjoy a berry dessert without much effort.

FRESH BLACKBERRY COBBLER

prep: 20 min. | bake: 25 min.

1/2 cup plus 1 tablespoon sugar, *divided*	1-1/2 teaspoons baking powder
1 tablespoon cornstarch	1/2 teaspoon salt
4 cups fresh blackberries	3 tablespoons shortening
1 teaspoon lemon juice	1/2 cup whole milk
1 cup all-purpose flour	Vanilla ice cream, optional

In a large saucepan, combine 1/2 cup sugar and cornstarch. Stir in the blackberries and lemon juice. Bring to a boil; cook and stir for 2 minutes or until thickened. Pour into a 1-1/2-qt. baking dish coated with cooking spray.

In a small bowl, combine the flour, baking powder, salt and remaining sugar; cut in shortening until crumbly. Add milk; stir into flour mixture just until moistened. Drop by tablespoonfuls onto hot fruit.

Bake at 400° for 25-30 minutes or until topping is golden brown. Serve warm with ice cream if desired. **YIELD: 6 SERVINGS.**

CRANBERRY ZUCCHINI WEDGES

prep: 15 min. | bake: 30 min. + cooling

1	can (20 ounces) pineapple chunks	1	cup canola oil
3	cups all-purpose flour	2	teaspoons vanilla extract
1-3/4	cups sugar	1	cup tightly packed shredded zucchini
1	teaspoon baking powder	1	cup fresh or frozen cranberries, halved
1	teaspoon baking soda	1/2	cup chopped walnuts
1	teaspoon salt		Confectioners' sugar
3	eggs		

Drain pineapple, reserving 1/3 cup juice (save remaining juice for another use). Place the pineapple and reserved juice in a blender; cover and process until smooth. Set aside.

In a large bowl, combine the flour, sugar, baking powder, baking soda and salt. In a small bowl, whisk eggs, oil, vanilla, pineapple mixture; stir into dry ingredients until blended. Fold in zucchini, cranberries and nuts.

Pour into two greased and floured 9-in. round baking pans. Bake at 350° for 30-35 minutes or until a toothpick inserted near the center comes out clean.

Cool for 10 minutes before removing from pans to wire racks to cool completely. Just before serving, dust with confectioners' sugar. **YIELD: 2 CAKES (8 WEDGES EACH).**

REDAWNA KALYNCHUK SEXSMITH, ALBERTA

I try to slip zucchini into as many dishes as possible. These cake wedges have wonderful flavor and a tender texture.

SAUCY POACHED PEARS

prep/total time: 30 min.

6	medium pears	1	package (10 ounces) frozen unsweetened strawberries, thawed
1/4	cup minced fresh mint		
1	can (11 ounces) mandarin oranges, drained	2	teaspoons sugar
		2	tablespoons finely chopped pistachios

Peel pears, leaving stems attached. Place in a Dutch oven and cover with water; add mint. Bring to a boil. Reduce heat; cover and simmer for 8-12 minutes or until pears are tender but firm. Remove with a slotted spoon. Refrigerate until serving.

For sauce, in a blender, combine the oranges, strawberries and sugar; cover and process until blended. Serve with poached pears; sprinkle with pistachios. **YIELD: 6 SERVINGS.**

AUDREY THIBODEAU GILBERT, ARIZONA

Need a showstopping dessert? My beautiful poached pears are dressed up enough to serve with the fanciest meal. They're as light as they are pretty.

ALAN MORTENSEN DWIGHT, ILLINOIS

I came up with this recipe because I love mousse, and because it's an easy way to enjoy rhubarb.

Fresh & Easy Tip

Look for rhubarb stalks that are crisp and brightly colored. At home, tightly wrap rhubarb in a plastic bag, and store it in the refrigerator for up to 3 days. Be sure to wash the stalks and remove the leaves before using. One pound of rhubarb yields about 3 cups chopped.

TANGY RHUBARB FOOL

prep: 30 min. + chilling

4 cups (32 ounces) plain yogurt	1 teaspoon white balsamic vinegar
3 cups chopped fresh *or* frozen rhubarb	Dash salt
3/4 cup sugar, *divided*	1 cup heavy whipping cream
2 tablespoons water	1/8 teaspoon vanilla extract

Line a strainer with four layers of cheesecloth; place over a bowl. Add the yogurt to strainer; cover yogurt with edges of cheesecloth. Refrigerate for 8 hours or overnight.

In a large saucepan, combine the rhubarb, 1/2 cup sugar, water, vinegar and salt; cook over medium heat for 12-15 minutes or until sugar is dissolved and rhubarb is tender. Transfer to a bowl; cover and refrigerate until chilled.

In a large bowl, beat cream until it begins to thicken. Add vanilla and remaining sugar; beat until stiff peaks form. Transfer yogurt from cheesecloth to a bowl (discard liquid from first bowl). Gradually fold cream mixture into yogurt.

Fold into the rhubarb mixture. Spoon into dessert dishes. Cover and refrigerate for at least 1 hour before serving. **YIELD: 5 SERVINGS.**

BUTTERNUT SQUASH LAYER CAKE

prep: 25 min. | bake: 25 min. + cooling

1/2 cup butter, softened	1/2 cup milk
1 cup sugar	1 cup chopped walnuts
1 cup packed brown sugar	**BROWN SUGAR FROSTING:**
2 eggs	1-1/2 cups packed brown sugar
1 cup mashed cooked butternut squash	3 egg whites
1 teaspoon maple flavoring	6 tablespoons water
3 cups cake flour	1/4 teaspoon cream of tartar
4 teaspoons baking powder	1/8 teaspoon salt
1/4 teaspoon baking soda	1 teaspoon vanilla extract

In a large bowl, cream butter and sugars until light and fluffy. Add eggs, one at a time, beating well after each addition. Beat in squash and maple flavoring. Combine the flour, baking powder and baking soda; add to creamed mixture alternately with milk. Stir in walnuts. Pour into two greased and floured 9-in. round baking pans.

Bake at 350° for 25-30 minutes or until a toothpick inserted near the center comes out clean. Cool 10 minutes before removing from pans to wire racks.

For frosting, in a heavy saucepan, combine the brown sugar, egg whites, water, cream of tartar and salt. With a portable mixer, beat on low speed for 1 minute. Continue beating over low heat until a thermometer reads 160°, about 8-10 minutes.

Pour into the bowl of a heavy-duty stand mixer; add vanilla. Beat on high speed until stiff peaks form, about 3 minutes. Spread between layers and over top and sides of cake. **YIELD: 10-12 SERVINGS.**

DEANNA RICHTER
FENTON, IOWA

The recipe for this lovely cake with its yummy, old-fashioned frosting has been in our family for as long as I can remember.

SUMMER MELON PARFAITS

prep/total time: 15 min.

1/4 cup thawed lemonade concentrate	1 carton (8 ounces) frozen whipped topping, thawed
Lemon, orange *or* raspberry yogurt	1 cup diced honeydew
	1 cup diced cantaloupe

In a large bowl, combine lemonade concentrate and yogurt; fold in whipped topping. In each of four dessert glasses, layer with 1/4 cup honeydew, 1/4 cup lemon mixture, 1/4 cup cantaloupe and the remaining lemon mixture. **YIELD: 4 SERVINGS.**

TASTE OF HOME
TEST KITCHEN

Even kids who don't care for fruit will gobble up this treat. It's sure to refresh in the heat of summer, no matter what time of day it's offered.

JODI TRIGG
TOLEDO, ILLINOIS

Adding fresh sliced peaches to a homemade praline sauce creates an irresistible topping for store-bought brownies and ice cream. The sundaes make a perfect ending to a summer supper.

PRALINE-PEACH BROWNIE SUNDAES
prep/total time: 20 min.

1/4	cup packed brown sugar	1/2	cup chopped pecans
1/4	cup heavy whipping cream	1	teaspoon vanilla extract
2	tablespoons butter	6	prepared brownies
1/4	teaspoon ground cinnamon	3	cups vanilla ice cream
2	medium peaches, peeled and sliced		Additional peach slices, optional

In a large saucepan, whisk brown sugar, cream, butter and cinnamon until smooth. Bring to a boil; cook and stir for 6-7 minutes or until thickened. Remove from the heat; stir in the peaches, pecans and vanilla. Cool for 10 minutes.

Place brownies in dessert dishes; top with ice cream and peach sauce. Garnish with additional peach slices if desired. **YIELD: 6 SERVINGS.**

TANGY LEMON-NUT TART
prep: 15 min. | bake: 20 min. + cooling

1	tube (8 ounces) refrigerated crescent rolls	1	tablespoon grated lemon peel
4	eggs	1	cup flaked coconut
1	cup sugar	1/2	cup chopped blanched almonds, hazelnuts or walnuts
2	tablespoons all-purpose flour		Confectioners' sugar
4	teaspoons lemon juice		

Separate crescent dough into eight triangles; place in an 11-in. fluted tart pan with a removable bottom with points toward the center. Press dough onto the bottom and up the sides of pan to form a crust; seal perforations. Bake at 350° for 5 minutes.

Meanwhile, in a small bowl, beat the eggs, sugar, flour, lemon juice and peel until blended. Stir in coconut and nuts.

Pour over hot crust. Bake for 20-25 minutes or until lightly browned. Cool on a wire rack. Sprinkle with confectioners' sugar. Refrigerate leftovers. **YIELD: 8 SERVINGS.**

MARY DETWEILER
MIDDLEFIELD, OHIO

I like to top wedges of this tasty tart with whipped cream or ice cream. Get ready to hand out copies of the recipe!

UPSIDE-DOWN APPLE CHEESE PIE

prep: 25 min. | bake: 45 min.

- 2/3 cup chopped pecans
- 1/2 cup packed brown sugar
- 3 tablespoons butter, melted
- Pastry for double-crust pie (9 inches)
- 1 package (8 ounces) cream cheese, softened
- 1/2 cup shredded cheddar cheese
- 1 tablespoon plus 1 cup sugar, *divided*
- 1 teaspoon vanilla extract
- 4 cups thinly sliced peeled tart apples
- 1/4 cup all-purpose flour
- 2 tablespoons lemon juice
- 2 teaspoons ground cinnamon
- 1/2 teaspoon ground ginger

In a small bowl, combine the pecans, brown sugar and butter; spread into a greased 9-in. pie plate. Roll out one pastry to fit the pie plate; place over pecan mixture. Trim pastry even with edge of plate.

In a small bowl, beat cream cheese, cheddar cheese, 1 tablespoon sugar and vanilla until blended; spread over pastry. In large bowl, combine the apples, flour, lemon juice, cinnamon, ginger and the remaining sugar; pour over cheese mixture.

Roll out remaining pastry to fit top of pie; place over filling. Trim, seal and flute edges. Cut slits in top.

Bake pie at 375° for 45-50 minutes or until golden brown. Cool for 5 minutes before inverting onto a serving plate. Serve warm. **YIELD: 6-8 SERVINGS.**

**LISA DILWORTH
GRAND RAPIDS, MICHIGAN**

When you want to serve something different for dessert, turn to my unique treat. The cheesecake-like dessert features slices of tart apples.

PERSIMMON RICE PUDDING

prep: 15 min. | bake: 45 min.

- 4 cups cooked long grain rice
- 2 cups ripe persimmon pulp
- 1-1/4 cups sugar
- 1-1/4 cups milk
- 1/3 cup all-purpose flour
- 1 egg, beaten
- 1 teaspoon vanilla extract
- 1/4 cup chopped walnuts
- 1/4 cup raisins

In a large bowl, combine the rice and persimmon pulp; set aside. Combine sugar, milk, flour, egg and vanilla; add to rice mixture and mix well. Stir in walnuts and raisins.

Pour into a greased 3-qt. baking dish. Bake, uncovered, at 350° for 45 minutes or until the pudding is set. Serve warm or cold. **YIELD: 10-12 SERVINGS.**

**OPAL AMIDON
GARDEN GROVE,
CALIFORNIA**

I often buy large quantities of persimmons, remove the pulp and freeze it. That way, I can enjoy this rice pudding all year long.

DIANE MANNIX
HELMVILLE, MONTANA

Since we are originally from Texas, we naturally love sweet potatoes. But this pound cake deserves to be a tradition in any home, whether you're from the South, East, North or West.

DONNA FRIEDRICH
FISHKILL, NEW YORK

Here's an easy, refreshing dessert. It's delicious with fresh berries, but it can be made using whatever fruit is available.

SWEET POTATO POUND CAKE

prep: 25 min. | bake: 50 min. + cooling

1	cup butter, softened	1/4	teaspoon salt
2	cups sugar	1/4	teaspoon ground nutmeg
4	eggs		
1	teaspoon vanilla extract	2	cups cold mashed sweet potatoes
3	cups all-purpose flour		

GLAZE:

2	teaspoons baking powder	1	cup confectioners' sugar
1	teaspoon ground cinnamon	1	teaspoon grated orange peel
1/2	teaspoon baking soda	3	to 5 teaspoons orange juice

In a large bowl, cream butter and sugar until light and fluffy. Add eggs, one at a time, beating well after each addition. Beat in vanilla. Combine the flour, baking powder, cinnamon, baking soda, salt and nutmeg; add to creamed mixture alternately with sweet potatoes. Beat just until combined (batter will be stiff).

Pour into a greased and floured 10-in. fluted tube pan. Bake at 350° for 50-60 minutes or until a toothpick inserted near the center comes out clean. Cool for 10 minutes before removing from pan to a wire rack to cool completely.

For glaze, in a small bowl, combine the confectioners' sugar, orange peel and enough juice to achieve desired consistency. Drizzle over the cake. **YIELD: 12 SERVINGS.**

FRUIT-TOPPED ALMOND CREAM

prep: 15 min. + chilling

1	package (3.4 ounces) instant French vanilla pudding mix	1/2	to 3/4 teaspoon almond extract
2-1/2	cups cold milk	3	cups assorted fruit (strawberries, grapes, raspberries, blueberries, mandarin oranges)
1	cup heavy whipping cream		

In a large bowl, combine pudding mix and milk. Beat on low speed for 2 minutes; set aside.

In a small bowl, beat cream and extract until stiff peaks form. Fold into pudding. Spoon into a shallow 2-qt. serving dish. Chill. Top with fruit just before serving. **YIELD: 8 SERVINGS.**

EASY STRAWBERRY NAPOLEONS

prep: 20 min. + chilling | bake: 10 min. + cooling

1	sheet puff pastry, thawed according to package directions	1	cup cold whole milk
1	quart fresh strawberries, sliced	1	package (3.4 ounces) instant vanilla pudding mix
2	tablespoons sugar	2	cups whipped topping
1/4	teaspoon vanilla extract	1/2	cup semisweet chocolate chips

Preheat oven to 400°. Unfold thawed puff pastry on cutting board. With a sharp knife, cut pastry into nine squares. Place on baking sheet coated with cooking spray. Bake 10-15 minutes or until golden brown. Remove from pan to wire rack to cool completely.

In a large bowl, combine the strawberries, sugar and vanilla; set aside. In another bowl, whisk milk and pudding mix for two minutes. Let stand for 2 minutes or until soft set. Stir in whipped topping and until thoroughly blended. Cover and refrigerate.

To assemble, split puff pastry squares horizontally for a total of 18 squares. Set aside six tops. Place six of the remaining puff pastry pieces on individual serving plates. Spread about 1/4 cup pudding mixture over each pastry square. Top with a spoonful of strawberries and another piece of puff pastry. Spread remaining pudding mixture over pastry pieces. Top with remaining strawberries and reserved pastry tops.

In a microwave, melt the chocolate; stir until smooth. Transfer to a small, heavy-duty plastic bag. Cut tiny corner from bag; squeeze chocolate over napoleons. **YIELD: 6 SERVINGS.**

SHIRLEY GLAAB
HATTIESBURG, MISSISSIPPI

This moist make-ahead spice cake, with its flavorful orange frosting, is popular at family gatherings. It's simple to prepare, and it tastes so good, everyone asks for the recipe.

DEANNA RICHTER
ELMORE, MINNESOTA

I make these delicious pops when the melons are ripening quickly in our cantaloupe patch.

PUMPKIN ORANGE CAKE
prep: 25 min. | bake: 30 min.

1/2	cup butter, softened	1/2	teaspoon salt
1-1/4	cups sugar	1/2	teaspoon ground ginger
2	eggs		
1	cup canned pumpkin	1/2	teaspoon ground allspice
1/2	cup orange juice		
1/4	cup milk	1/2	cup chopped walnuts

ORANGE FROSTING:

1	tablespoon grated orange peel	1/3	cup butter, softened
2	cups all-purpose flour	3	cups confectioners' sugar
3	teaspoons baking powder	3	tablespoons milk
1	teaspoon ground cinnamon	2	teaspoons orange juice
1/2	teaspoon baking soda	4-1/2	teaspoons grated orange peel

Candied orange peel, optional

In a large bowl, cream butter and sugar until light and fluffy. Add eggs, one at a time, beating well after each addition. In another bowl, beat pumpkin, orange juice, milk and orange peel. Combine dry ingredients; add to creamed mixture alternately with pumpkin mixture, beating well after each addition. Fold in nuts.

Pour batter into a greased 13-in. x 9-in. baking pan. Bake at 350° for 30 minutes or until a toothpick inserted near the center comes out clean. Cool on a wire rack.

For frosting, in a large bowl, beat butter and confectioners' sugar until smooth. Beat in the milk, orange juice and peel. Frost the cake. Garnish with candied peel if desired. **YIELD: 12 SERVINGS.**

CREAMY CANTALOUPE POPS
prep: 10 min. | cook: 10 min. + freezing

1-1/2	cups cubed cantaloupe	8	Popsicle molds *or* plastic cups (3 ounces)
1	cup heavy whipping cream		
1/2	cup sugar	8	Popsicle sticks

Place cantaloupe in a blender. Cover and process until smooth; set aside. In a small saucepan, combine the cream and sugar. Cook and stir over low heat until sugar is dissolved. Remove from the heat.

Stir in pureed cantaloupe. Pour 1/4 cup into each mold; insert the Popsicle sticks. Freeze until firm. **YIELD: 8 SERVINGS.**

GRILLED PEACHES 'N' BERRIES

prep/total time: 30 min.

3	medium ripe peaches, halved and pitted	2	tablespoons brown sugar
1	cup fresh blueberries	2	tablespoons butter
		1	tablespoon lemon juice

Place two peach halves, cut side up, on each of three double thicknesses of heavy-duty foil (12 in. square). Sprinkle each with blueberries, brown sugar, butter and lemon juice. Fold foil around peaches and seal tightly.

Grill, covered, over medium-low heat for 18-20 minutes or until tender. Open foil carefully to allow steam to escape. **YIELD: 3 SERVINGS.**

**SHARON BICKETT
CHESTER, SOUTH CAROLINA**

With only five ingredients, this treat is so easy to prepare. Just halve the peaches and sprinkle with fresh berries and a brown sugar mixture. Because they're grilled in foil, there are no messy dishes to wash.

ORANGE APPLESAUCE CUPCAKES

prep: 20 min. | bake: 20 min. + cooling

6	tablespoons butter, softened	1	teaspoon baking powder
1	cup packed brown sugar	1/2	teaspoon salt
		1/4	teaspoon baking soda
1	egg	1/2	cup chopped pecans
1/2	cup unsweetened applesauce	**FROSTING:**	
1	teaspoon vanilla extract	1/4	cup butter, softened
		2	cups confectioners' sugar
1	teaspoon grated orange peel	1-1/2	teaspoons grated orange peel
1	cup all-purpose flour	2	to 4 teaspoons orange juice

In a large bowl, cream the butter and brown sugar until light and fluffy. Beat in egg. Beat in the applesauce, vanilla and orange peel. Combine the flour, baking powder, salt and baking soda; gradually add to creamed mixture and mix well. Stir in pecans.

Fill paper-lined muffin cups half full. Bake at 350° for 20-25 minutes or until a toothpick comes out clean. Cool for 10 minutes before removing from pan to a wire rack to cool completely.

For frosting, in a small bowl, cream butter and confectioners' sugar until light and fluffy. Add orange peel and enough orange juice to achieve spreading consistency. Frost cupcakes. **YIELD: 1 DOZEN.**

**JANIS PLOURDE
SMOOTH ROCK FALLS,
ONTARIO**

Kids of all ages rave about these fruity cupcakes. I've made them for 25 years to serve at potlucks, church picnics and family suppers alike.

LIME POPPY SEED SHORTCAKES
prep: 20 min. | bake: 20 min. + cooling

3 cups fresh blueberries	1-1/2 teaspoons grated lime peel
1 cup chopped peeled mango	1/2 teaspoon salt
2 tablespoons brown sugar	1 cup heavy whipping cream
BISCUITS:	1/2 cup plus 1 tablespoon butter, melted, *divided*
2 cups all-purpose flour	**TOPPING:**
1/4 cup plus 1 tablespoon sugar, *divided*	1 cup (8 ounces) sour cream
4 teaspoons poppy seeds	1/4 cup packed brown sugar
3 teaspoons baking powder	

In a small bowl, combine blueberries, mango and brown sugar; cover and refrigerate until serving.

In a large bowl, combine the flour, 1/4 cup sugar, poppy seeds, baking powder, lime peel and salt. In a small bowl, combine cream and 1/2 cup butter; stir into dry ingredients until a thick batter forms.

Drop by 1/3 cupfuls onto a greased baking sheet. Brush with the remaining butter; sprinkle with the remaining sugar. Bake at 375° for 18-20 minutes or until golden brown. Remove to wire racks to cool.

In a small bowl, combine the topping ingredients. Cut biscuits in half horizontally. Spoon about 1/3 cup fruit mixture and 2 tablespoons topping onto the biscuit bottoms; replace the tops. Serve immediately. **YIELD: 8 SERVINGS.**

GINGER-LIME PEAR COBBLER

prep: 25 min. | bake: 50 min. + cooling

3/4	cup sugar
1/8	teaspoon ground ginger
5	cups sliced peeled fresh pears
2	tablespoons finely chopped crystallized ginger
2	tablespoons lime juice
1/2	cup butter, melted

BATTER:

3/4	cup all-purpose flour
1/2	cup sugar
2	teaspoons baking powder
1	teaspoon grated lime peel
1/8	teaspoon salt
Pinch	ground ginger
3/4	cup milk

In a large bowl, combine sugar and ground ginger. Stir in the pears, crystallized ginger and lime juice; set aside.

Pour butter into an ungreased 11-in. x 7-in. baking dish. In a small bowl, combine the flour, sugar, baking powder, lime peel, salt and ginger. Stir in milk. Pour over butter (do not stir). Spoon pear mixture over the top.

Bake at 350° for 50-55 minutes or until bubbly and golden brown. Cool for 10 minutes before serving. **YIELD: 8-10 SERVINGS.**

HEATHER NAAS
LOMPOC, CALIFORNIA

We have a huge pear tree in our yard, which is why I came up with this recipe. The tart lime, sweet pears and tangy ginger are a winning combination.

STRAWBERRY-BANANA ANGEL TORTE

prep/total time: 20 min.

1	prepared angel food cake (8 to 10 ounces)
1/2	cup sour cream
1/4	cup sugar
1/4	cup pureed fresh strawberries

3/4	cup sliced ripe bananas
1/2	cup sliced fresh strawberries
1	cup heavy whipping cream, whipped
Halved fresh strawberries	

Split cake horizontally into three layers; place the bottom layer on a serving plate. In a large bowl, combine the sour cream, sugar and pureed strawberries; fold in bananas and sliced strawberries. Fold in whipped cream.

Spread a third of the filling between each layer; spread the remaining filling over top. Cover and refrigerate until serving. Garnish with halved strawberries. **YIELD: 8-10 SERVINGS.**

MILLIE VICKERY
LENA, ILLINOIS

Readers of the "Cooking with Millie" newspaper food column I've written for many years share their best recipes, like this tasty dessert from Cheryl Rife.

**SHARON DELANEY-CHRONIS
SOUTH MILWAUKEE,
WISCONSIN**

When I first prepared this change-of-pace soup for a party, everyone called it a hit! My husband always likes it warmed up, but I prefer it chilled. We drizzle leftovers frozen custard for a fresh, fruity topping.

**JANICE BRADY
DES MOINES, WASHINGTON**

To use up an abundance of garden zucchini, try these wholesome soft-textured cookies.

STRAWBERRY DESSERT SOUP

prep: 20 min. + chilling

1	cup water, *divided*	2	cups fresh strawberries, hulled
1	cup unsweetened apple juice	2	cups strawberry yogurt
2/3	cup sugar	2	to 3 drops red food coloring, optional
1/2	teaspoon ground cinnamon	1/4	cup sour cream
1/8	teaspoon ground cloves	2	tablespoons whole milk

In a large saucepan, combine 3/4 cup water, apple juice, sugar, cinnamon and cloves. Bring to a boil, stirring occasionally. Remove from the heat.

Place the strawberries and remaining water in a blender; cover and process until smooth. Pour into apple juice mixture. Stir in yogurt and food coloring if desired. Cover and refrigerate for at least 2 hours or until chilled.

Ladle soup into bowls. Combine sour cream and milk; spoon about 2-1/2 teaspoons into the center of each bowl. Using a toothpick, pull mixture out, forming a flower design. **YIELD: 7 SERVINGS.**

ZUCCHINI GRANOLA COOKIES

prep: 10 min. | bake: 10 min./batch

3/4	cup butter, softened	3	cups granola without raisins
1-1/2	cups packed brown sugar	1	teaspoon baking soda
1	egg	1	teaspoon salt
1	tablespoon grated orange peel	3	cups shredded zucchini
1	teaspoon vanilla extract	1	package (10 to 12 ounces) semisweet chocolate *or* butterscotch chips
3-1/2	cups all-purpose flour		

In a large bowl, cream butter and brown sugar until light and fluffy. Beat in the egg, orange peel and vanilla. Combine flour, granola, baking soda and salt; add to creamed mixture and mix well. Stir in zucchini and chips.

Drop by tablespoonfuls 2 in. apart onto greased baking sheets. Bake at 350° for 8-10 minutes or until lightly browned. Remove to wire racks to cool. **YIELD: 6-1/2 DOZEN.**

NANTUCKET CRANBERRY TART

prep: 15 min. | bake: 40 min. + cooling

1	package (12 ounces) fresh *or* frozen cranberries, thawed	3/4	cup butter, melted
1	cup sugar, *divided*	1	teaspoon almond extract
1/2	cup sliced almonds	1	cup all-purpose flour
2	eggs	1	tablespoon confectioners' sugar

In a small bowl, combine the cranberries, 1/2 cup sugar and almonds. Transfer to a greased 11-in. fluted tart pan with a removable bottom. Place on a baking sheet.

In a small bowl, beat the eggs, butter, extract and remaining sugar. Beat in flour just until moistened (batter will be thick). Spread evenly over berries.

Bake at 325° for 40-45 minutes or until a toothpick inserted near the center comes out clean. Cool on a wire rack. Dust with confectioners' sugar. Refrigerate leftovers. **YIELD: 12 SERVINGS.**

JACKIE ZACK
RIVERSIDE, CONNECTICUT

While everyone enjoys a hearty meal, this eye-catching tart can be baking to perfection in the oven. I love it because it calls for very few ingredients and is a snap to assemble.

SQUASH-STUFFED BAKED APPLES

prep: 25 min. | bake: 1-1/2 hours

8	medium tart apples	2	tablespoons butter
1/2	cup plus 1 tablespoon packed brown sugar, *divided*	2-1/2	cups mashed cooked butternut squash
1/2	cup orange juice	1/4	teaspoon salt
1/2	cup water	1/2	teaspoon ground nutmeg, *divided*

Core apples, leaving bottoms intact. Peel the top third of each apple. Remove apple pulp, leaving a 1/2-in. shell. Chop the removed apple; set aside.

Place the cored apples in an ungreased 13-in. x 9-in. baking dish. Combine 1/2 cup brown sugar, orange juice and water; pour mixture over the apples. Bake, uncovered, at 325° for 1 hour or until tender, basting occasionally.

In a large saucepan, saute chopped apple in butter until tender. Add the squash; bring to a boil. Reduce the heat; cover and simmer for 5 minutes, stirring often. Stir in the salt, 1/4 teaspoon nutmeg and remaining brown sugar. Spoon into the baked apples; sprinkle with remaining nutmeg.

Bake 30-35 minutes longer or until heated through, basting occasionally. Drizzle with pan juices before serving. **YIELD: 8 SERVINGS.**

CAROLYN BUSCHKAMP
EMMETSBURG, IOWA

My husband and our four children like my baking creations, such as apples filled with squash and festive spices. The apples make a healthy and delicious accompaniment to a winter meal.

LUCILLE MEAD
ILION, NEW YORK

If you're craving some comfort food, give this pie a try. Served warm and a la mode, it just can't be beat!

SPICED PLUM PIE

prep: 20 min. | bake: 45 min. + cooling

Pastry for double-crust pie (9 inches)	1/4 teaspoon ground nutmeg
4-1/2 cups sliced fresh plums	1 egg, lightly beaten
2/3 cup sugar	1/2 cup orange juice
1/4 cup all-purpose flour	1 teaspoon grated orange peel
1 teaspoon ground cinnamon	2 tablespoons butter
1/4 teaspoon salt	Vanilla ice cream, optional

Line a 9-in. pie plate with bottom pastry; trim even with the edge. Arrange plums in crust. In a small bowl, combine the sugar, flour, cinnamon, salt and nutmeg. Stir in the egg, orange juice and peel. Pour over plums; dot with butter.

Roll out remaining pastry to fit top of pie; place over filling. Trim, seal and flute edges. Cut slits in pastry.

Bake at 400° for 45-50 minutes or until crust is golden brown and filling is bubbly (cover edges with foil during the last 15 minutes to prevent overbrowning if necessary). Cool the pie on a wire rack for 10 minutes before cutting. Serve pie warm with vanilla ice cream if desired. **YIELD: 8 SERVINGS.**

MONICA GROSS
DOWNEY, CALIFORNIA

I use the first ripe berries of the season to make this fruity pie.

GLAZED BLACKBERRY PIE

prep: 25 min. + chilling

5 cups fresh blackberries, *divided*	3/4 cup sugar
1 pastry shell (9 inches), baked	3 tablespoons cornstarch
1 cup water, *divided*	Red food coloring, optional
	Whipped topping

Place 2 cups blackberries in pastry shell; set aside. In a saucepan, crush 1 cup berries. Add 3/4 cup water. Bring to a boil over medium heat, stirring constantly. Cook and stir for 2 minutes. Press berries through a sieve. Set juice aside and discard pulp.

In a saucepan, combine the sugar and cornstarch. Stir in remaining water and reserved juice until smooth. Bring to a boil; cook and stir for 2 minutes or until thickened. Remove from the heat; stir in food coloring if desired. Pour half of glaze over berries in pastry shell. Stir remaining berries into remaining glaze; carefully spoon over filling.

Refrigerate for 3 hours or until set. Garnish with whipped topping. Refrigerate leftovers. **YIELD: 6-8 SERVINGS.**

PHYLLIS SCHMIDT MANITOWOC, WISCONSIN

I am 90 years old and have been baking this cake every Christmas for 65 years! My sister-in-law gave me the recipe in 1941 and it has been in demand since. My grandchildren have never been able to figure out why it's called a potato cake since it doesn't taste like potatoes.

CARAMEL-FROSTED POTATO CAKE

prep: 20 min. | bake: 55 min. + cooling

3/4 cup butter, softened	1 teaspoon ground cloves
2 cups sugar	1/2 cup whole milk
4 eggs, *separated*	1 cup chopped walnuts
1 cup mashed potatoes (without added milk and butter)	**FROSTING:**
2 ounces German sweet chocolate, melted	1/4 cup butter
2 cups all-purpose flour	1/2 cup packed brown sugar
2 teaspoons baking soda	1-1/4 cups confectioners' sugar
1 teaspoon ground nutmeg	1/4 teaspoon vanilla extract
	2 to 4 tablespoons whole milk

In a large bowl, cream butter and sugar until light and fluffy. Beat in the egg yolks, potatoes and chocolate. Combine the flour, baking soda, nutmeg and cloves; gradually add to creamed mixture alternately with milk, beating well after each addition. Stir in walnuts.

In a small bowl, beat egg whites until stiff peaks form; fold into batter. Pour into a greased and floured 10-in. fluted tube pan.

Bake at 350° for 55-60 minutes or until cake springs back when lightly touched. Cool for 10 minutes before removing from pan to a wire rack to cool completely.

For frosting, in a small saucepan, melt butter. Add brown sugar; cook and stir over low heat for 2 minutes. Remove from the heat; cool for 3 minutes. Stir in the confectioners' sugar, vanilla and enough milk to achieve a thick pouring consistency. Pour over cake. **YIELD: 12-16 SERVINGS.**

MARION KARLIN
WATERLOO, IOWA

My south-of-the-border treats are meal-ending favorites. You'll love the presentation of strawberries, apricots, peaches and plums in chocolate-drizzled tortilla cups.

MIA WERNER
WAUKEGAN, ILLINOIS

Try this easy, sauce spooned over pound cake, ice cream, pancakes or waffles.

FRUITY CHOCOLATE TORTILLA CUPS

prep/total time: 30 min.

1	to 2 tablespoons butter, softened	2	tablespoons honey
8	flour tortillas (6 inches), warmed	1-1/2	cups halved fresh strawberries
3/4	cup semisweet chocolate chips	3	small plums, sliced
1	teaspoon shortening	2	medium peaches, sliced
FILLING:		1/2	cup heavy whipping cream
1	pound fresh apricots, halved	2	tablespoons confectioners' sugar

Spread butter over one side of each tortilla. Press tortillas, butter side down, into ungreased 8-oz. custard cups. Place on a 15-in. x 10-in. x 1-in. baking pan. Bake at 400° for 10-12 minutes or until golden brown. Remove tortilla cups from custard cups; cool on wire racks.

In a microwave, melt the chocolate chips and shortening; stir until smooth. Drizzle over the insides of tortilla cups; refrigerate for 3-4 minutes or until set.

For filling, in a food processor, combine apricots and honey; cover and process until smooth. In a large bowl, combine strawberries, plums and peaches; add apricot mixture and gently toss to coat. Spoon 1/2 cup into each tortilla cup.

In a small bowl, beat the cream until it begins to thicken. Add the confectioners' sugar; beat until stiff peaks form. Dollop onto fruit. **YIELD: 8 SERVINGS.**

STRAWBERRY RHUBARB SAUCE

prep/total time: 15 min.

2	cups halved fresh strawberries	2/3	cup sugar
1	cup sliced fresh *or* frozen rhubarb	1	tablespoon cornstarch
		2	tablespoons cold water

In a small saucepan, combine the strawberries, rhubarb and sugar. Bring to a boil over medium heat. Combine cornstarch and water until smooth; stir into fruit mixture. Cook and stir for 1-2 minutes or until thickened. Serve warm or chilled. **YIELD: 1-3/4 CUPS.**

EDITOR'S NOTE: If using frozen rhubarb, measure rhubarb while still frozen, then thaw completely. Drain in a colander, but do not press liquid out.

GINGERED CRANBERRY PEAR CRISP

prep: 25 min. | bake: 25 min.

1/2	cup sugar
2	tablespoons all-purpose flour
2	tablespoons lemon juice
4	cups sliced peeled fresh pears
1-1/2	cups fresh *or* frozen cranberries
3	tablespoons finely chopped crystallized ginger

TOPPING:

3/4	cup packed brown sugar
3/4	cup old-fashioned oats
2/3	cup all-purpose flour
6	tablespoons cold butter

In a large bowl, combine sugar and flour; stir in lemon juice. Add the pears, cranberries and ginger; toss to coat. Divide among six greased 10-oz. ramekins or custard cups.

In a small bowl, combine the brown sugar, oats and flour; cut in butter until mixture resembles coarse crumbs. Sprinkle over fruit.

Bake at 400° for 25-30 minutes or until the topping is golden brown. Serve warm. **YIELD: 6 SERVINGS.**

VIRGINIA MIRACLE
MENASHA, WISCONSIN

This is a dessert so elegant-looking, you will be proud to serve it to weekend guests. Best of all, it comes together fast for weekday snack.

CARROT CHOCOLATE CHIP COOKIES

prep/total time: 30 min.

1	cup packed brown sugar
1/3	cup canola oil
2	eggs
1/3	cup fat-free milk
2	cups all-purpose flour
1	teaspoon baking powder
1/2	teaspoon salt
1/2	teaspoon ground cinnamon

1/4	teaspoon baking soda
1/4	teaspoon ground nutmeg
1	cup (6 ounces) semisweet chocolate chips
1	cup quick-cooking oats
1	cup grated carrots
1	cup raisins

KARIN WOODBURY
OCALA, FLORIDA

The recipe for these delicious cookies was handwritten in a book I received from my husband's grandmother. She told my husband when he was young that the bites were a good way to eat carrots. He loved then anyway!

In a large bowl, beat brown sugar and oil until blended. Beat in eggs, then milk. Combine the flour, baking powder, salt, cinnamon, baking soda and nutmeg; gradually add to egg mixture and mix well. Stir in the chips, oats, carrots and raisins.

Drop by heaping teaspoonfuls onto baking sheets coated with cooking spray; flatten slightly. Bake at 350° for 10-13 minutes or until golden. Remove to wire racks to cool. **YIELD: ABOUT 7 DOZEN.**

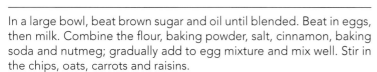

**JUDY BOND
DUNCAN,
BRITISH
COLUMBIA**

*I make these
delectable treats
in early summer
when the
cherries are ripe
and plentiful.
An all-time
favorite, they
freeze very
nicely and are a
wonderful treat
to serve guests.*

STUFFED CHERRIES DIPPED IN CHOCOLATE

prep: 40 min. + standing

1-1/2	pounds fresh dark sweet cherries with stems		2	tablespoons maple syrup
1	package (8 ounces) cream cheese, softened		2	cups white baking chips
2	tablespoons ground hazelnuts		12	teaspoons shortening, *divided*
			1-1/2	cups milk chocolate chips
			1-1/2	cups semisweet chocolate chips

Pit cherries through the sides, leaving stems intact. In a small bowl, beat cream cheese until smooth. Stir in hazelnuts and syrup. Pipe into cherries.

In a small microwave-safe bowl, melt the white chips and 5 teaspoons shortening at 70% power. Microwave at additional 10- to 20-second intervals, stirring until smooth. In another bowl, repeat with milk chocolate chips and 3-1/2 teaspoons shortening. Repeat with the semisweet chips and remaining shortening.

Holding stems, dip a third of the stuffed cherries into melted white chocolate; allow excess to drip off. Place on waxed paper; let stand until set. Repeat with remaining cherries and milk chocolate and semisweet chocolate. Dip the white-coated cherries a second time to completely cover; let stand until set.

Reheat remaining melted chocolate if necessary. Drizzle white chocolate over cherries dipped in milk or semisweet chocolate. Drizzle milk or semisweet chocolate over white chocolate-dipped cherries. Store in an airtight container in the refrigerator. **YIELD: 5 DOZEN.**

PEAR-CRANBERRY LATTICE PIE
prep: 25 min. | bake: 55 min. + cooling

Pastry for double-crust pie (9 inches)

3/4	cup sugar
3	tablespoons cornstarch
1	teaspoon ground cinnamon
1/4	teaspoon ground allspice

5	cups sliced peeled fresh pears
2	cups fresh or frozen cranberries, thawed
2	tablespoons butter
1	egg
1	tablespoon whole milk

Additional sugar

Line a 9-in. pie plate with bottom pastry; set aside. In a large bowl, combine the sugar, cornstarch, cinnamon and allspice. Add pears and cranberries; toss to coat. Spoon into crust; dot with butter.

With a fluted pastry wheel, pizza cutter or sharp knife, cut remaining pastry into eight 1-in. strips. Twist the strips; position parallel to each other and about 1/2 in. to 3/4 in. apart over filling. Trim strips evenly with pastry edge. Seal and flute edges.

In a small bowl, whisk egg and milk; brush over pastry. Sprinkle with additional sugar. Cover pie loosely with foil to prevent overbrowning.

Bake at 450° for 15 minutes. Reduce heat to 350° and remove foil; bake for 40-45 minutes or until crust is golden brown and filling is bubbly. Cool on a wire rack. **YIELD: 6-8 SERVINGS.**

MARIAN PLATT
SEQUIM, WASHINGTON

This flavorful pie makes any gathering a celebration. It's a delightful choice for Thanksgiving or even Christmas.

BERRY SMOOTHIE PIE
prep: 10 min. + chilling

1	package (.3 ounce) sugar-free strawberry gelatin
1/3	cup reduced-calorie reduced-sugar cranberry juice
3/4	cup (6 ounces) raspberry yogurt

3	cups chopped fresh strawberries
1	reduced-fat graham cracker crust (8 inches)

Fat-free whipped topping, optional

In a small microwave-safe bowl, sprinkle gelatin over cranberry juice; let stand for 1 minute. Microwave on high for 40 seconds; stir. Let stand for 1 minute or until gelatin is completely dissolved.

In a blender, combine the gelatin mixture, yogurt and strawberries; cover and process until blended. Pour mixture into the crust. Refrigerate for 4 hours or until set. Serve with the whipped topping if desired. **YIELD: 6 SERVINGS.**

JILL BONANNO
PRINEVILLE, OREGON

This light dessert is so beautiful and tastes sensational. Your family will love it, just like mine!

CHOCOLATE CHIP STRAWBERRY SHORTCAKES

prep: 20 min. | bake: 20 min. + cooling

3 cups sliced fresh strawberries	1/2 teaspoon salt
1/4 cup sugar	1 cup heavy whipping cream
BISCUITS:	1/2 cup plus 1 tablespoon butter, melted, *divided*
2 cups all-purpose flour	
3 tablespoons sugar, *divided*	1/2 cup miniature semisweet chocolate chips
3 teaspoons baking powder	Whipped cream, optional

In a small bowl, combine strawberries and sugar; cover and refrigerate until serving.

In a large bowl, combine flour, 2 tablespoons sugar, baking powder and salt. In a small bowl, combine the cream and 1/2 cup butter; stir into the dry ingredients until a thick batter forms. Gently stir in the chocolate chips.

Drop by 1/3 cupfuls onto a greased baking sheet. Brush with the remaining butter; sprinkle with the remaining sugar. Bake at 375° for 18-20 minutes or until golden brown. Remove to wire racks to cool.

Cut the biscuits in half horizontally. Spoon fruit onto bottom halves. Top with whipped cream if desired; replace the biscuit tops. Serve immediately. **YIELD: 8 SERVINGS.**

TASTE OF HOME TEST KITCHEN

Nothing goes better with juicy strawberries than whipped cream and chocolate. This tasty combo is decadent and fun, so it's ideal for kids and adults alike!

BERRIES AND CREAM WONTON CUPS

prep: 20 min. | bake: 10 min. + cooling

24 wonton wrappers	1 cup whipped topping
1 tablespoon butter, melted	3/4 cup (6 ounces) raspberry yogurt
2 tablespoons sugar	1/2 cup fresh blueberries
1-1/2 cups fresh raspberries, *divided*	Confectioners' sugar and fresh mint, optional

Brush wonton wrappers with butter and sprinkle with sugar. Press sugar side up into ungreased miniature muffin cups. Bake at 350° for 8-10 minutes or until lightly browned. Cool completely.

Place 1/2 cup raspberries in a small bowl; mash slightly. Stir in whipped topping and yogurt. Spoon into wonton cups. Top with blueberries and remaining raspberries. Garnish with confectioners' sugar and mint if desired. **YIELD: 2 DOZEN.**

HEIDI HOSKINSON CONIFER, COLORADO

Feel free to use different flavored yogurt and fruit to make my wonderful little desserts.

BLUEBERRY LEMON CAKE

prep: 15 min. | bake: 30 min. + cooling

1/4	cup butter, cubed	2	cups fresh *or* frozen blueberries
1/2	cup sugar	1	package (9 ounces) yellow cake mix
2	teaspoons grated lemon peel, *divided*		Whipped cream, optional

In a small saucepan, melt butter; stir in sugar until dissolved. Add 1 teaspoon lemon peel. Pour into a greased 8-in. square baking dish. Arrange blueberries in a single layer over top; set aside.

Prepare cake batter according to package directions. Stir in the remaining lemon peel. Carefully pour over blueberries.

Bake at 350° for 30-35 minutes or until a toothpick inserted near the center of cake comes out clean. Cool on a wire rack. Serve with whipped cream if desired. **YIELD: 9 SERVINGS.**

EDITOR'S NOTE: If using frozen blueberries, do not thaw.

**LEONA LUECKING
WEST BURLINGTON, IOWA**

I always set aside some of my fresh-picked blueberries to make this quick and easy cake.

CAKE AND FRUIT KABOBS

prep/total time: 30 min.

1	large red apple, cut into 16 chunks	8	seedless green grapes
1	large green apple, cut into 16 chunks	3	slices pound cake, cut into 1-inch cubes
1	large firm banana, cut into eight chunks		**SAUCE:**
2	tablespoons lemon juice	1-1/2	cups semisweet chocolate chips
16	fresh strawberries	2/3	cup sweetened condensed milk
8	seedless red grapes	1/4	cup orange juice

In a small bowl, combine the apples and banana; add lemon juice and toss gently. Thread the fruit and the cake alternately onto eight wooden skewers.

For sauce, in a microwave-safe bowl, combine semisweet chips and milk on high for about 1 minute; stir. Microwave at additional 10- to 20-second intervals, stirring until smooth. Stir in orange juice. Serve with kabobs. **YIELD: 8 SERVINGS (1 CUP SAUCE).**

EDITOR'S NOTE: This recipe was tested in a 1,100-watt microwave.

**ROBIN SPIRES
TAMPA, FLORIDA**

I've served these no-fuss kabobs at many parties. You can use any combination of fruit you like, depending on what's in season. The thick chocolate sauce has just the right hint of orange.

BANANA ICE CREAM

prep: 15 min. + chilling | process: 20 min./batch + freezing

4 cups half-and-half cream	1 can (5 ounces) evaporated milk
2-1/2 cups sugar	1 tablespoon vanilla extract
Dash salt	2 cups mashed ripe bananas (4 to 5 medium)
4 eggs, lightly beaten	
4 cups heavy whipping cream	

In a large heavy saucepan, heat half-and-half to 175°; stir in sugar and salt until dissolved. Whisk a small amount of hot mixture into eggs. Return all to the pan, whisking constantly. Cook and stir over low heat until mixture reaches 160° and coats the back of a metal spoon.

Remove from the heat. Cool quickly by placing pan in a bowl of ice water; stir for 2 minutes. Stir in the whipping cream, milk and vanilla. Press plastic wrap onto surface of custard. Refrigerate for several hours or overnight.

Stir in bananas. Fill cylinder of ice cream freezer two-thirds full; freeze according to manufacturer's directions. Refrigerate remaining mixture until ready to freeze. When ice cream is frozen, transfer to a freezer container; freeze for 2-4 hours before serving. **YIELD: 3 QUARTS.**

**DONNA ROBBINS
SKIATOOK, OKLAHOMA**

My son-in-law says this is the best ice cream he's ever had. It's always requested at family gatherings.

**PEGGY WEST
GEORGETOWN, DELAWARE**

For a finger-licking finale to any meal, I turn to this light and luscious sweet potato pie laced with just a hint of lemon. Funny how folks always seem able to find room for this delectable dessert!

LEMONY SWEET POTATO PIE

prep: 20 min. | bake: 50 min.

2 cups mashed sweet potatoes	1-1/2 teaspoons vanilla extract
3 eggs	1/2 teaspoon lemon extract
1 can (5 ounces) evaporated milk	1 cup sugar
1/4 cup water	1 unbaked pastry shell (9 inches)
1/4 cup butter, melted	Whipped cream

Press mashed sweet potatoes through a sieve or food mill. In a large bowl, whisk the eggs, milk, water, butter and extracts. Stir in the sugar and sweet potatoes. Pour into crust.

Bake at 375° for 50 -60 minutes or until a knife inserted near the center comes out clean. Cover edges with foil during the last 20 minutes to prevent overbrowning if necessary. Cool on a wire rack. Serve pie with whipped cream Refrigerate leftovers. **YIELD: 6-8 SERVINGS.**

MARLENE MUCKENHIRN DELANO, MINNESOTA

Be ready to share the recipe for this do-ahead dessert. Perfect for a large group, it's a real eye-catcher.

KIWI DESSERT SQUARES

prep: 15 min. | bake: 20 min. + chilling

2 cups all-purpose flour	1/4 teaspoon orange extract
1/2 cup confectioners' sugar	**TOPPING:**
1 cup cold butter, cubed	2 packages (8 ounces *each*) cream cheese, softened
CITRUS GLAZE:	2/3 cup sugar
6 tablespoons sugar	1-1/2 teaspoons orange extract
2 teaspoons cornstarch	4 kiwifruit, peeled
1/2 cup cold water	14 fresh strawberries, halved

In a large bowl, combine flour and confectioners' sugar. Cut in the butter until crumbly. Press into a greased 15-in. x 10-in. a 1-in. baking pan. Bake at 350° for 16-19 minutes or until golden brown. Cool on a wire rack.

In a small saucepan, combine the sugar and cornstarch. Stir in water until smooth. Bring to a boil over medium heat; cook and stir for 2 minutes or until thickened. Remove from the heat; stir in orange extract. Cool completely.

In a large bowl, beat the cream cheese, sugar and orange extract until smooth. Spread over crust. Cover and refrigerate for 45 minutes. Cut into 28 squares.

Cut each kiwi into seven slices. Place a kiwi slice in middle of each square; top each with a strawberry half. Brush with glaze; refrigerate until set. **YIELD: 28 SERVINGS.**

STRAWBERRY SUNDAE SAUCE
prep: 25 min. + standing

2	quarts fresh strawberries	1/3	cup chocolate syrup
6	cups sugar	1/3	cup raspberry liqueur, optional
1	pouch (3 ounces) liquid fruit pectin		Vanilla ice cream

Wash and mash strawberries, measuring out enough mashed berries to make 4 cups. In a Dutch oven, combine strawberries and sugar. Bring to a full rolling boil over high heat, stirring constantly. Stir in pectin. Boil 1 minute longer, stirring constantly. Remove from the heat. Stir in syrup and liqueur if desired. Skim off foam.

Pour into jars or freezer containers, leaving a 1/2-in. headspace. Cool to room temperature, about 1 hour. Cover and let stand overnight or until set. Refrigerate for up to 3 weeks or freeze for up to 1 year. Serve with ice cream. **YIELD: 8 CUPS.**

PEGGY TOWNSEND
FLORENCE, COLORADO

My husband simply loves this sauce over ice cream and banana splits. If you choose not to use liqueur, replace 1-1/2 cups of the mashed strawberries with 1-1/2 cups mashed raspberries instead.

PEACH UPSIDE-DOWN CAKE
prep: 15 min. | bake: 45 min. + cooling

1/3	cup butter, melted	1/2	teaspoon vanilla extract
1/2	cup packed brown sugar	1-1/3	cups all-purpose flour
2	cups sliced peeled fresh peaches	2	teaspoons baking powder
1/3	cup shortening	1/2	teaspoon salt
1	cup sugar	2/3	cup milk
1	egg		Whipped cream, optional
1/2	teaspoon lemon juice		

Pour butter into an ungreased 9-in. square baking pan; sprinkle with brown sugar. Arrange peach slices in a single layer over brown sugar.

In a small bowl, cream shortening and sugar until light and fluffy. Beat in egg. Beat in lemon juice and vanilla. Combine the flour, baking powder and salt; add to the creamed mixture alternately with milk, beating well after each addition. Spoon over peaches.

Bake at 350° for 45-50 minutes or until a toothpick inserted near the center comes out clean. Cool for 10 minutes before inverting onto a serving plate. Serve cake warm with the whipped cream if desired. **YIELD: 6 SERVINGS.**

SUSIE FISHER
LOGANTON, PENNSYLVANIA

Here is a family favorite and great summertime dessert using fresh peaches. We like the cake served warm with whipped cream.

DELECTABLE RASPBERRY CREAM CAKE
prep: 25 min. + chilling | bake: 25 min. + cooling

1	package (18-1/4 ounces) yellow cake mix

FILLING:

2	tablespoons all-purpose flour
2/3	cup whole milk
6	tablespoons butter, softened
1/3	cup shortening
2/3	cup sugar
3/4	teaspoon vanilla extract

2	cups fresh raspberries, *divided*

GLAZE:

1	cup (6 ounces) semisweet chocolate chips
3	tablespoons half-and-half cream
2	tablespoons butter
2	tablespoons light corn syrup

Prepare and bake cake according to package directions, using two 9-in. round baking pans. Cool for 10 minutes before removing from pans to wire racks to cool completely.

For filling, in a small saucepan, combine flour and milk until smooth. Bring to a boil; cook and stir for 1-2 minutes or until thickened. Cool to room temperature. In a small bowl, cream the butter, shortening, sugar and vanilla; beat in milk mixture until sugar is dissolved, about 5 minutes.

Place one cake layer on a serving plate. Spread with 1 cup filling. Place remaining filling in a pastry bag with star tip #195; pipe filling around outside edge of cake. Sprinkle 1-3/4 cups raspberries over filling. Top with second cake layer. Chill.

For glaze, combine chocolate chips, cream, butter and corn syrup in a small saucepan. Cook over low heat until chocolate is melted, stirring occasionally. Remove from heat; stir until smooth. Spread enough glaze over the top of cake to cover. Chill for 10 minutes. Repeat with remaining glaze, allowing glaze to drape over sides. Chill for 1 hour.

Arrange the remaining raspberries on top of the cake. Refrigerate leftovers. **YIELD: 10-12 SERVINGS.**

CREAM-TOPPED GRAPES
prep/total time: 10 min.

1	pound seedless grapes
1	cup (8 ounces) sour cream

1/4	cup packed dark brown sugar

Place grapes in six serving cups. Combine sour cream and brown sugar until smooth. Refrigerate until ready to serve. Spoon over the grapes. **YIELD: 6 SERVINGS.**

TASTE OF HOME
TEST KITCHEN

For a cake to impress, try this delicious snack. The filling makes it so yummy with raspberries. Your guests will surely ask for the recipe.

JOYCE KEY
SNELLVILLE, GEORGIA

You need just three ingredients to enjoy the rich taste of this treat. The sweet sauce looks lovely over red or green grapes when served in sherbet glasses.

**VICKI AYRES
WAPPINGERS
FALLS,
NEW YORK**

*Golden biscuits
with a tart
lemon flavor
float on a ruby
raspberry sauce
in my dessert.
I love serving
it to guests. My
children also
like it with
blackberries.*

LEMON WHIRLIGIGS WITH RASPBERRIES

prep: 35 min. | bake: 25 min.

2/3 cup sugar	2 teaspoons baking powder
2 tablespoons cornstarch	1/2 teaspoon salt
1/4 teaspoon ground cinnamon	3 tablespoons shortening
1/8 teaspoon ground nutmeg	1 egg, lightly beaten
1/8 teaspoon salt	2 tablespoons half-and-half cream
1 cup water	1/4 cup sugar
3 cups fresh raspberries	2 tablespoons butter, melted
WHIRLIGIGS:	1 teaspoon grated lemon peel
1 cup all-purpose flour	Heavy whipping cream and additional raspberries, optional

In a small saucepan, combine the sugar, cornstarch, cinnamon, nutmeg and salt. Stir in water until smooth. Bring to a boil; cook and stir for 2 minutes or until thickened.

Place raspberries in an ungreased 1-1/2-qt. shallow baking dish; pour hot sauce over top. Bake, uncovered, at 400° for 10 minutes. Remove from the oven; set aside.

For whirligigs, combine the flour, baking powder and salt in a small bowl. Cut in shortening until crumbly. Combine egg and half-and-half; stir into crumb mixture to form a stiff dough.

Shape into a ball. On a lightly floured surface, roll out into a 12-in. x 6-in. rectangle. Combine the sugar, butter and lemon peel; spread over dough to within 1/2 in. of edges. Roll up, jelly roll style, starting at a long side. Cut into 10 slices; pat each slice slightly to flatten. Place on berry mixture.

Bake, uncovered, at 400° for 15 minutes or until whirligigs are golden. Garnish servings with cream and raspberries if desired. **YIELD: 10 SERVINGS.**

WATERMELON SORBET

prep: 25 min. + freezing

4 cups water	1 can (12 ounces) frozen pink lemonade concentrate, thawed
2 cups sugar	
8 cups cubed seedless watermelon	

In a large saucepan, bring water and sugar to a boil. Cook and stir until sugar is dissolved. Cool slightly. In batches, process the sugar syrup and watermelon in a food processor. Transfer to a large bowl; stir in lemonade concentrate. Cover and refrigerate until chilled.

Fill the cylinder of an ice cream freezer two-thirds full; freeze according to the manufacturer's directions. Refrigerate the remaining mixture until ready to freeze. Allow to ripen in the ice cream freezer or firm up in the refrigerator freezer for 2-4 hours before serving. **YIELD: ABOUT 2-1/2 QUARTS.**

HEIDE GRABLE
RALEIGH, NORTH CAROLINA

After scooping out the watermelon for this pretty pink sorbet, I freeze the rind shell to use as an eye-fetching serving bowl.

MAJESTIC CHERRY PIE

prep: 20 min. + standing | bake: 45 min. + cooling

1 cup plus 1 tablespoon sugar, *divided*	1 cup halved pitted fresh Bing cherries
2 tablespoons all-purpose flour	1 tablespoon lemon juice
2 tablespoons quick-cooking tapioca	4-1/2 teaspoons butter
1/8 teaspoon salt	Pastry for double-crust pie (9 inches)
3-1/2 cups pitted fresh Rainier cherries	2 teaspoons whole milk

In a large bowl, combine 1 cup sugar, flour, tapioca and salt. Add cherries and lemon juice; toss to coat. Let stand for 15 minutes.

Line a 9-in. pie plate with bottom pastry; trim even with edge of plate. Add filling; dot with butter. Roll out remaining pastry to fit top of pie; place over filling. Trim, seal and flute edges. Cut slits in pastry. Brush with milk and sprinkle with remaining sugar.

Bake at 400° for 45-50 minutes or until the crust is golden brown and filling is bubbly. Cover the edges with foil during the last 15 minutes to prevent overbrowning if necessary. Cool the pie on a wire rack. **YIELD: 6-8 SERVINGS.**

LOUISE PIPER
GARNER, IOWA

Cherries are my favorite fruit so creating this pie was a hit in my book!

**GAYNELLE HENRY
NEWLAND,
NORTH CAROLINA**

This is my favorite fruit pizza and my family loves it. I make it often for a cool, pretty and delicious dessert.

**JEANNIE FRITSON
KEARNEY, NEBRASKA**

My mother often made this pie when we were growing up. The beaten egg whites give it a delicate texture and make this custard pie unique! It's a great way to top off any meal.

FRUIT PIZZA
prep: 30 min. + chilling

1	tube (16-1/2 ounces) refrigerated sugar cookie dough	1	teaspoon grated orange peel
1	cup sugar, *divided*	2/3	cup heavy whipping cream
2	tablespoons cornstarch	1-1/2	cups halved fresh strawberries
1/2	cup orange juice		
1/4	cup lemon juice	1	medium peach, thinly sliced
1	package (8 ounces) cream cheese, softened	1	small banana, sliced
		1	small apple, thinly sliced
1	tablespoon milk	1/2	cup fresh blueberries

Let dough stand at room temperature for 5-10 minutes to soften. Press onto an ungreased 14-in. pizza pan. Bake at 350° for 15-18 minutes or until deep golden brown. Cool on a wire rack.

In a small saucepan, combine 1/2 cup sugar, cornstarch and juices. Bring to a boil; cook and stir for 2 minutes or until thickened. Remove from the heat; set aside to cool.

In a large bowl, beat cream cheese, milk, orange peel and remaining sugar until blended.

In a small bowl, beat cream until soft peaks form; fold into cream cheese mixture. Spread over crust. Arrange fruit over filling; spread with reserved glaze. Refrigerate until chilled. **YIELD: 12 SERVINGS.**

MOM'S LEMON CUSTARD PIE
prep: 20 min. | bake: 1 hour

1	cup sugar	1/8	teaspoon salt
1	tablespoon butter, softened	1/4	cup lemon juice
2	eggs, *separated*	2	teaspoons grated lemon peel
1	cup milk	1	unbaked pie pastry (9 inches)
3	tablespoons all-purpose flour		

In a large bowl, beat sugar and butter until well blended. Add the egg yolks, one at a time, beating well after each addition. Add the milk, flour and salt; mix well. Stir in lemon juice and peel; set aside. In a small bowl, beat egg whites until stiff peaks form; gently fold into lemon mixture.

Pour into pie shell. Bake at 325° for 1 hour or until lightly browned and a knife inserted near center comes out clean. Cool. Garnish as desired. Store in the refrigerator. **YIELD: 6-8 SERVINGS.**

WARM BANANA CREPES
prep/total time: 10 min.

1/2	cup butter, cubed
1/2	cup packed brown sugar
4	medium ripe bananas, halved lengthwise
4	prepared crepes (9 inches)

In a large skillet, melt the butter. Add the brown sugar; heat and stir until sugar is dissolved. Add bananas; cook until light golden brown, turning once.

In a small ungreased skillet, heat crepes for 10 seconds on each side or until warm.

Place two banana halves in the center of each crepe. Fold the sides over filling and roll up; drizzle with the brown sugar mixture. **YIELD: 4 SERVINGS.**

LIME KIWI CLOUD
prep: 20 min. + freezing | cook: 10 min. + chilling

12	cups cubed angel food cake (about 12 ounces)
1-1/2	cups (12 ounces) vanilla yogurt
1/4	cup lime juice
2	teaspoons grated lime peel
1	carton (8 ounces) frozen reduced-fat whipped topping, thawed
6	medium kiwifruit, peeled and sliced
1	package (24 ounces) frozen unsweetened whole strawberries, thawed
2	tablespoons sugar
1	tablespoon cornstarch

Arrange half the cake cubes in an ungreased 13-in. x 9-in. dish. In a large bowl, combine the yogurt, lime juice and peel; fold in whipped topping. Spread half the yogurt mixture over the cake, pressing down to make a smooth layer. Layer with kiwi slices. Top with the remaining cake and yogurt mixture. Cover, refrigerate for 2-3 hours or until set.

Meanwhile, drain the strawberries, reserving juice. In a small bowl, combine the sugar, cornstarch and reserved juice until smooth; set aside. Place strawberries in a saucepan; bring to a boil over medium heat, mashing strawberries.

Stir in cornstarch mixture; cook and stir for 2 minutes or until thickened. Remove from the heat; cool. Cover and refrigerate until serving. Scoop cake into dessert dishes; drizzle with the strawberry sauce. **YIELD: 12 SERVINGS.**

TASTE OF HOME TEST KITCHEN

This yummy breakfast dish is so quick—what looks like a weekend-only treat can be served any day of the week. Ready-to-use crepes speed it along. You can find them near the berries in the produce section of your local grocery store.

BERNICE JANOWSKI STEVENS POINT, WISCONSIN

I enjoy serving this delicious dessert any time of the year. Prepared angel food cake, fruit and a few other items are all it takes to whip up the tangy delight.

EDNA HOFFMAN
HEBRON, INDIANA

When nectarines are in season at their sweet, juicy peak, we treat ourselves to this homemade ice cream. The fresh-fruit flavor and hint of almond make it very special.

PATRICIA NIEH
PORTOLA VALLEY, CALIFORNIA

I've made this recipe by toasting the bread on a grill at cookouts, but any way I prepare it, I never have any leftovers. The bruschetta is sweet instead of savory and guests enjoy the change.

NECTARINE ICE CREAM
prep: 10 min. | process: 20 min. + freezing

2	cups whole milk	1-1/2	cups heavy whipping cream
3/4	cup sugar		
1-1/2	cups mashed fresh nectarines (about 6 medium)	1/2	teaspoon vanilla extract
		1/8	teaspoon almond extract
1-1/2	teaspoons lemon juice	1/8	teaspoon salt

In a small saucepan, heat milk to 175°; stir in sugar until dissolved. Cool quickly by placing pan in a bowl of ice water; stir for 2 minutes.

In a small bowl, combine nectarines and lemon juice. In a large bowl, combine the milk mixture, whipping cream, extracts and salt; stir in the nectarine mixture.

Fill cylinder of ice cream freezer two-thirds full; freeze according to manufacturer's directions. Transfer to a freezer container; freeze for 2-4 hours before serving. **YIELD: ABOUT 1 QUART.**

 # SWEET BERRY BRUSCHETTA
prep/total time: 20 min.

10	slices French bread (1/2 inch thick)	3/4	cup fresh blackberries
5	teaspoons sugar, *divided*	3/4	cup fresh raspberries
		1/4	cup slivered almonds, toasted
6	ounces fat-free cream cheese	2	teaspoons confectioners' sugar
1/2	teaspoon almond extract		

Place bread on an ungreased baking sheet; lightly coat with cooking spray. Sprinkle with 2 teaspoons sugar. Broil 3-4 in. from the heat for 1-2 minutes or until lightly browned.

In a small bowl, combine the cream cheese, almond extract and remaining sugar. Spread over toasted bread. Top with berries and almonds; dust with confectioners' sugar. **YIELD: 10 PIECES.**

MURIEL BOYD ROSCOE, ILLINOIS

I put winter in its place with this light and lovely, orange meringue pie that tastes as sun-kissed as it looks.

FLORIDA PIE

prep: 25 min. | bake: 15 min. + chilling

1	cup sugar		1	tablespoon grated orange peel
5	tablespoons cornstarch		1	tablespoon lemon juice
1-1/2	cups orange juice		1	pastry shell (9 inches), baked
3	egg yolks, lightly beaten		**MERINGUE:**	
2	large navel oranges, peeled, sectioned and finely chopped		3	egg whites
2	tablespoons butter		2	tablespoons sugar

In a small saucepan, combine sugar and cornstarch. Stir in orange juice until smooth. Cook and stir over medium-high heat until thickened and bubbly. Reduce heat; cook and stir 2 minutes longer.

Remove from the heat. Stir a small amount of hot filling into egg yolks; return all to the pan, stirring constantly. Bring to a gentle boil; cook and stir for 2 minutes. Remove from the heat. Stir in the oranges, butter and orange peel. Gently stir in lemon juice. Pour into pastry shell.

In a small bowl, beat egg whites on medium speed until soft peaks form. Gradually add the sugar, 1 teaspoon at a time, beating on high until stiff glossy peaks form and sugar is dissolved. Spread evenly over hot filling, sealing edges to crust.

Bake at 350° for 15 minutes or until the meringue is golden brown. Cool on a wire rack for 1 hour. Refrigerate for at least 3 hours before serving. Refrigerate leftovers. **YIELD: 8 SERVINGS.**

CHOCOLATE CARAMEL APPLES
prep: 15 min. + cooling

1	package (14 ounces) caramels	1	cup (6 ounces) semisweet chocolate chips
2	tablespoons water	1	teaspoon shortening
4	wooden sticks	1	cup English toffee bits *or* almond brickle chips
4	large tart apples		
2	cups chopped pecans *or* peanuts		

In a large microwave-safe bowl, combine the caramels and water. Microwave, uncovered, on high for 45 seconds; stir. Microwave 20-40 seconds longer or until the caramels are melted; stir until smooth.

Insert wooden sticks into apples; dip apples into the caramel mixture, turning to coat. Coat with nuts; set on waxed paper to cool.

Meanwhile, melt chocolate chips and shortening; stir until smooth. Drizzle over apples. Sprinkle with toffee bits. Place on waxed paper to cool. Cut into wedges to serve. **YIELD: 8 SERVINGS.**

EDITOR'S NOTE: This recipe was tested in a 1,100-watt microwave.

LINDA SMITH
FREDERICK, MARYLAND

Caramel apples get dressed up for the harvest with chocolate, nuts and toffee bits. Cut into wedges, the scrumptious apples are easy to share.

PEAR SORBET WITH RASPBERRY SAUCE
prep: 30 min. + freezing

2	pounds pears, peeled and halved	5-1/2	teaspoons lemon juice, *divided*
2	cups water	1	package (10 ounces) frozen sweetened raspberries, thawed
1-1/2	cups sugar		

In a large saucepan, combine pears, water, sugar and 4-1/2 teaspoons lemon juice. Cook and stir over medium heat for 15-20 minutes or until pears are tender. Cool slightly.

In a blender, process pear mixture for 1-2 minutes or until smooth. Transfer to a 13-in. x 9-in. dish. Cover and freeze for 45 minutes or until edges begin to firm; stir.

Freeze 2 hours longer or until firm. Just before serving, process again in a blender for 2-3 minutes or until smooth.

For sauce, press raspberries through a sieve; discard seeds. Stir in remaining lemon juice. Serve with sorbet. **YIELD: 10 SERVINGS.**

LAURIE FISHER
EVANS, COLORADO

I clipped this recipe out of the newspaper years ago and then modified it to suit my family's taste. It serves as a casual dessert or it makes a lovely presentation in pretty dishes with the raspberry sauce drizzled over it.

OLD-FASHIONED CHEESECAKE

prep: 20 min. | bake: 50 min. + chilling

1-1/3 cups whole almonds, toasted and ground

3/4 cup crushed vanilla wafers

1/3 cup butter, melted

3 packages (8 ounces *each*) cream cheese, softened

1 cup sugar

3 eggs, lightly beaten

2 teaspoons vanilla extract

3/4 teaspoon grated lemon peel

TOPPING:

2 cups (16 ounces) sour cream

3 tablespoons sugar

1 teaspoon vanilla extract

Assorted fresh fruit

In a small bowl, combine almonds and wafer crumbs; stir in butter. Press onto the bottom and 2 in. up the sides of an ungreased 9-in. springform pan. Bake at 350° for 5 minutes. Cool on a wire rack.

In a large bowl, beat cream cheese and sugar until smooth. Add eggs; beat on low speed just until combined. Beat in vanilla and lemon peel just until blended. Pour into crust. Place pan on a baking sheet. Bake at 350° for 40-45 minutes or until center is almost set.

Combine the sour cream, sugar and vanilla; carefully spread over the filling. Bake 10 minutes longer or until edges appear dry. Cool on a wire rack for 10 minutes. Carefully run a knife around the edge of the pan to loosen; cool 1 hour longer. Cover the cheesecake and chill overnight. Remove sides of pan. Top with fresh fruit. Refrigerate the leftovers. **YIELD: 12 SERVINGS.**

**MARIAN LEVIN
LOS ALTOS, CALIFORNIA**

A variety of fresh fruit makes my cheesecake oh-so impressive. Use whatever fruits and berries you enjoy most.

BANANA CARAMEL TOPPING

prep/total time: 10 min.

1 jar (12-1/4 ounces) caramel ice cream topping

2 tablespoons lemon juice

1/2 teaspoon ground cinnamon

1/2 teaspoon grated lemon peel

5 medium firm bananas, cut into 1/4-inch slices

1 teaspoon rum extract

Vanilla ice cream

In a large saucepan, combine the ice cream topping, lemon juice, cinnamon and lemon peel. Cook and stir over medium heat until heated through.

Just before serving, stir in bananas and extract. Serve over ice cream. **YIELD: 3-1/2 CUPS.**

**ANGIE CASSADA
MONROE, NORTH CAROLINA**

This dessert was made famous in New Orleans because the recipe came from a Louisiana chef. Guests rave about it when I make it, but it is very easy and quick.

SHIRLEY
BRAITHEWAITE
ONAWAY,
ALBERTA

I found this recipe in a cookbook years ago. It's easy to make, and my family loves how moist it is.

COCONUT CARROT CAKE

prep: 25 min. | bake: 35 min. + cooling

2	cups sugar		2	cups grated carrots
1	cup canola oil		1-1/2	cups flaked coconut
4	eggs		**FROSTING:**	
4	cups all-purpose flour		1	package (8 ounces) cream cheese, softened
2	teaspoons baking powder		1/2	cup butter, softened
2	teaspoons ground cinnamon		1	teaspoon vanilla extract
1-1/2	teaspoons baking soda		2-1/2	cups confectioners' sugar
1	teaspoon salt			Orange paste food coloring
1	can (8 ounces) crushed pineapple			Parsley sprig

In a large bowl, beat the sugar, oil and eggs until well blended. In another large bowl, combine the flour, baking powder, cinnamon, baking soda and salt; gradually beat into sugar mixture until blended. Drain pineapple, reserving juice; set juice aside. Stir in the pineapple, carrots and coconut (batter will be thick).

Transfer to three greased and floured 9-in. round baking pans. Bake at 350° for 35-40 minutes or until a toothpick inserted near the center comes out clean. Cool for 10 minutes before removing from pans to wire racks.

For frosting, in a large bowl, beat the cream cheese, butter and vanilla until fluffy. Gradually add confectioners' sugar and enough of the reserved pineapple juice to achieve desired spreading consistency. Tint 1/4 cup frosting orange; place in a small resealable plastic bag. Cut a small hole in a corner of the bag; set aside.

Place one cake layer on a serving plate; spread with a third of the white frosting. Repeat layers twice. With orange frosting, pipe carrots on top; add parsley sprig for carrot top. Cover and store in the refrigerator. **YIELD: 12-14 SERVINGS.**

APPLE BREAD PUDDING

prep: 20 min. | bake: 40 min.

1/4 cup butter, cubed	1/2 cup chopped walnuts
2 cups chopped peeled tart apples	4 eggs
1/3 cup packed brown sugar	3 cups half-and-half cream
8 cups cubed French bread	1 teaspoon vanilla extract
1/2 cup butterscotch chips	Additional cinnamon baking chips, melted, optional
1/2 cup cinnamon baking chips	

In a large skillet, melt butter. Stir in the apples and brown sugar. Cook over medium heat for 6-7 minutes or until the apples are tender, stirring occasionally.

Place bread cubes in a greased 13-in. x 9-in. baking dish. Add the apple mixture, chips and walnuts; toss to coat. In a large bowl, whisk the eggs, cream and vanilla; pour over bread mixture.

Bake at 350° for 40-45 minutes or until a knife inserted near center comes out clean. Drizzle with melted cinnamon chips if desired. Serve warm. Refrigerate leftovers. **YIELD: 12 SERVINGS.**

**SALLY SIBTHORPE
SHELBY TOWNSHIP, MICHIGAN**

My bread pudding, which features apples and walnuts, uses a unique combination of cinnamon and butterscotch chips to create a yummy flavor. It's perfect for chilly winter mornings.

CRANBERRY APPLE CRISP

prep: 20 min. | bake: 40 min.

6 cups chopped peeled tart apples (about 7 medium)	1 cup sugar
1/2 cup fresh *or* frozen cranberries, thawed	1/2 teaspoon salt
2 tablespoons maple syrup	1 egg, lightly beaten
1 teaspoon lemon juice	1/2 cup butter, melted
1 cup all-purpose flour	1-1/2 teaspoons ground cinnamon
	Vanilla ice cream

In a large bowl, combine apples and cranberries. Add syrup and lemon juice; toss to coat. Transfer to a greased 11-in. x 7-in. baking dish.

In a small bowl, combine the flour, sugar and salt. Stir in egg until blended. Sprinkle over the fruit. Drizzle with butter; sprinkle with cinnamon. Bake, uncovered, at 350° for 40-45 minutes or until the topping is golden brown and fruit is tender. Serve warm with ice cream. **YIELD: 8 SERVINGS.**

**SUSIE VAN ETTEN
CHAPMANSBORO, TENNESSEE**

Both my sister-in-law and I make this for the holidays, even though we know each other will have it on one another's menus. It's a family favorite.

**ALMA MOSHER
MOHANNES,
NEW BRUNSWICK**

The wild blueberries on our property spark new recipe ideas, including this ice cream. The many children in our family just love it.

**LILY JULOW
GAINESVILLE, FLORIDA**

My gang enjoys Italian purple plums so I look for dishes that feature them. This recipe has become a favorite dessert.

BLUEBERRY ICE CREAM

prep: 15 min. + chilling | process: 20 min./batch + freezing

4 cups fresh *or* frozen blueberries	2 tablespoons water
2 cups sugar	4 cups half-and-half cream

In a large saucepan, combine the blueberries, sugar and water. Bring to a boil. Reduce heat; simmer, uncovered, until sugar is dissolved and berries are softened. Strain mixture; discard seeds and skins. Stir in cream. Cover and refrigerate overnight.

Fill cylinder of ice cream freezer two-thirds full; freeze according to manufacturer's directions. Refrigerate the remaining mixture until ready to freeze.

Allow to ripen in ice cream freezer or firm up in the refrigerator freezer for 2-4 hours before serving. **YIELD: ABOUT 1-3/4 QUARTS.**

PLUM CRISP

prep: 15 min. | bake: 20 min.

3-1/2 cups chopped fresh plums (about 2 pounds)	Pinch ground nutmeg
	Pinch ground cloves
6 tablespoons brown sugar, *divided*	2/3 cup old-fashioned oats
5 teaspoons all-purpose flour, *divided*	2 tablespoons butter, melted
1/8 teaspoon pepper	1-1/2 teaspoons finely grated orange peel

In a large bowl, combine the plums and 3 tablespoons brown sugar. Combine 2 teaspoons flour, pepper, nutmeg and cloves; sprinkle over the plums and toss to coat. Transfer to a greased shallow 1-qt. baking dish.

In a small bowl, combine the oats with remaining brown sugar and flour. Stir in the butter and orange peel until crumbly. Sprinkle over plum mixture.

Bake at 375° for 20-25 minutes or until topping is golden brown and plums are tender. Serve warm. **YIELD: 6 SERVINGS.**

PEACH DELIGHT

prep: 25 min. | bake: 15 min. + chilling

1/4 cup butter, softened
1/2 cup sugar
1 cup all-purpose flour
1/4 cup chopped walnuts

FILLING:

1 package (8 ounces) reduced-fat cream cheese
3/4 cup confectioners' sugar

1 carton (8 ounces) frozen reduced-fat whipped topping, thawed, *divided*
7 medium peaches, thinly sliced

GLAZE:

3 tablespoons cornstarch
2 cups water
1 package (.3 ounce) sugar-free lemon gelatin

In a bowl, cream butter and sugar until light and fluffy. Gradually add the flour (mixture will be crumbly). Stir in walnuts. Press into a 13-in. x 9-in. baking dish coated with cooking spray. Bake at 350° for 14-16 minutes or until lightly browned. Cool on a wire rack.

For filling, in a large bowl, beat the cream cheese and confectioners' sugar until smooth. Fold in half of the whipped topping. Carefully spread over crust. Top with peaches.

For glaze, in a small saucepan, combine cornstarch and water until smooth. Bring to a boil; cook and stir for 2 minutes or until thickened. Gradually stir in gelatin until dissolved. Cool to room temperature. Spoon over peaches. Cover and refrigerate until firm. Dollop with remaining whipped topping. **YIELD: 15 SERVINGS.**

CLARA HUNT
LEXINGTON, NORTH CAROLINA

Colorful peach slices, a nutty crust and refreshing lemon gelatin take center stage in my creamy treat.

ORANGE DREAM CUPS

prep: 20 min. + freezing

4 large navel oranges
1 package (3 ounces) orange gelatin

1 cup boiling water
1-1/2 cups fat-free frozen vanilla yogurt

Cut each orange in half widthwise; carefully remove fruit from both halves, leaving shells intact. Set shells aside. Section orange pulp, then dice (discard orange juice or save for another use).

In a large bowl, dissolve gelatin in boiling water. Add frozen yogurt; stir until melted. Fold in orange pulp. Refrigerate until thickened. spoon into reserved orange shells. Cover and freeze for 3 hours. **YIELD: 8 SERVINGS.**

ELIZABETH ALVAREZ
BEDFORD, TEXAS

Hollowed-out orange "cups" make this recipe fun...and the light fluffy filling is so refreshing. These cute cups are always a hit with company.

APPLE FRITTERS

prep/total time: 20 min.

1 cup cake flour	1 tablespoon orange juice
1 tablespoon sugar	2 teaspoons grated orange peel
3/4 teaspoon baking powder	
1/4 teaspoon salt	1/4 teaspoon vanilla extract
1 egg	3/4 cup chopped peeled tart apple
1/3 cup whole milk	
4 teaspoons butter, melted	Oil for frying
	Confectioners' sugar

In a large bowl, combine the flour, sugar, baking powder and salt. In another bowl, combine the egg, milk, butter, orange juice, peel and vanilla. Add to dry ingredients just until moistened. Fold in apples.

In an electric skillet or deep-fat fryer, heat 1/4 in. of oil to 375°. Drop batter by rounded tablespoons into oil. Fry until golden brown on both sides. Drain on paper towels. Dust with confectioners' sugar. Serve warm. **YIELD: 2-3 SERVINGS.**

**JOHN ROBBINS
SPRINGDALE,
PENNSYLVANIA**

This is an old Southern dish. When we got home from a trip through the South years ago, I found the recipe among the brochures I brought back. I've been making the fritters ever since.

FRESH APRICOT PIE

prep: 15 min. | bake: 45 min. + cooling

4 cups sliced fresh apricots (about 1-3/4 pounds)	Pinch ground nutmeg
	Pastry for double-crust pie (9 inches)
1 tablespoon lemon juice	Milk
1 cup sugar	Additional sugar
1/3 cup all-purpose flour	

In a large bowl, sprinkle the apricots with lemon juice. Combine the sugar, flour and nutmeg. Add to apricots; toss gently to coat.

Line a 9-in. pie plate with bottom pastry; trim to 1 in. beyond edge of pie plate. Add filling. Roll out remaining pastry to make a lattice crust. Trim, seal and flute edges. Brush with milk and sprinkle with additional sugar.

Cover edges of pastry loosely with foil. Bake at 375° for 45-55 minutes or until crust is golden brown and filling is bubbly. Cool on a wire rack. **YIELD: 6-8 SERVINGS.**

**RUTH PETERSON
JENISON, MICHIGAN**

This is a nice change of pace from the more traditional apple or cherry pies. It's easier, too.

**MAXINE SMITH
OWANKA,
SOUTH DAKOTA**

*When I want
something very
special, I turn to
this recipe given
to me by a friend.
Even those who
often pass up
rhubarb desserts
rave over the
creamy squares.*

COOL RHUBARB DESSERT
prep: 40 min. + chilling

1-1/2	cups all-purpose flour
3/4	cup butter, melted
1/4	cup finely chopped walnuts

FILLING:

1	cup sugar
3	tablespoons cornstarch
2	tablespoons water
4	cups chopped fresh *or* frozen rhubarb

TOPPING:

1	cup heavy whipping cream
2	tablespoons confectioners' sugar
1	cup miniature marshmallows
1-1/2	cups cold whole milk
1	package (3.4 ounces) instant vanilla pudding mix
1/4	cup flaked coconut, toasted

In a small bowl, combine the flour, butter and walnuts. Press into an ungreased 13-in. x 9-in. baking dish. Bake at 350° for 20-25 minutes or until lightly browned. Cool on a wire rack.

In a large saucepan, combine the sugar, cornstarch, water and rhubarb until blended. Bring to a boil. Reduce the heat; simmer, uncovered, for 5 minutes or until rhubarb is tender. Cool; pour over the crust. Chill.

In a large bowl, beat cream until thickened. Add confectioners' sugar and beat until soft peaks form. Fold in marshmallows. Spread over rhubarb layer.

In a small bowl, whisk milk and pudding mix for 2 minutes. Let stand for 2 minutes or until soft-set. Spread over cream layer; sprinkle with coconut. Cover and refrigerate for 4-5 hours or until set. Remove from the refrigerator 30 minutes before cutting. **YIELD: 16 SERVINGS.**

**GENEVA BAIRD
BASIN,
WYOMING**

Make the most of your rhubarb harvest with this tender spice cake. The sweet, crunchy topping is a definite palate-pleaser.

COCONUT-RHUBARB SPICE CAKE

prep: 20 min. | bake: 40 min. + cooling

1/2	cup shortening
1-1/2	cups packed brown sugar
1	egg
1-1/4	teaspoons vanilla extract
2	cups all-purpose flour
1-1/2	teaspoons ground cinnamon
1	teaspoon baking soda
1/4	teaspoon salt
1/4	teaspoon ground allspice
1/4	teaspoon ground cloves
1	cup buttermilk
2	cups finely chopped fresh *or* frozen rhubarb, thawed

TOPPING:

1/2	cup sugar
1/2	cup flaked coconut
1/2	cup chopped pecans
1	teaspoon ground cinnamon

In a large bowl, cream shortening and brown sugar until light and fluffy. Beat in egg. Beat in vanilla. Combine the flour, cinnamon, baking soda, salt, allspice and cloves; add to the creamed mixture alternately with buttermilk, beating well after each addition. Fold in rhubarb.

Pour into a greased 13-in. x 9-in. baking dish. Combine the topping ingredients; sprinkle over the top. Bake at 350° for 40-45 minutes or until a toothpick inserted near the center comes out clean. Cool on a wire rack. **YIELD: 12-15 SERVINGS.**

EDITOR'S NOTE: If using frozen rhubarb, measure rhubarb while still frozen, then thaw completely. Drain in a colander, but do not press liquid out.

APPLE PEAR PIE

prep: 20 min. | bake: 1 hour

Pastry for double-crust pie (9 inches)

- 3 medium ripe pears, peeled and thinly sliced
- 3 medium tart apples, peeled and thinly sliced
- 1 cup plus 1 teaspoon sugar, *divided*
- 1 teaspoon lemon juice
- 1 teaspoon ground cinnamon
- 1/4 teaspoon ground nutmeg
- 3 tablespoons butter
- 1 teaspoon whole milk

Line a 9-in. pie plate with bottom pastry; trim to 1 in. beyond edge of plate. In a large bowl, combine the pears, apples, 1 cup sugar, lemon juice, cinnamon and nutmeg. Transfer mixture to crust; dot with butter.

Roll out the remaining pastry to fit top of pie; cut slits or decorative cutouts in pastry. Place over filling; trim, seal and flute edges. Add decorative cutouts if desired. Brush with milk; sprinkle with remaining sugar. Cover edges loosely with foil.

Bake at 350° for 30 minutes. Remove foil; bake 30-35 minutes longer or until crust is golden. Cool on a wire rack. **YIELD: 6-8 SERVINGS.**

**GRACE CAMP
OWINGSVILLE, KENTUCKY**

This fruit pie, brimming with apples and pears, really says "fall." What a yummy way to use your backyard bounty or the pickings from local orchards! I've made plenty of pies over the years, and this is a real standout.

CLEMENTINE TAPIOCA

prep: 25 min. + chilling

- 2 cups fat-free milk
- 1/4 cup quick-cooking tapioca
- 3 tablespoons sugar
- 1/2 teaspoon vanilla extract
- 1/8 teaspoon ground nutmeg
- 1/2 cup clementine juice (about 5 clementines)
- 1/2 cup reduced-fat whipped topping
- 2 clementines, peeled and sectioned

In a small saucepan, combine the milk, tapioca and sugar; let stand for 5 minutes. Cook and stir over medium heat until mixture comes to a full boil. Transfer to a small bowl; stir in vanilla and nutmeg. Cool for 20 minutes. Stir in the clementine juice; cover and refrigerate until chilled.

Fold in whipped topping. Spoon into four dessert dishes, 2/3 cup in each. Top with clementine segments. **YIELD: 4 SERVINGS.**

**TASTE OF HOME
TEST KITCHEN**

Made from the cassava plant, which is a staple food source in Africa, tapioca can be found in your grocery store's baking section. Because tapioca doesn't have a lot of flavor on its own, the other tasty ingredients in this recipe really shine through.

ALPHABETICAL RECIPE INDEX

Refer to this index for a complete alphabetical listing of all the recipes in this book.

GENERAL RECIPE INDEX

This handy index lists every recipe by its food category, major ingredient and/or cooking method.

FISH & SEAFOOD
(continued)
Cod with Rhubarb
 Sauce, 140
Crab Bruschetta, 24
Crab-Stuffed Celery, 20
Dressed-Up Tuna Salad, 44
Fennel Stuffed Cod, 109
Grilled Salmon with
 Nectarines, 118
Jamaican Shrimp, 15
Lemony Grilled Salmon, 142
Mango Couscous with
 Salmon, 119
Pasta Primavera with
 Shrimp, 138
Shrimp Gazpacho, 76
Shrimp in Herbs, 109
Smoked Salmon Cucumber
 Canapes, 10
Snappy Eggplant
 Spaghetti, 116
Steak and Shrimp
 Kabobs, 106
Tuna Melt on Corn
 Bread, 90
Tuna-Stuffed Potatoes, 147
Veggie-Topped Tilapia, 132
Veggie Tuna Burgers, 82

FRUIT *(also see specific kinds)*
Cake and Fruit Kabobs, 223
Chicken Breasts with Fruit
 Salsa, 130
Christmas Fruit Kabobs, 29
Favorite Turkey Salad, 54
Fresh Fruit Compote, 52
Frozen Fruit Slush, 37
Fruit 'n' Spinach Salad, 42
Fruit Pizza, 230
Fruit Salsa, 15
Fruit-Topped Almond
 Cream, 208
Fruited Cabbage Salad, 48
Fruited Turkey Wraps, 82
Grapefruit Avocado Salad, 58
Meringue Nests, 202
Mixed Fruit with Lemon-Basil
 Dressing, 57
Old-Fashioned
 Cheesecake, 235
Persimmon Rice
 Pudding, 207

GRAPES
Cream-Topped Grapes, 227
Dijon Chicken with
 Grapes, 137
Green Grape Salad, 41

GREENS
Chicken Florentine Panini, 98
Chicken Lettuce Wraps, 14
Cran-Orange Swiss
 Chard, 173
Dressed-Up Tuna Salad, 44
Fruit 'n' Spinach Salad, 42
Garlicky Kale, 193
Greek Spinach Pizza, 134
Green Salad with Herb
 Vinaigrette, 47
Greens and Roasted
 Beets, 45
Grilled Romaine Salad, 37
Grilled Steak Tossed Salad, 43
Kiwi-Strawberry Spinach
 Salad, 46
Layered Tortellini Salad, 47
Mashed Potato Spinach
 Bake, 183
Mushroom Steak 'n'
 Linguine, 114
Pear Chicken Salad, 36
Raspberry Tossed Salad, 49
Roasted Onion Salad, 53
Sausage and Kale Soup, 62
Sausage Garden Quiche, 129
Spinach Feta Burgers, 93
Spinach Feta Pizza, 17
Spinach Po'Boys, 84
Spinach-Stuffed
 Portobellos, 140
Swiss Chard Bean Soup, 74
Texas Toast Steak
 Sandwiches, 93
Tossed Salad with Carrot
 Dressing, 39
Warm Asparagus-Spinach
 Salad, 59

HERBS
Basil
 Artichoke Caprese
  Platter, 19
 Basil Butter, 175
 Basil-Cheese Bread
  Strips, 159
 Basil-Tomato Grilled
  Cheese, 97
 Basil Tomato Soup, 64
 Basil Tuna Steaks, 141
 Bruschetta Pizza, 124
 Mixed Fruit with
  Lemon-Basil
  Dressing, 57
 Mozzarella Basil
  Bruschetta, 29
 Pesto Rice-Stuffed Pork
  Chops, 108

Cilantro & Parsley
 Grilled Veggie Sandwiches
  with Cilantro Pesto, 99
 Perky Parsleyed
  Tomatoes, 34
 Pesto Rice-Stuffed Pork
  Chops, 108
Cornucopia
 Easy Grilled Flank
  Steak, 107
 Four-Herb Bread, 163
 Fresh Herb Flatbread, 8
 Green Salad with Herb
  Vinaigrette, 47
 Herb-Buttered Baby
  Carrots, 192
 Herb-Crusted Pork
  Roast, 117
 Herbed Cheese Spread, 31
 Lemon Herb Chicken, 126
 Melon with Minted Lime
  Dip, 27
 Oregano Olive
  Chicken, 121
 Shrimp in Herbs, 109
Dill
 Dilled Cabbage Soup, 78
 Zucchini Patties with Dill
  Dip, 11
Fennel
 Fennel Stuffed Cod, 109
 Fennel Waldorf Salad, 52
 Garlic Fennel Bisque, 66
Garlic
 Garlic-Butter Parmesan
  Corn, 188
 Garlic Fennel Bisque, 66
 Garlicky Kale, 193
 Pork Medallions with
  Garlic-Strawberry
  Sauce, 118
Ginger
 Ginger-Lime Pear
  Cobbler, 213
 Gingered Cranberry Pear
  Crisp, 219
 Gingered Green Bean
  Salad, 45
 Gingered Orange
  Beets, 180
 Gingered Peach
  Chutney, 193
Rosemary
 Rosemary-Skewered
  Artichoke Chicken, 141
 Rosemary Zucchini
  Sticks, 25
 Tomato Rosemary
  Focaccia, 160

Tarragon
 Artichokes with Tarragon
  Butter, 178
 French Tarragon
  Burgers, 83
 Tarragon Cheese Loaf, 165
 Tarragon-Lemon Turkey
  Breast, 128

KIWIFRUIT
Halibut with Kiwi Salsa, 134
Kiwi Dessert Squares, 225
Kiwi-Strawberry Spinach
 Salad, 46
Kiwifruit Muffins, 163
Lime Kiwi Cloud, 231

KOHLRABI
Creamed Kohlrabi, 170
Kohlrabi 'n' Carrot Bake, 190

LEMON & LIME
Blueberry Lemon Cake, 223
Broccoli Timbales with
 Lemon Sauce, 194
Ginger-Lime Pear
 Cobbler, 213
Jamaican Shrimp, 15
Lemon Blueberry
 Muffins, 150
Lemon Herb Chicken, 126
Lemon Parsley
 Potatoes, 192
Lemon Whirligigs with
 Raspberries, 228
Lemony Grilled Salmon, 142
Lemony Sweet Potato
 Pie, 224
Lime Kiwi Cloud, 231
Lime Poppy Seed
 Shortcakes, 212
Melon with Minted Lime
 Dip, 27
Mixed Fruit with Lemon-Basil
 Dressing, 57
Mom's Lemon Custard
 Pie, 230
Tangy Lemon-Nut Tart, 206
Tarragon-Lemon Turkey
 Breast, 128

MANGOES
Broiled Pork Chops with
 Mango Sauce, 105
Halibut with Kiwi Salsa, 134
Jamaican Shrimp, 15
Lime Poppy Seed
 Shortcakes, 212
Mango Colada Scones, 150

Substitutions & Equivalents

Equivalent Measures

3 teaspoons	=	1 tablespoon	16 tablespoons	=	1 cup
4 tablespoons	=	1/4 cup	2 cups	=	1 pint
5-1/3 tablespoons	=	1/3 cup	4 cups	=	1 quart
8 tablespoons	=	1/2 cup	4 quarts	=	1 gallon

Food Equivalents

Grains

Macaroni	1 cup (3-1/2 ounces) uncooked	=	2-1/2 cups cooked
Noodles, Medium	3 cups (4 ounces) uncooked	=	4 cups cooked
Popcorn	1/3 to 1/2 cup unpopped	=	8 cups popped
Rice, Long Grain	1 cup uncooked	=	3 cups cooked
Rice, Quick-Cooking	1 cup uncooked	=	2 cups cooked
Spaghetti	8 ounces uncooked	=	4 cups cooked

Crumbs

Bread	1 slice	=	3/4 cup soft crumbs, 1/4 cup fine dry crumbs
Graham Crackers	7 squares	=	1/2 cup finely crushed
Buttery Round Crackers	12 crackers	=	1/2 cup finely crushed
Saltine Crackers	14 crackers	=	1/2 cup finely crushed

Fruits

Bananas	1 medium	=	1/3 cup mashed
Lemons	1 medium	=	3 tablespoons juice, 2 teaspoons grated peel
Limes	1 medium	=	2 tablespoons juice, 1-1/2 teaspoons grated peel
Oranges	1 medium	=	1/4 to 1/3 cup juice, 4 teaspoons grated peel

Vegetables

Cabbage	1 head	=	5 cups shredded	Green Pepper	1 large	=	1 cup chopped
Carrots	1 pound	=	3 cups shredded	Mushrooms	1/2 pound	=	3 cups sliced
Celery	1 rib	=	1/2 cup chopped	Onions	1 medium	=	1/2 cup chopped
Corn	1 ear fresh	=	2/3 cup kernels	Potatoes	3 medium	=	2 cups cubed

Nuts

Almonds	1 pound	=	3 cups chopped	Pecan Halves	1 pound	=	4-1/2 cups chopped
Ground Nuts	3-3/4 ounces	=	1 cup	Walnuts	1 pound	=	3-3/4 cups chopped

Easy Substitutions

When you need...	Use...	
Baking Powder	1 teaspoon	1/2 teaspoon cream of tartar + 1/4 teaspoon baking soda
Buttermilk	1 cup	1 tablespoon lemon juice or vinegar + enough milk to measure 1 cup (let stand 5 minutes before using)
Cornstarch	1 tablespoon	2 tablespoons all-purpose flour
Honey	1 cup	1-1/4 cups sugar + 1/4 cup water
Half-and-Half Cream	1 cup	1 tablespoon melted butter + enough whole milk to measure 1 cup
Onion	1 small, chopped (1/3 cup)	1 teaspoon onion powder or 1 tablespoon dried minced onion
Tomato Juice	1 cup	1/2 cup tomato sauce + 1/2 cup water
Tomato Sauce	2 cups	3/4 cup tomato paste + 1 cup water
Unsweetened Chocolate	1 square (1 ounce)	3 tablespoons baking cocoa + 1 tablespoon shortening or oil
Whole Milk	1 cup	1/2 cup evaporated milk + 1/2 cup water

Guide to Cooking with Popular Herbs

HERB	APPETIZERS SALADS	BREADS/EGGS SAUCES/CHEESE	VEGETABLES PASTA	MEAT POULTRY	FISH SHELLFISH
BASIL	Green, Potato & Tomato Salads, Salad Dressings, Stewed Fruit	Breads, Fondue & Egg Dishes, Dips, Marinades, Sauces	Mushrooms, Tomatoes, Squash, Pasta, Bland Vegetables	Broiled, Roast Meat & Poultry Pies, Stews, Stuffing	Baked, Broiled & Poached Fish, Shellfish
BAY LEAF	Seafood Cocktail, Seafood Salad, Tomato Aspic, Stewed Fruit	Egg Dishes, Gravies, Marinades, Sauces	Dried Bean Dishes, Beets, Carrots, Onions, Potatoes, Rice, Squash	Corned Beef, Tongue Meat & Poultry Stews	Poached Fish, Shellfish, Fish Stews
CHIVES	Mixed Vegetable, Green, Potato & Tomato Salads, Salad Dressings	Egg & Cheese Dishes, Cream Cheese, Cottage Cheese, Gravies, Sauces	Hot Vegetables, Potatoes	Broiled Poultry, Poultry & Meat Pies, Stews, Casseroles	Baked Fish, Fish Casseroles, Fish Stews, Shellfish
DILL	Seafood Cocktail, Green, Potato & Tomato Salads, Salad Dressings	Breads, Egg & Cheese Dishes, Cream Cheese, Fish & Meat Sauces	Beans, Beets, Cabbage, Carrots, Cauliflower, Peas, Squash, Tomatoes	Beef, Veal Roasts, Lamb, Steaks, Chops, Stews, Roast & Creamed Poultry	Baked, Broiled, Poached & Stuffed Fish, Shellfish
GARLIC	All Salads, Salad Dressings	Fondue, Poultry Sauces, Fish & Meat Marinades	Beans, Eggplant, Potatoes, Rice, Tomatoes	Roast Meats, Meat & Poultry Pies, Hamburgers, Casseroles, Stews	Broiled Fish, Shellfish, Fish Stews, Casseroles
MARJORAM	Seafood Cocktail, Green, Poultry & Seafood Salads	Breads, Cheese Spreads, Egg & Cheese Dishes, Gravies, Sauces	Carrots, Eggplant, Peas, Onions, Potatoes, Dried Bean Dishes, Spinach	Roast Meats & Poultry, Meat & Poultry Pies, Stews & Casseroles	Baked, Broiled & Stuffed Fish, Shellfish
MUSTARD	Fresh Green Salads, Prepared Meat, Macaroni & Potato Salads, Salad Dressings	Biscuits, Egg & Cheese Dishes, Sauces	Baked Beans, Cabbage, Eggplant, Squash, Dried Beans, Mushrooms, Pasta	Chops, Steaks, Ham, Pork, Poultry, Cold Meats	Shellfish
OREGANO	Green, Poultry & Seafood Salads	Breads, Egg & Cheese Dishes, Meat, Poultry & Vegetable Sauces	Artichokes, Cabbage, Eggplant, Squash, Dried Beans, Mushrooms, Pasta	Broiled, Roast Meats, Meat & Poultry Pies, Stews, Casseroles	Baked, Broiled & Poached Fish, Shellfish
PARSLEY	Green, Potato, Seafood & Vegetable Salads	Biscuits, Breads, Egg & Cheese Dishes, Gravies, Sauces	Asparagus, Beets, Eggplant, Squash, Dried Beans, Mushrooms, Pasta	Meat Loaf, Meat & Poultry Pies, Stews & Casseroles, Stuffing	Fish Stews, Stuffed Fish
ROSEMARY	Fruit Cocktail, Fruit & Green Salads	Biscuits, Egg Dishes, Herb Butter, Cream Cheese, Marinades, Sauces	Beans, Broccoli, Peas, Cauliflower, Mushrooms, Baked Potatoes, Parsnips	Roast Meat, Poultry & Meat Pies, Stews & Casseroles, Stuffing	Stuffed Fish, Shellfish
SAGE		Breads, Fondue, Egg & Cheese Dishes, Spreads, Gravies, Sauces	Beans, Beets, Onions, Peas, Spinach, Squash, Tomatoes	Roast Meat, Poultry, Meat Loaf, Stews, Stuffing	Baked, Poached & Stuffed Fish
TARRAGON	Seafood Cocktail, Avocado Salads, Salad Dressings	Cheese Spreads, Marinades, Sauces, Egg Dishes	Asparagus, Beans, Beets, Carrots, Mushrooms, Peas, Squash, Spinach	Steaks, Poultry, Roast Meats, Casseroles & Stews	Baked, Broiled & Poached Fish, Shellfish
THYME	Seafood Cocktail, Green, Poultry, Seafood & Vegetable Salads	Biscuits, Breads, Egg & Cheese Dishes, Sauces, Spreads	Beets, Carrots, Mushrooms, Onions, Peas, Eggplant, Spinach, Potatoes	Roast Meat, Poultry & Meat Loaf, Meat & Poultry Pies, Stews & Casseroles	Baked, Broiled & Stuffed Fish, Shellfish, Fish Stews